Carlton Ware
Catalogue & Price Guide

Dr Czes & Yvonne Kosniowski

ckyk publishing

Acknowledgments

We would like to thank everyone that has supplied us with information or photographs, or allowed us to photograph their Carlton Ware. It's not possible to name everyone but we would particularly like to thank Steve Jessup, Harvey Pettit, Ian Harwood, Jerome Wilson and Frank Salmon.

Published by ckyk publishing, a division of ckyk ltd.

ISBN 0-9549558-1-1

Contents

Introduction

This book is a *must have* for Carlton Ware collectors and enthusiasts alike. It will appeal to all collectors and dealers, large or small, whether veterans or those new to collecting or dealing. The long awaited and up to date information provided in this Catalogue and Price Guide will be a benefit to all collectors and dealers worldwide.

Our aim with this book is to provide valuable and relevant up to date information about the embossed and related range of Carlton Ware. We have concentrated on the Carlton Ware produced from the 1930's onwards and the contents of this book provide a comprehensive source of some previously unpublished information on shape numbers and names of Carlton Ware.

Our ultimate goal is to catalogue the complete and diverse ranges that were produced by Carlton Ware throughout its entire history. Our enthusiasm for Carlton Ware and the thirst for correct information fuelled the conception of our Web site www.carltonware.com several years ago, which to date has not been equalled. This is an important reference site of information, including over six thousand photographs with relevant names, descriptions, pattern numbers and shape numbers which span the entire history of Carlton Ware.

The collation of this information was developed further with the publishing of the book *A Pocket Guide to Carlton Ware*, which was avidly greeted with delight and fervour by all in the Carlton Ware world. This book complements our first book rather than replacing it as further research uncovers, clarifies and provides links, which aids our aim to quench the thirst for information of the Carlton Ware produced.

We have included some archival black and white photographs that show the 1959 retail prices of Carlton Ware. Furthermore pages 11 and 12 of this book, shown in vivid green, are a reproduction of the original cover of a 1959 Carlton Ware retail catalogue. These advertisements and the price lists have been included in the appropriate sections of this book along with some original colour advertising photographs produced for Carlton Ware.

We have endeavoured to present the information about Carlton Ware in a correct way. Occasionally mistakes may be made and we apologise in advance for any error that may occur. Please let us know if you believe or know of any error. Our current email address may be found on the www.carltonware.com web site.

Guide to Pricing

This catalogue includes a price guide. Prices are, of course, very subjective and very fluid. They can change enormously with demand and fashion. Our price estimates assume that the pieces are complete and "perfect". We have tried to reflect the prices that you might find being used by reputable antique dealers. These prices may seem higher than some other mediums but good dealers have their reputations to maintain and usually provide some guarantee of satisfaction.

The internet is a relatively easy way to buy almost anything nowadays and this includes Carlton Ware. Prices on Internet auction sites such as eBay may be quite a bit lower, particularly if there is any doubt about condition. Before you buy, ask for a detailed condition report and check the seller's feedback for any negative comments. Remember there is often a risk involved with using this method and this may be reflected in the final price. A bargain that is too good to be true can sometimes be too good to be true.

If you buy from an auction house you should view the items carefully and ask for condition reports. This may be your only means of redress should you find any damage or restoration after the auction, otherwise you will still be liable to pay for the items. Also, remember to add the buyer's premium of up to 17.5% into the equation as this is added to the selling price upon winning the bid.

Prices do vary from country to country. Also, you may find price fluctuations between regions of a country. For example, prices in the Northern regions of the UK may be lower than the prices in the Southern regions.

Frequently a shape may have been produced in a number of sizes and colours. In this case we have indicated a wider price range within the price guides. Larger pieces nearly always demand higher prices as do certain colours. Where the latter applies we have indicated this in the text. Occasionally we have placed a question mark for a price, this is where we believe a piece may exist but we have not seen it for sale!

Damaged and restored pieces are obviously worth less than "perfect" pieces. And, good restoration can sometimes be difficult to spot, so it's very important that you are able to trust the seller to inform you of the presence of any restoration work. It's unlikely that many embossed pieces have been restored but chips, firing faults and hairline cracks can be an issue to consider.

Compiling a price guide on such a large variety and spectrum of wares that Carlton Ware produced has been a daunting task. We were aware that we weren't going to please everyone. But, we felt it was important to take on this challenging project. Our task was compounded by the fact that this is the first time that such a comprehensive guide has been written. Please accept our apologies in advance for any seemingly obvious errors or inaccuracies. Our intention was never to cause any offence or in any way inflate or devalue your stock or collection.

Please be assured that the price guide will be an ongoing project that will be subject to amendments and/or corrections in future updated editions.

A Brief History of Carlton Ware

Carlton Ware began life in 1890, with a partnership by J. F. Wiltshaw and J. A. & W. H. Robinson. This gave birth to a company that lasted for more than a century albeit with several changes of ownership. Nowadays Carlton Ware is well known all over the world where it is collected and sold.

The early Carlton Ware products were the *Victorian Blush Ware* which were, and remain, very popular. At the turn of the century, the *Crested Ware* line was introduced followed by matt black ware with floral decorations and a range of *Cloisonne* that was outlined in gilt to resemble the well known jewellery range. The *Oriental* designs were introduced between the two World Wars. This, combined with a series of lustre finishes, put Carlton Ware at the forefront of the market.

In 1925 the first of the embossed *Salad Wares* appeared, these contained vivid red painted Crabs and Lobsters amongst other things. By the late 1920's, the range of Carlton Ware had expanded to include more modestly priced tableware, and Carlton Ware was the first manufacturer to offer the very popular *Oven to Table* wares in 1929.

In the early 1930's beautiful embossed patterns such as *Fruit Basket, Anemone, Gum Nut, Oak Tree* and *Rock Garden* were introduced. These were multi-coloured and very popular.

By the mid 1930's, the Japanese had become very proficient at copying good quality wares and Carlton Ware became a target for them. Their prices for the imitations were much lower than the genuine originals. Carton Ware discovered a clause in the *South East Asia Treaty Organisation* which concerned Australia and Japan. This treaty stated that the Japanese could not copy designs registered in Australia. Carlton Ware took advantage of this treaty and registered a large number of designs in Australia. This explains the *Registered Australian Design* back stamp on many of these wares.

World War II effectively stopped the production of anything except utility wares. However, during this period, new production methods were introduced and the lustre ranges were produced in the *Royale* range of colours. New hand-painted decorations were also added to include *Spider's Web, New Mikado* and *New Storks*. In parallel with these finer wares, fruit and floral designs also continued to be made and the range was expanded to include *Hydrangea, Vine, Grape, Poppy* and *Daisy.*

The 1950's was probably the most productive period in the Carlton Ware history. Most of the Carlton Ware being produced now contained the word *Handpainted* on the back stamp, regardless of whether it was or wasn't. *Windswept, Leaf* and *Pinstripe* were added to the range and a steady production of lustre wares was maintained. In 1958, the company officially changed its name to Carlton Ware Ltd. The 1970's led to the introduction of the *Walking Ware* range. This novelty ware gained immediate popularity.

With the recession in the early 1980's the Receivers were called into the Copeland Street works in 1989. Although there was a short period of production of Carlton Ware between 1990 and 1992, the name then remained dormant until 1997 when Francis Joseph acquired it together with a number of moulds and a few pre-production models.

Shape Numbers and Dates

Most, but not all, Carlton Ware has an impressed number on the base which is known as the "shape" of the piece. The following table indicates approximately when a shape was first introduced. These dates will only indicate how old the item might be but cannot be a guarantee of its age. Some shapes were re-introduced at a later date and this is indicated in the table.

Shape Number	Date when first introduced	
Upto 1000	upto 1934	Crab and Lobster Salad Ware, Fruit Basket, Cottage
1000 - 1100	1934	Gum nut, Anemone, Bluebell, Crinoline Lady
1100 - 1200	1934 - 1935	Oak Tree, Lemon
1200 - 1300	1935	Rock Garden, Moderne, Crab, Musical Mugs & Jugs
1300 - 1400	1935 - 1936	Curled Lettuce, Buttercup
1400 - 1500	1936 - 1937	Tulip, Daisy, Blackberry, Raspberry, Pear
1500 - 1600	1937 - 1938	Water Lily, Wild Rose, Crocus, Musical Mugs & Jugs, Thistle
1600 - 1700	1938 - 1939	Red Currant, Apple Blossom
1700 - 1800	1939	Water Lily, Crocus, Pyrethrum, Clover, Shamrock, Narcissus, Begonia, Campion, Crinoline Lady, Bell, Daffodil, Arum Lily, Gladioli, Forget me not
1800 - 1900	1939 - 1940	Lily, Margarite, Foxglove
1900 - 2000	1940 - 1945	Basket, Chestnut, Clematis, Primula, Cherry, Wallflower, Dogshead
2000 - 2100	1945 - 1950	Delphinium, Apple Blossom, Poppy, Late Buttercup or Buttercup Garland, New Daisy, Poppy and Daisy, Hydrangea, Salad Ware
2100 - 2200	1950 - 1953	Wild Rose, Card Series, Langouste
2200 - 2300	1953 - 1955	Grape
2300 - 2400	1955 - 1958	Guinness figures, Hazel Nut, Leaf Salad
2400 - 2500	1958 - 1959	Windswept, Pinstripe, Langouste, Convolvulus, Fruit Ware, Novelty Cruet, Linen
2500 - 2600	1959 - 1964	Magnolia, Orchid, Aladdin's Lamp
2600 - 2700	1964 - 1968	Guinness Penguin Lamp, Carlton Village, Orbit, Floral Spray
2700 - 2800	1968	Guinness, Tapestry, Onion, Daisy Chain
2800 - 2900	1968 - 1969	Military, Athena, Skye, Vine
2900 - 3000	1969 - 1970	Wellington, Sunflower, Money Box - Flat
3000 - 3100	1970 - 1971	New Buttercup, Somerset, Money Box, Money Box - Bug Eyes
3100 - 3200	1971 - 1976	Early Walking Ware, Apple Blossom, Later Walking Ware, Flow Blue
3200 - 3300	1976 - 1980	Dovecote, Hovis, Pig
3300 - 3400	1980 - 1985	Charles & Di, Walking Ware Big Feet
3400 - 3500	1985 - 1986	Robertson Golly
3500+	1986+	Coronation Street

Carlton Ware Back-Stamps

For completeness we have included the full range of Carlton Ware Back-Stamps. These provide an approximate indication of the date that a piece of Carlton Ware might have been made. Some fake pieces of Carlton Ware have a back-stamp from the wrong date period.

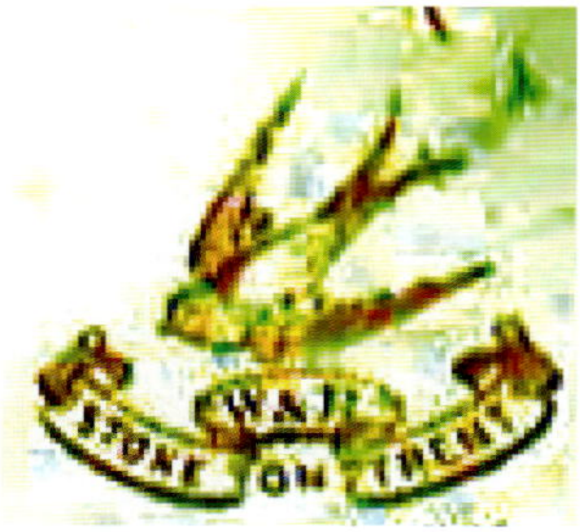

Ribbon or Blue Bird
1890 - 1894

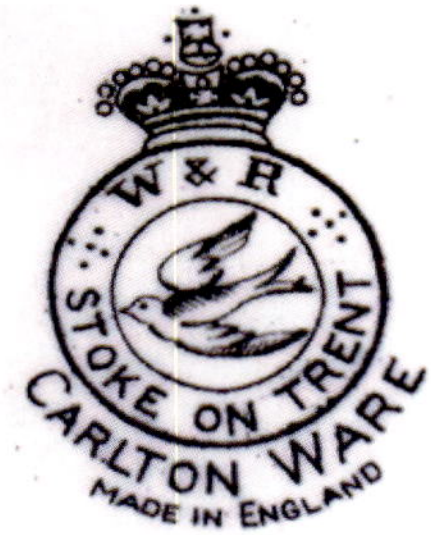

Crown
1894 - 1927

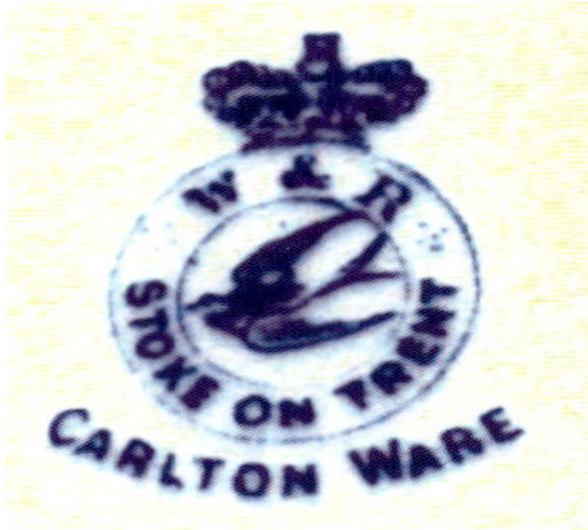

Crown variation
1906 - 1927

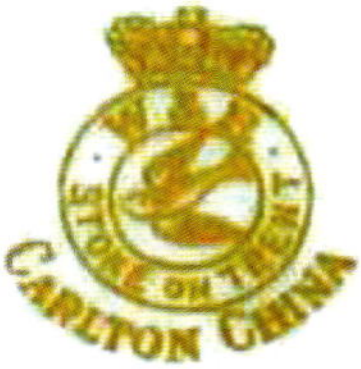

Carlton China Crown
1906 - 1927

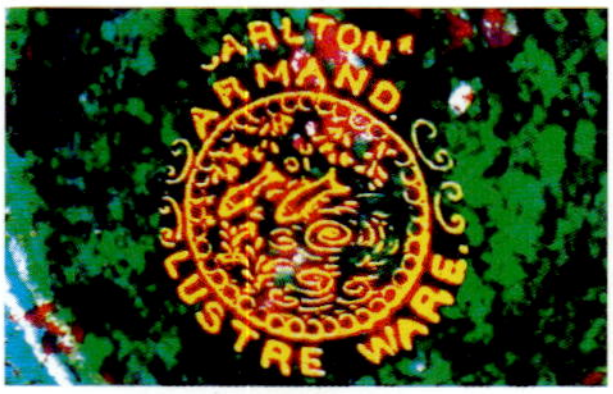

Armand Lustre,
Late 1910's - early 1920's

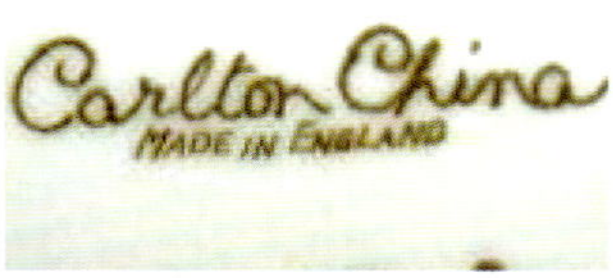

Carlton China
1925 - 1957

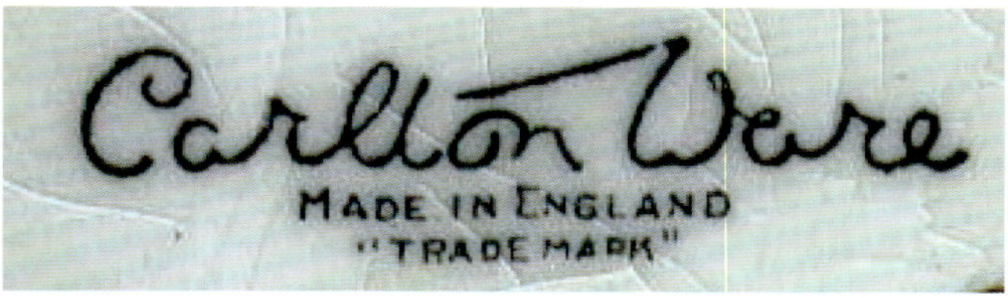

Script
1925 - 1970

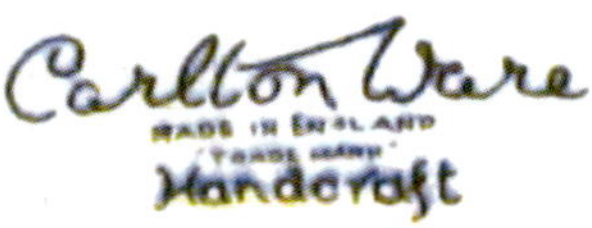

Handcraft
1929 - 1939

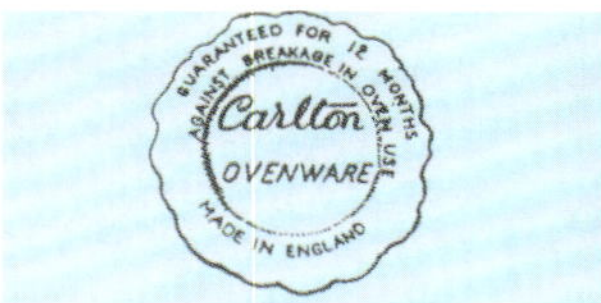

Ovenware
1929 - 1942

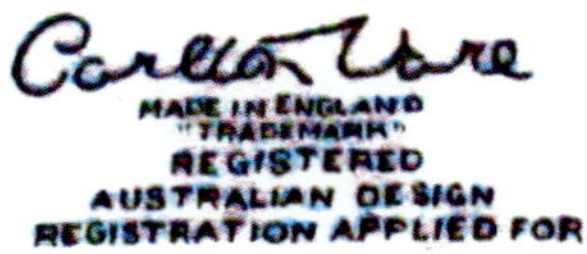

Australian
1935 - 1961

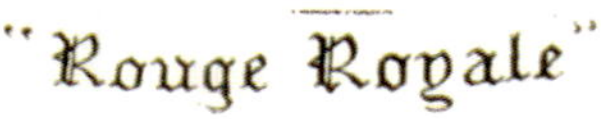

Rouge Royale (Red).
1940+

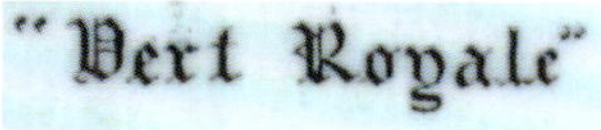

Vert Royale (Green).
1940+

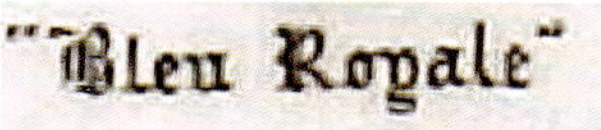

Bleu Royale (Blue).
1940+

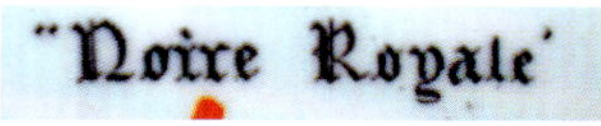

Noire Royale (Black).
1940+

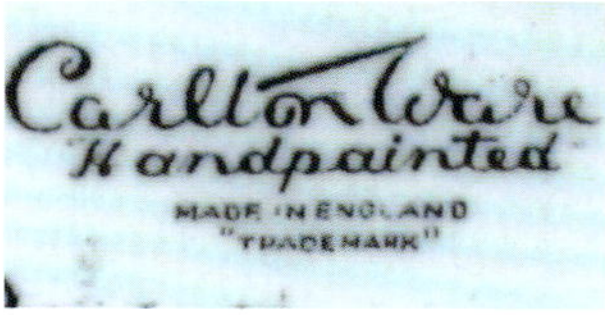

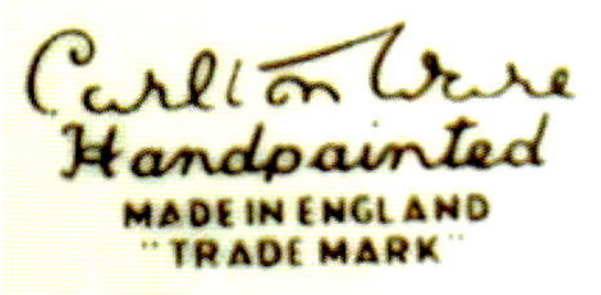

Handpainted
1952 - 1962

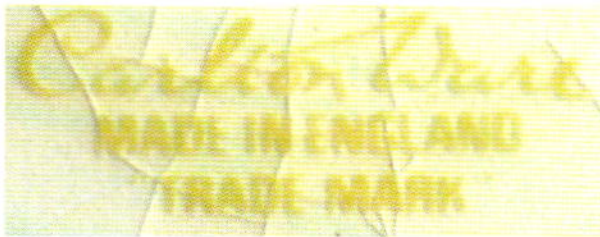

Yellow Script
1967-1987

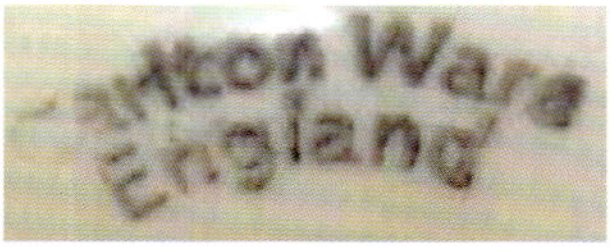

Curved
1967 - 1989

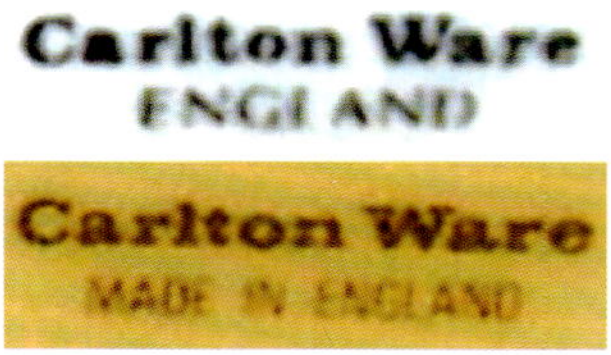

Plain
1968 - 1990

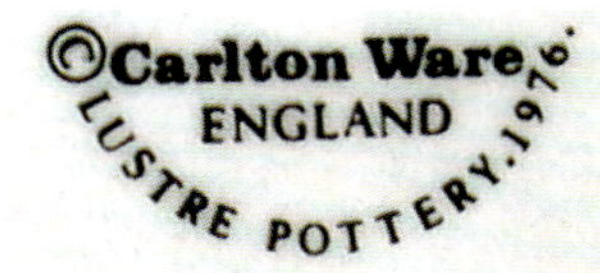

Lustre Pottery
1973 - 1989

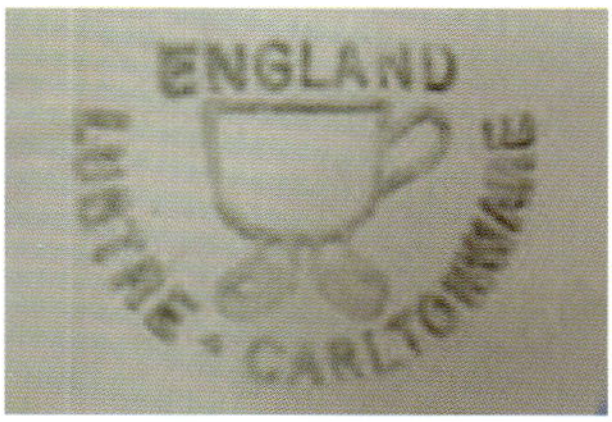

Walking Lustre
Used on Walking Ware
1973 - 1989

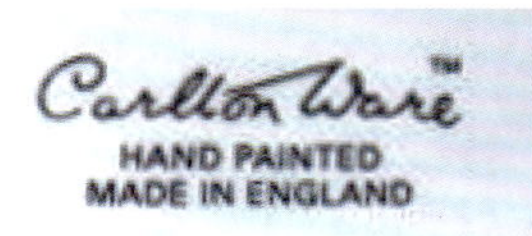

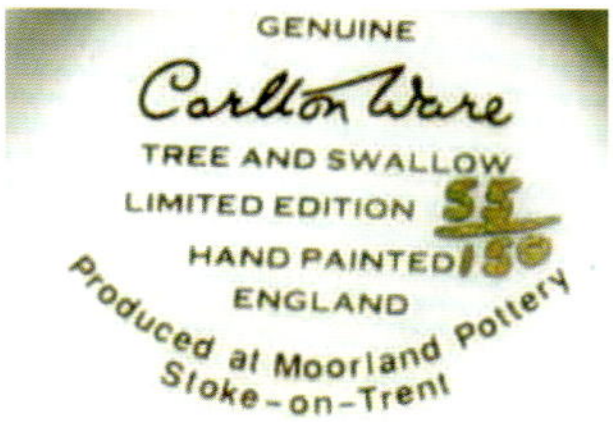

Recent Francis Joseph Back Stamps
1997 -

British Registered Design Number

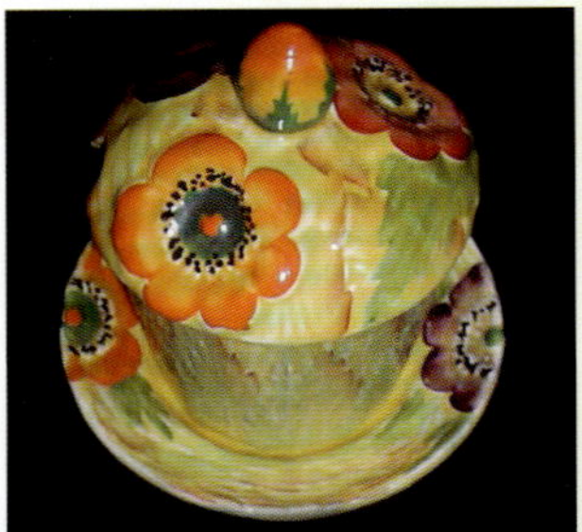

Rd No 786475
Registered in 1933

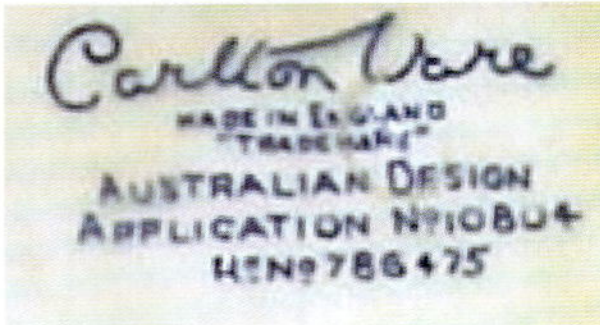

Registered Design numbers are a consecutive numbering system which was first introduced in Britain in 1884. The Registered Design number, usually written as Rd followed by the number gives the date when that design was registered. Original designs were usually registered to help prevent copying. The number was shown on the base of some pieces of Carlton Ware, particularly the older W & R pieces.

Details of when Rd numbers were registered may be found in the table. Note that for simplicity we have rounded off the Registered numbers to the nearest hundred. The date of registration does not necessarily mean the date of manufacture since production might have started a few years later. Also, a particular design may have been in continuous production for many years after being registered, so dates should not be taken as the exact date of manufacture.

Year	Rd No	Year	Rd No	Year	Rd No	Year	Rd No
1884	1 -	1909	535200 -	1934	789000 -	1959	891700 -
1885	19700 -	1910	552000 -	1935	799100 -	1960	895000 -
1886	40500 -	1911	574800 -	1936	808800 -	1961	899900 -
1887	64500 -	1912	594200 -	1937	817300 -	1962	904600 -
1888	90500 -	1913	612400 -	1938	825200 -	1963	909400 -
1889	116600 -	1914	630200 -	1939	832600 -	1964	914500 -
1890	141300 -	1915	644900 -	1940	837500 -	1965	919600 -
1891	163800 -	1916	653500 -	1941	838600 -	1966	924500 -
1892	185700 -	1917	659000 -	1942	839200 -	1967	929300 -
1893	205200 -	1918	662900 -	1943	840000 -	1968	934500 -
1894	224700 -	1919	666100 -	1944	841000 -	1969	939900 -
1895	247000 -	1920	673700 -	1945	842700 -	1970	944900 -
1896	268400 -	1921	680100 -	1946	845500 -	1971	950000 -
1897	291200 -	1922	687100 -	1947	849700 -	1972	955300 -
1898	311700 -	1923	695000 -	1948	853300 -	1973	960700 -
1899	331700 -	1924	702700 -	1949	857000 -	1974	965200 -
1900	351200 -	1925	710200 -	1950	860900 -	1975	969200 -
1901	368200 -	1926	718100 -	1951	863100 -	1976	973800 -
1902	385200 -	1927	726300 -	1952	866300 -	1977	978400 -
1903	402200 -	1928	734400 -	1953	869300 -	1978	982800 -
1904	424400 -	1929	742700 -	1954	872500 -	1979	987900 -
1905	447800 -	1930	751200 -	1955	876100 -	1980	993000 -
1906	471800 -	1931	760600 -	1956	879300 -	1981	998300 -
1907	494000 -	1932	769700 -	1957	882900 -	1982	1004500-
1908	518600 -	1933	779300 -	1958	887100 -		

Carlton Ware LTD.

FORMERLY Wiltshaw & Robinson Ltd

CARLTON WORKS
STOKE-ON-TRENT
ENGLAND

CATALOGUE & PRICE GUIDE by Dr Czes & Yvonne Kosniowski

CARLTON WARE LIMITED

From January 1st 1959, all prices are strictly nett.

Orders of £25 and over will be sent carriage and cartons free.

Fruit Basket

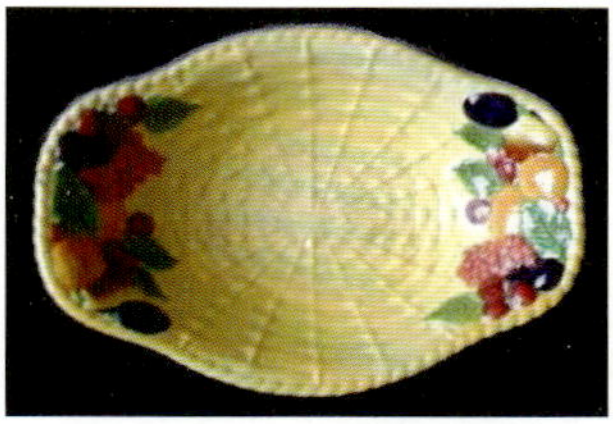

Carlton Ware introduced the embossed *Fruit Basket* range in the early 1930's; making it one of the very early embossed ranges. It was introduced after the *Salad ware* range and around the time of other brightly coloured and bold designs.

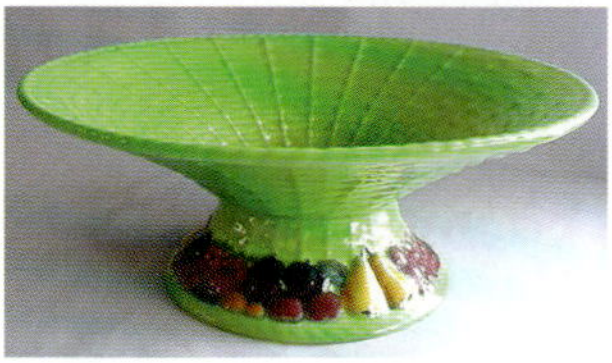

Fruit Basket is highly coloured and appears in vivid yellow and a paler yellow, green and a vivid orange colour. The variations of vivid and pale colours could be attributable to items being made for the home and the Australian market; the pieces destined for the Australian market were often coloured with more depth to compensate for the bright sunshine there.

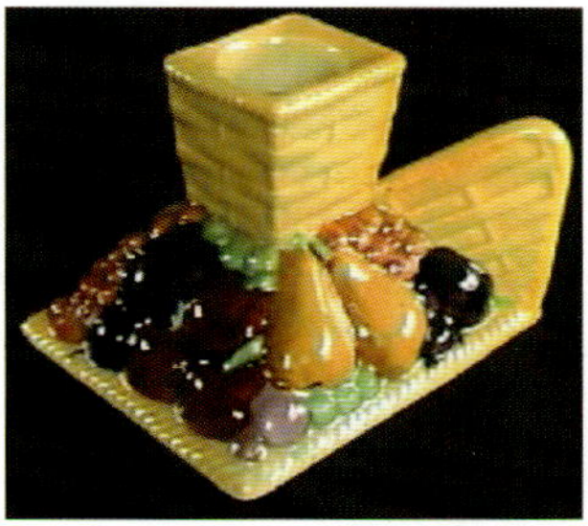

The look achieved is an accurate depiction of a basket weave. The embossed fruit is a variety of brightly coloured fruits that are interspersed with sprigs of leaves. The finish of the design is very highly glazed which at the time was considered quite an expensive format to create. This range is quite a rare find and is perhaps attributable to the fact that it did not continue in production for many years.

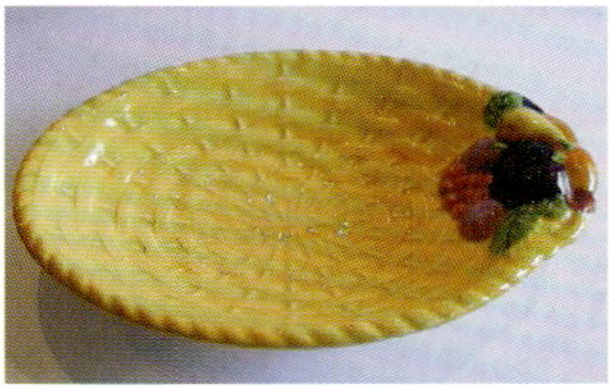

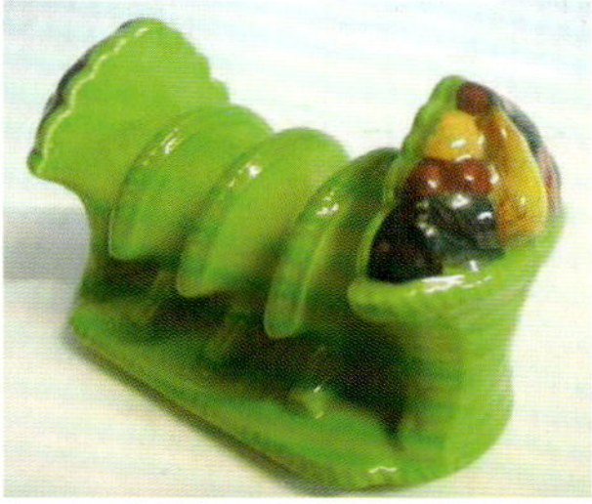

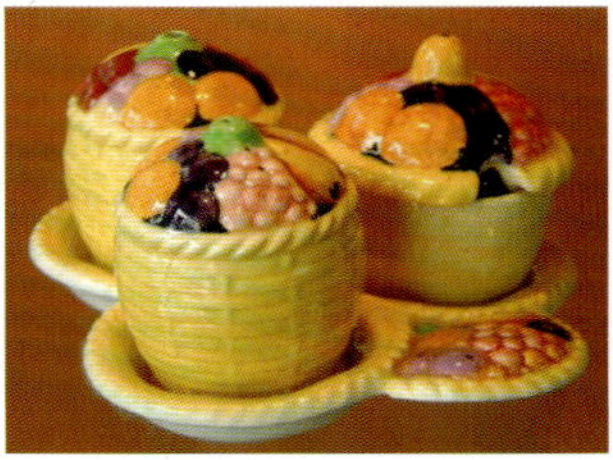

245 Small Preserve Pot £45 - £65
711 Preserve Pot £55 - £75
760 Bowl £30 - £45
761 Cruet £120 - £170
830 Jug and Stand £70 - £90
876 Comport £50 - £80
995 Pitcher £75 - £95
Basket, handled £65 - £85
Biscuit Barrel £100 - £140
Candlestick £55 - £80
Covered Cheese £175 - £225
Creamer £40 - £60 Large Milk Jug £75 - £95
Grapefruit £50 - £70
Jug, narrow waist £50 - £75
Napkin Ring £30 - £50
Oval Tray £30 - £45
Plate £25 - £35
Reamer (Lemon Squeezer) £60 - £80
Round Bowl £30 - £45
Round Tray £35 - £50
Salad Bowl £50 - £75
Sugar Bowl £40 - £60 Sugar Shaker £80 - £110
Toast Rack, 3 bar £55 - £75
Toast Rack, 5 bar £60 - £85
Toast Rack, combination £120 - £160
Tri-dish £45 - £65
Vase £30 - £45

Cottage Ware

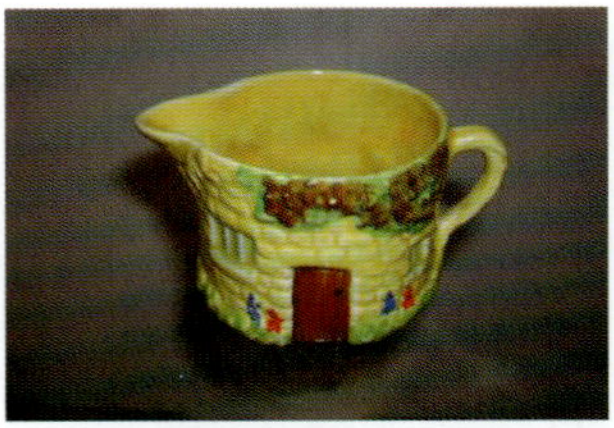

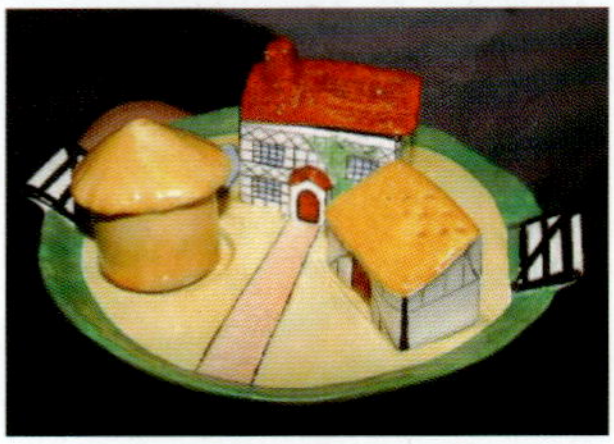

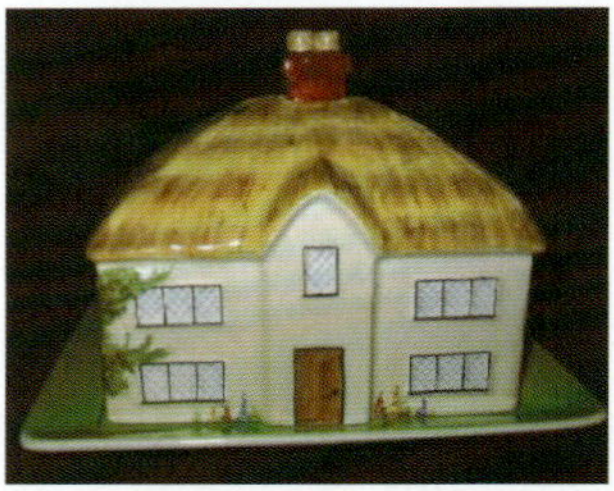

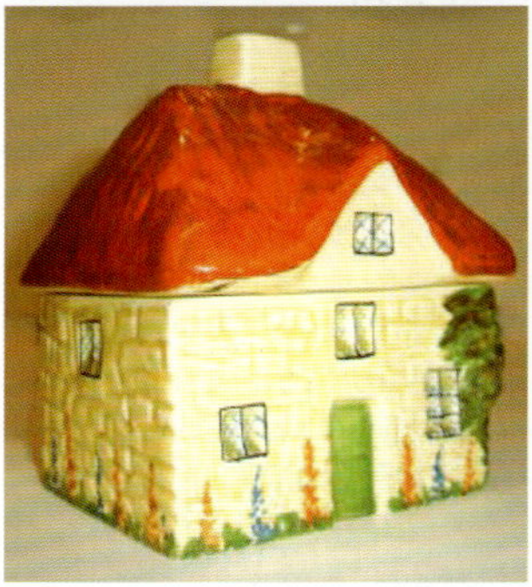

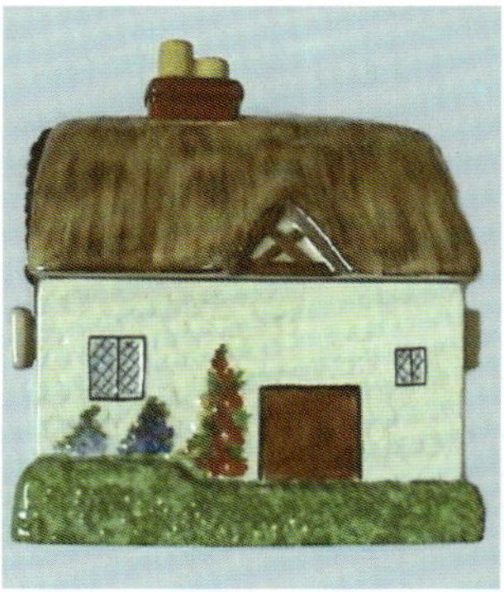

Carlton Ware registered this range in the early 1930's and may have produced them some time around that date or within a few years of that date. The British Registered Design Number sometimes appears on the base of a piece. It indicates when the design was registered but does not validate the actual production date.

Cottage Ware is a lovely depiction of quaint old English country cottages that were hand painted. The logo that can be found on most pieces is the black script mark, which ties in with the 1930's date.

There are seven pieces in this range. The photograph of the Jug shows this without a lid but this would render it as the only piece in the range without a roof! That seems unlikely and we feel that it would have been designed with some sort of a lid to make it look more like a complete cottage. The colourway is a creamy beige.

The Cruet set came in at least two different styles, one in a delightful display of three cottages shown in a copse with a small pathway and edged with a hedge and two gates on a circular stand. The other design is of the more conventional rectangular style with a cottage mustard pot, which is flanked by two topiary style trees for the salt and pepper pots.

The cheese or butter dish can be found in the usual yellow with a green base and a matt cream colourway.

The preserve pots come in two different styles, one a more unusual round shape like a bee hive in a brown colourway and the other is a square shape cottage in a yellow colourway.

The other shapes in this range consist of a biscuit barrel, toast rack and the more unusual sugar shaker. The Sugar Shaker comes in four colours representing Spring, Summer, Autumn and Winter.

Milk Jug £40 - £60
Cruet Set, 2 styles £100 - £200
Cheese or Butter Dish £70 - £95
Preserve Pot, 2 styles £70 - £95
Biscuit Barrel £80 - £120
Toast Rack £60 - £80
Sugar Shaker £80 - £100

Anemone

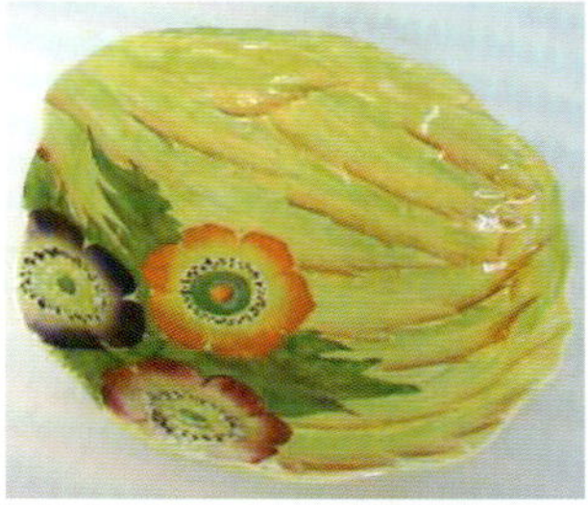

The story behind the name "anemone" is of life and death. The word comes from the Greek language and means "windflower". According to Greek Mythology the anemone flower sprang up from the blood of Aphrodite's slain lover, Adonis. The word "windflower" signifies that the wind that blows the petal open will also blow the dead petals away.

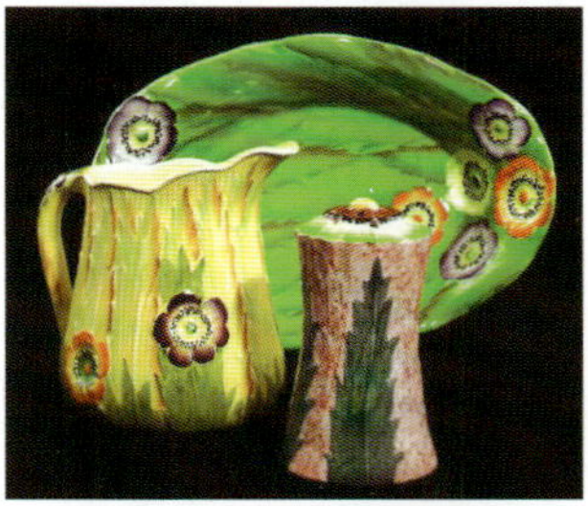

Carlton Ware introduced the *Anemone* range in 1934. It was one of the first of the "floral embossed" range made by Carlton Ware. It is very collectable.

The pattern was produced in three colours: yellow, green and pink; all with many different coloured flower heads.

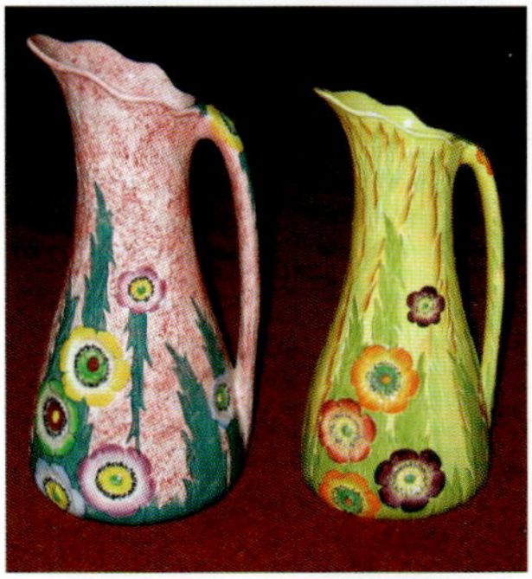

925, 979, 1174 Preserve Cover, Base & Pot £120 - £175
928 Tray £75 - £110
932 or 935 Plate £75 - £110
933 Leaf Tray, one hole for handle £80 - £150
945 Biscuit Barrel £250 - £350
946 Square Salad Bowl & Servers £350 - £450
970 Small Bowl £45 - £70
975 Flower Jug, Pitcher, 3 sizes £200 - £400
976 Bowl £75 - £110
978 Jug £100 - £130
983 Cress Dish and Tray £150 - £190
1014, 1015 Round Plate 4", 8" £75 - £110
1026 Tea Pot £300 - £420
1027 Sugar £60 - £85
1028 Cream £60 - £85
1029 & 1030 Cup & Saucer £150 - £200

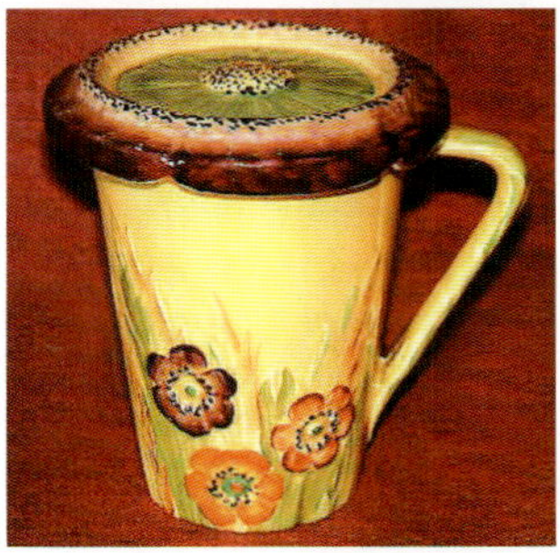

1031 Puff (Bowl with feet plus lid) £160 - £190
1032 Mayonnaise (Puff with spoon) £185 - £265
1033 Sugar Sifter £90 - £125
1041 Trinket Tray £75 - £110
1042 Bee Box £100 - £120
1067 Vase £100 - £120
1068 Covered Mug £190 - £250
1069 Flower Pot £70 - £100
1096 Butter, small £45 - £70
1097 & 1029 Morning Tray & Cup £100 - £125
1753, 1761, 1762 Butter, Spoon, Knife £75 - £110
Candle Holder £120 - £150

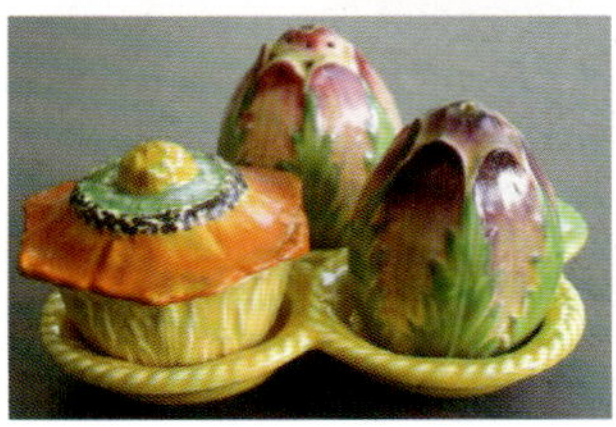

Comport £190 - £250
Covered Cheese £230 - £325
Cruet £190 - £225
Goblet £80 - £110

Gum Nut

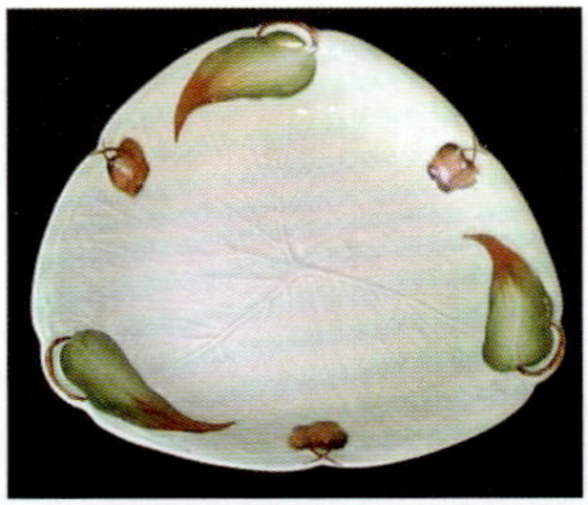

Carlton Ware introduced the embossed *Gum Nut* pattern in 1934. The only colourway it was produced in was green; it is highly glazed. The design incorporates the realistic veins of a leaf embossed into the finish and the design often resembles the shape of a leaf where appropriate (such as a plate or tray). It has realistic brown nuts or seeds hanging from brownish tinted stems. The accompanying green leaves are tinged with brown similar to a maturing leaf.

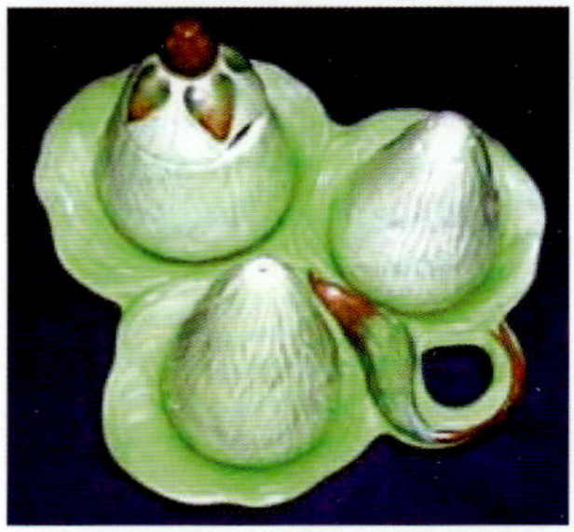

It is possible that the *Gum Nut* pattern was inspired by the Eucalyptus tree; possibly a variety such as the blue gum eucalyptus.

One of the features of Carlton Ware was the fact that they always included a lot of attention to detail within the design and that is probably why their hallmark is synonymous with quality.

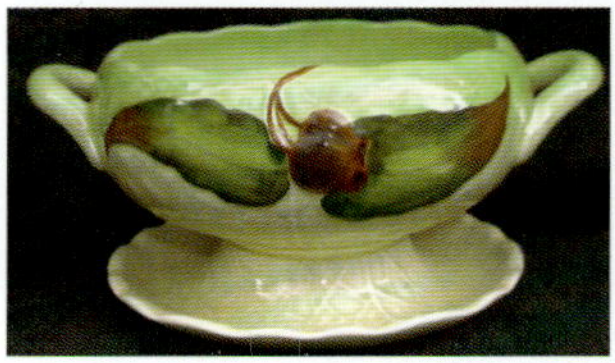

A design that is probably similar to and could be confused with *Gum Nut* is *Gum Tree*. This was produced around the mid to late 1930's and was made in a similar green colourway. The pattern of *Gum Tree* is more decorative and includes beautiful seed flowers. It is not an embossed pattern and so is smooth in finish and doesn't have the veins of a leaf embossed into the pieces.

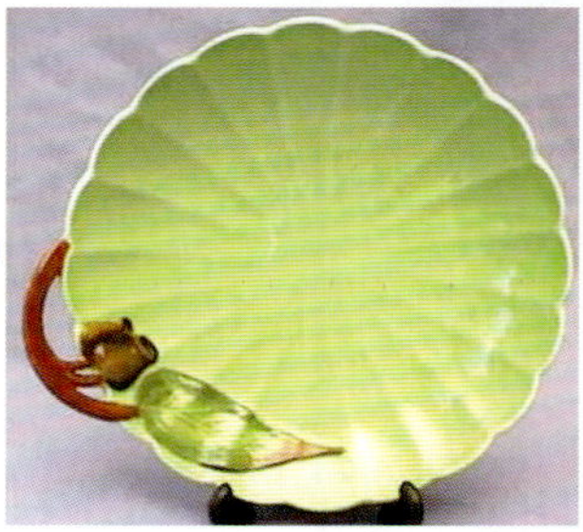

949 Round Plate £20 - £35
950 Long Tray £25 - £40
952 Preserve Pot £40 - £60
1009, 1010, 1011, 1084 Triangular Tray 9", 7", 6", 8" £25 - £40
1035 Grapefruit £30 - £60
1036 Toast Rack, 3 bar £30 - £50
1037 & 1038 Sauceboat & Stand £30 - £50
1040 Sauce Container £30 - £50
1043 Sugar Bowl £15 - £30
1044 Milk or Creamer £15 - £30
1045 Cruet Set £35 - £60
1063, 1064, 1066 Salad Spoon, Fork & Bowl £50 - £70
1082 Toast Rack, 5 bar £40 - £60
1086 Rectangular Tray £25 - £40
1089 Leaf Butter £25 - £45
1100, 1101 Sauceboat & Stand, Large Size £30 - £50
1120 Mayonnaise £35 - £55
Cup & Saucer £20 - £40
Jug & Lemon Squeezer £40 - £60

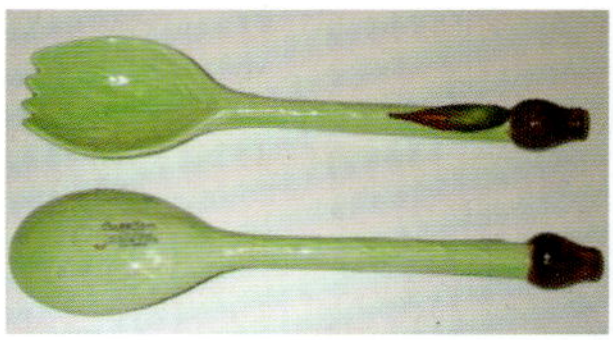

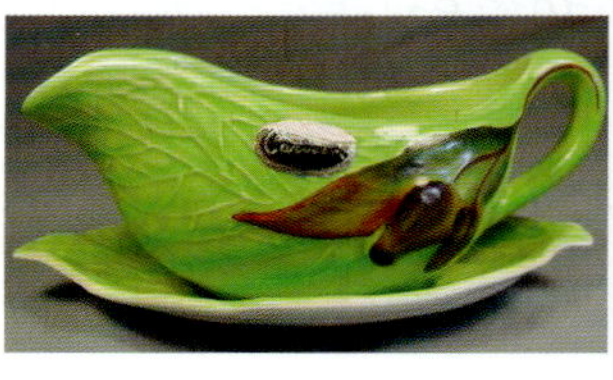

Crinoline Lady

In Victorian times feminine underclothing was fancy, frilly and lacy. It was also, often, outlandish. Ladies wore lots of flounces beneath their outer clothing. Well, that was the case for the rich and wealthy but the poorer women would have dispensed with the adornments of lace and ribbons. During this time, women were made to feel unimportant by society and useless apart from mothering children. So psychologically, the more space that women took up helped to make them feel more important.

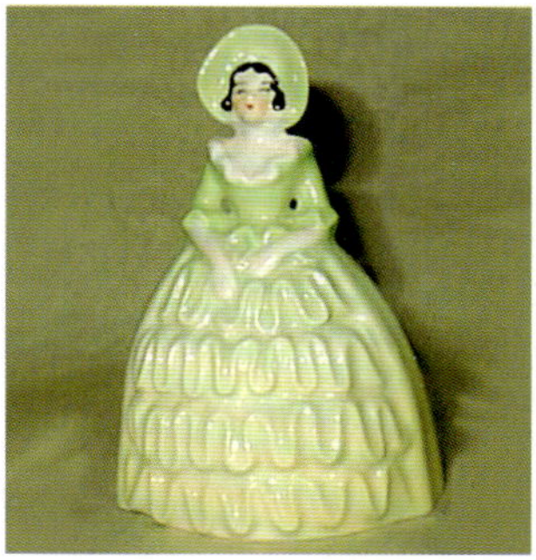

The crinoline made its appearance in the early 1840's. Because it had an excessively large skirt the crinoline made the waist appear comparatively small. It was made from a band or braid of horsehair, *crin* being the French word for horsehair and *linum* means linen or cotton.

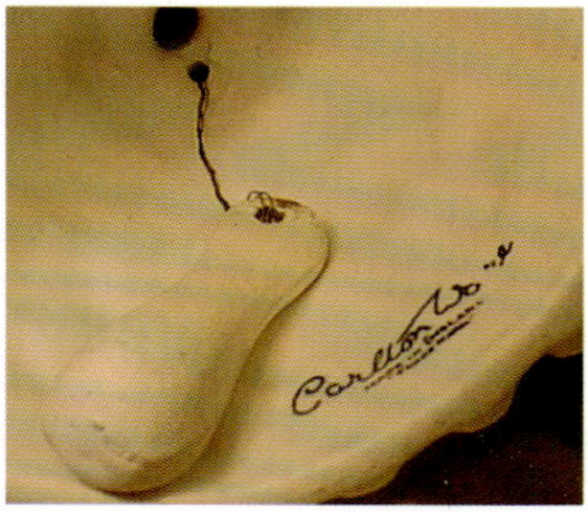

In the mid 1850's the hoop skirt was invented. This was hailed as a liberating device for women - they no longer would have to wear layer upon layer of hot, heavy and itchy horsehair to hold out their skirts in the fashionable bell shape. Although they still had the corset!

The new hoop skirt or cage crinoline was made out of watch-spring or steel. It was light and airy and the lady could walk around without having numerous petticoats wrap and tangle around her legs! Crinolines in various forms lasted until about 1887.

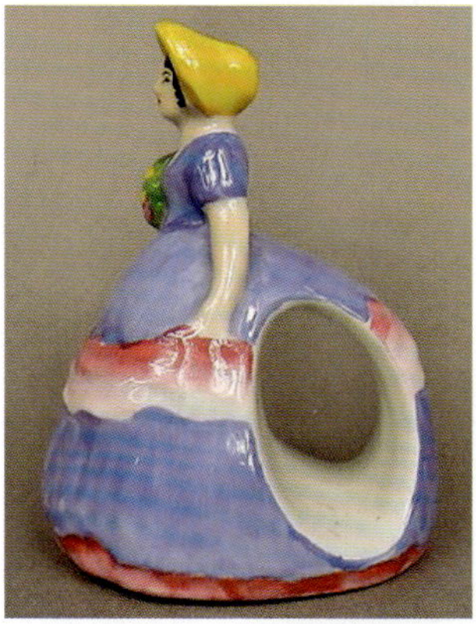

There are several Carlton Ware items showing Crinolines. These include Napkin Holders, Bells and Cruet Sets.

The Napkin Holders and Bells were made in the 1930's. The Bell is very much rarer than the Napkin Holders.

The Cruet Set comes with a lady and 3 condiment pieces. You can see the largeness of the Crinoline. We are aware of two colourways - pink and green. Warning: There are fake versions of these sets in both colourways. These fake pieces are usually painted in just one colour and have no facial or hair details on the lady.

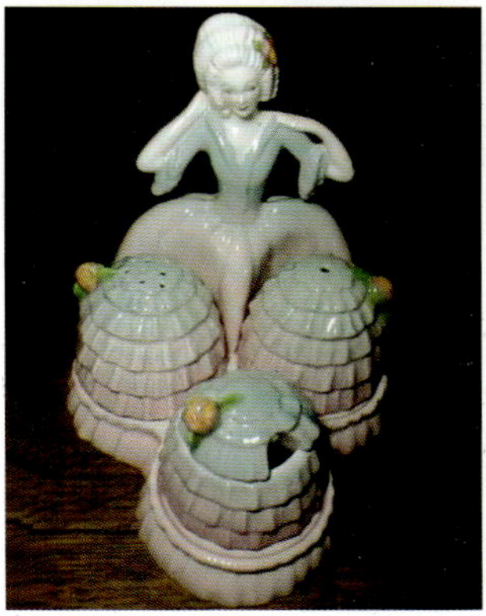

1012 Bell £110 - £160
1138 Napkin Holder £60 - £90
1705 Cruet Set £120 - £180

Bluebell

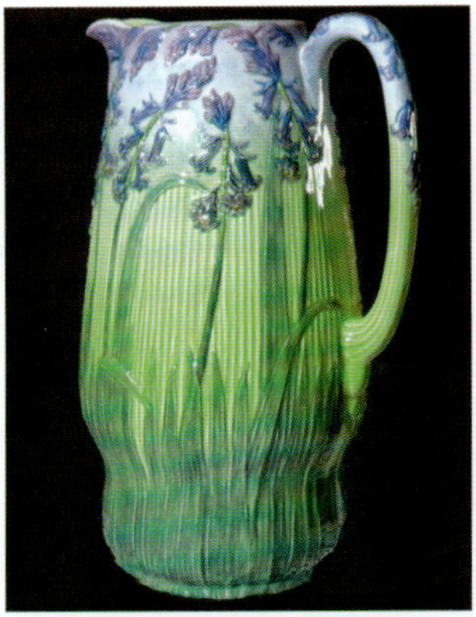

This seems to be a one-off pattern which was only produced in a jug.

We have also seen "uncoloured" pieces, unlike the blue and green in the picture here.

1099 Jug £200 - £300

Lemon

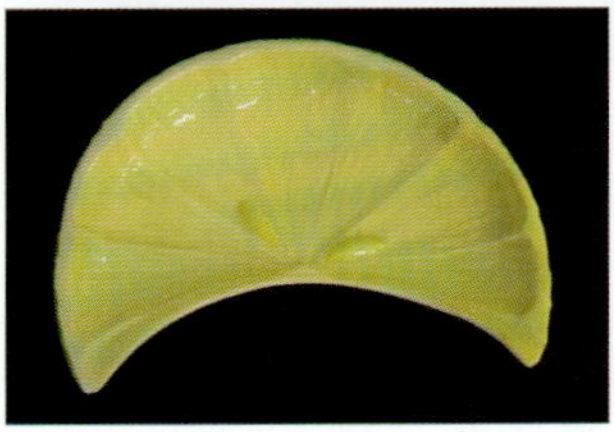

The main range of Fruit Ware was introduced in the 1950's. This *Lemon Wedge* dish appears to have been made in the mid 1930's.

1170 Segmented Dish £40 - £60

Moderne

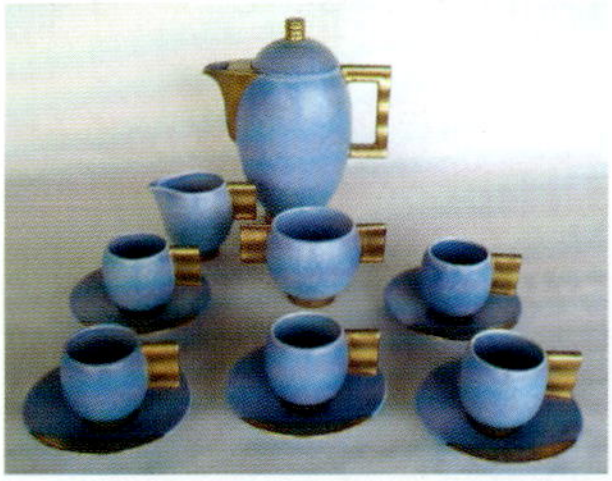

This Set was introduced in the mid 1930's. It was made in a variety of colours, usually two-tone. These colours include gold with blue, pink with grey, blue with grey and black with white.

It is quite common for Art-Deco Furniture dealers to use this coffee set to adorn their furniture.

1245 Tea Set £300 - £400
1246 Coffee Set £300 - £400

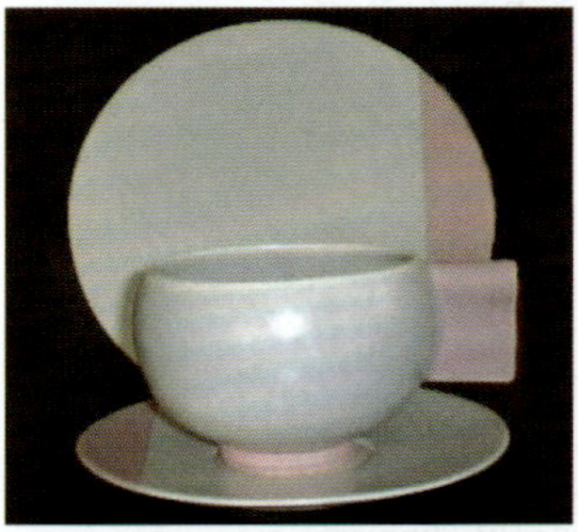

Crab and Crab & Lobster

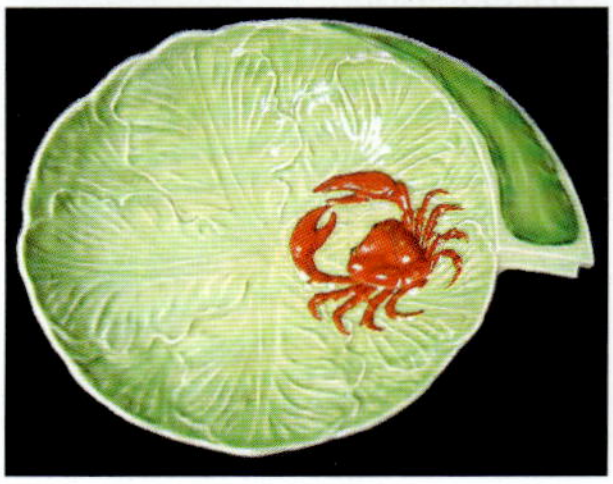

Carlton Ware introduced their first *Salad Ware* range in the 1920's. Some of these were reintroduced in the 1930's. This piece has a red painted *Crab*. See later on for information about the *Curled Lettuce* range.

1270 (Crab) Butter £20 - £40
1280 (Crab & Lobster) Butter £20 - £40

Oak Tree

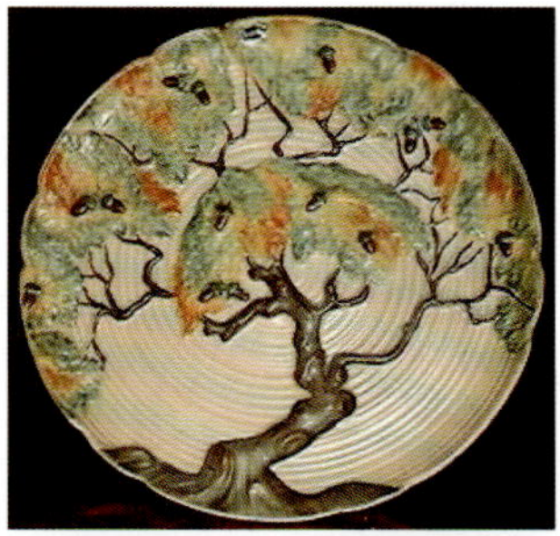

Oak trees are deciduous - broad-leaved trees that shed all their leaves each year. They can grow into huge spreading trees reaching 130 feet or 40 metres high. In Britain they can live for over 1,000 years. The lobed oblong leaves are familiar to most people and they are often represented in art. And, of course, Carlton Ware produced an embossed form of the oak.

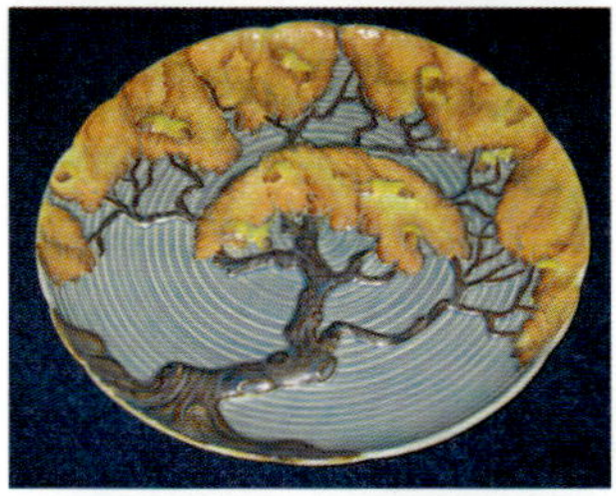

They introduced their *Oak Tree* range in the mid 1930's. They were produced in only two colourways: Pattern 3810 Blue ground, and Pattern 3811 Fawn ground. Many collectors claim that the two versions represent daytime and nighttime. Others claim that the fawn coloured pieces show an autumnal oak tree in greens and yellows with the acorns clearly visible. The acorns on the blue pieces are less visible. Carlton Ware produced 31 different shapes as listed below; many were produced in a variety of sizes.

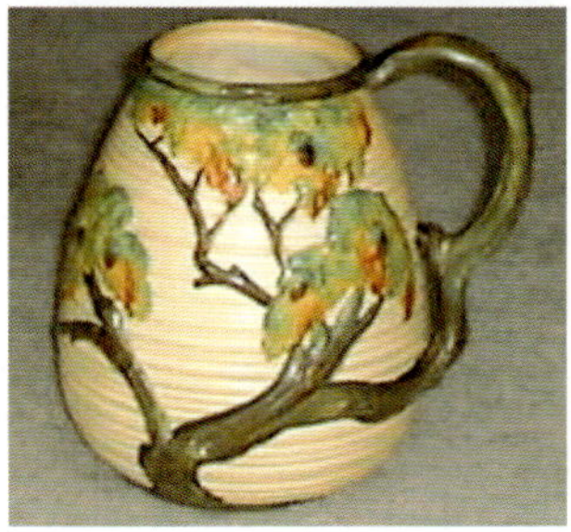

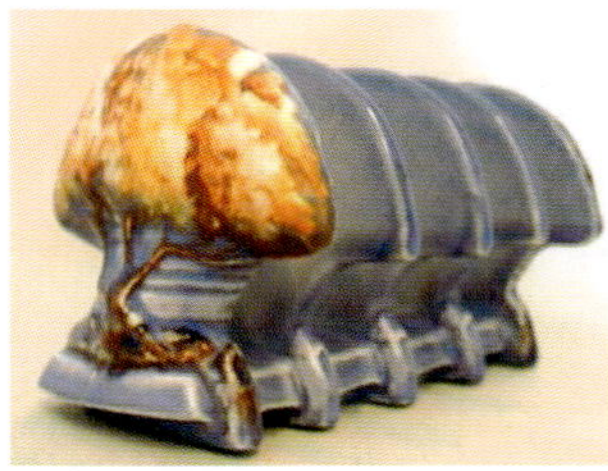

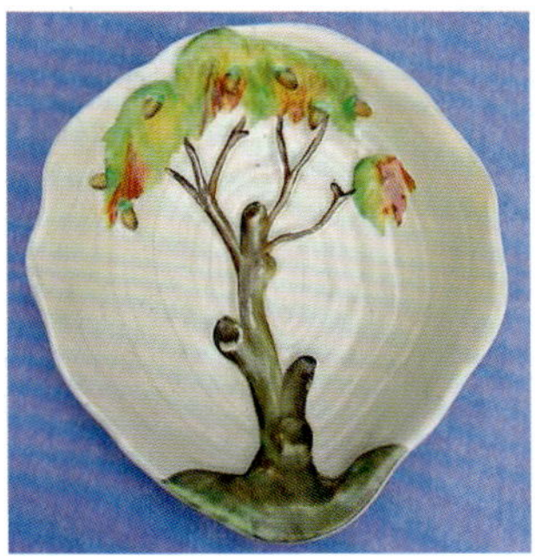

1098 Jug or Pitcher £120 - £160
1143 Ashtray £40 - £60
1144 Charger £100 - £150
1145 Candlestick, single £50 - £60
1146 Jug, 8" £100 - £130
1147 Cigarette Box £40 - £70
1148 Bowl, handled £60 - £90
1149 Toast Rack, 3 bar £40 - £50
1155 Match Holder £45 - £60
1162 Vase £50 - £70
1163 Vase, two handled £80 - £110
1164 Book Ends £140 - £170
1165 Oval Bowl £30 - £45
1166 Toast Rack, 5 bar £50 - £60
1167 Cheese Dish and Cover £80 - £100
1168 Butter, covered, square £60 - £80
1169 Leaf Butter £25 - £35
1175 Preserve with Base £60 - £80
1183 Cruet Set £130 - £160
1185 Cream £35 - £50
1186 Sugar £35 - £50
1187 Leaf Tray (s, m, l) £25 - £60
1188 Biscuit £70 - £100
1189 Sauceboat and Stand £40 - £60
1190 Sugar Sifter £70 - £90
1191 Jug, 6", 1 pint £120 - £150
1192 Double Candlestick £60 - £70
1193 Cigarette Holder and Ashtray £45 - £70
1194 Triple Tray £50 - £70
1208 Bon-bon dish £30 - £50
1214 Bowl, 3" £40 - £70

Mugs & Jugs, Musical

Carlton Ware made a number of *Musical Jugs* and *Mugs.* These have a removable music mechanism in the base that plays a tune. The tune is usually associated with the theme on the item. Some of the jugs and mugs have a relief mould while others have a smooth surface.

Carlton Ware introduced most of their *Musical Jugs* and *Mugs* in the 1930's. The first one was the *Humpty Dumpty Jug* which was made in about 1935. Some of the *Musical Jugs* and *Mugs* produced by Carlton Ware have the following shape numbers.

1213 Humpty Dumpty £100 - £200
1260 Hunting Scene Jug £40 - £80
1284 Hangsman £150 - £250
1289 Hunting Scene Mug £40 - £80
1543 Flower Mug £80 - £120
1549 Ghoules £100 - £200
1685 Grandfather Clock £150 - £250

The *Hunting Scene* Jug and Mug has a huntsman and hounds. It also has an ornately carved handle.

The *Hangsman* Mug has a red Mephistopheles handle. Many counterfeit copies are circulating, usually the counterfeit mug has a Wiltshaw and Robinson Crown Mark on the base.

The *Ghouls, Flower* and *Grandfather Clock* have one or more roses on the handle. The *Grandfather Clock* Jug has a single rose on the handle and a transfer print of a Grandfathers clock. This was made for Guinness.

The *Hangsman* Mug was also produced with no musical box. Two shape numbers are:

1285 Hangsman £80 - £150
1972 Hangsman, Plain Handle £40 - £80

The musical movements are easy to remove and many jugs and mugs nowadays have no musical movement. Carlton Ware did also sell the same shape jugs and mugs with or without any movements. An old Carlton Ware catalogue lists four of these jugs and mugs with prices for the items "with music" and "no music".

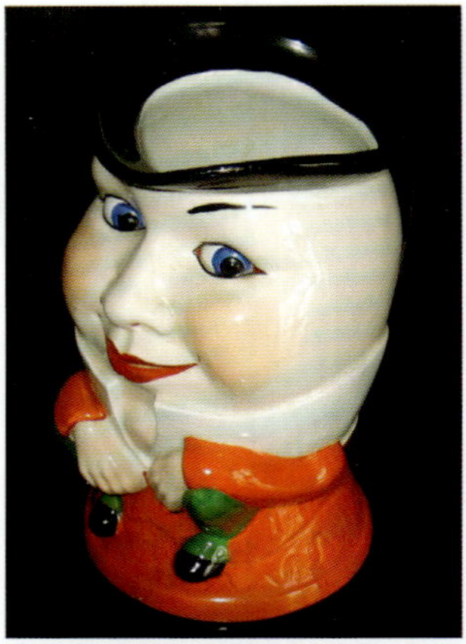

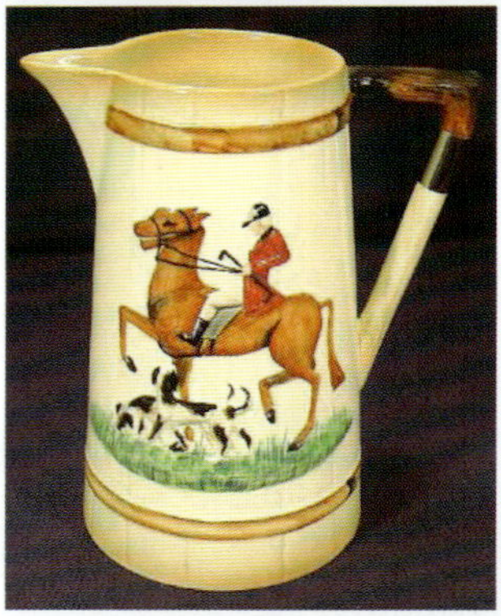

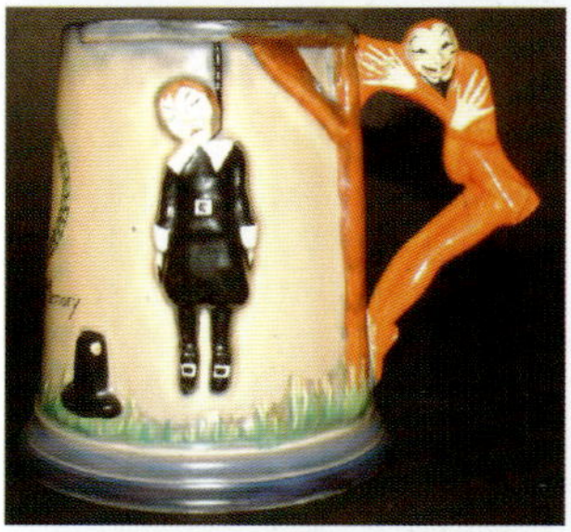

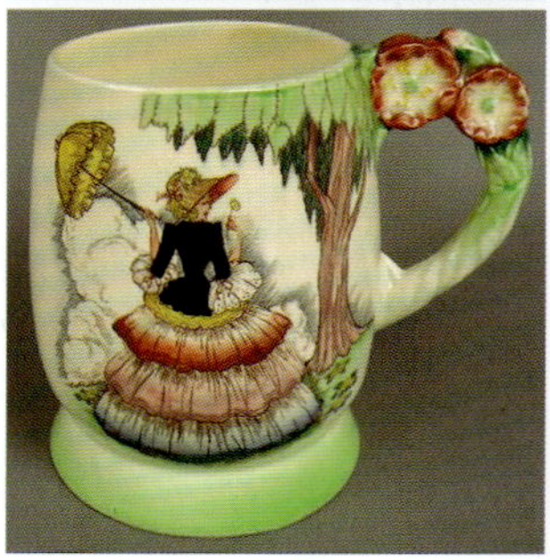

Rock Garden

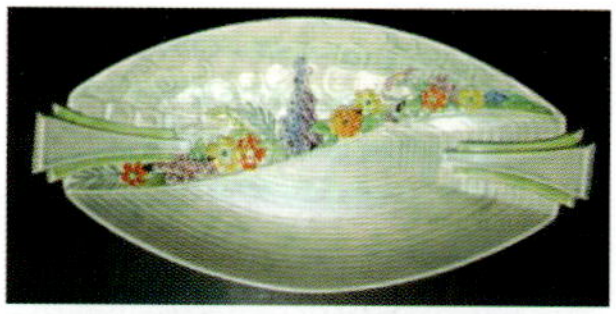

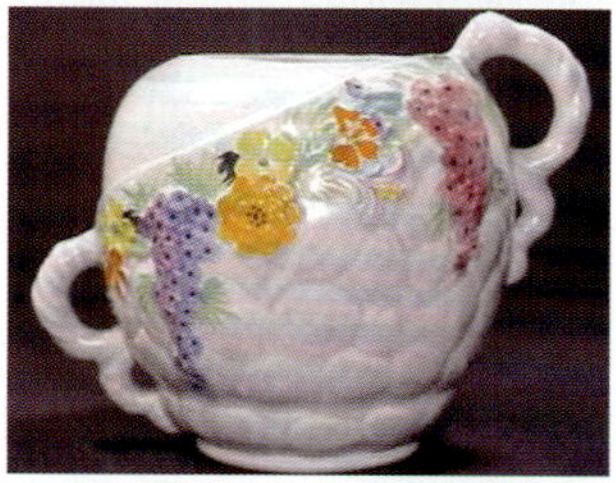

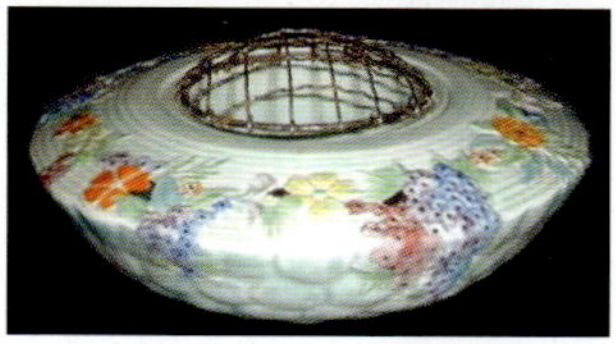

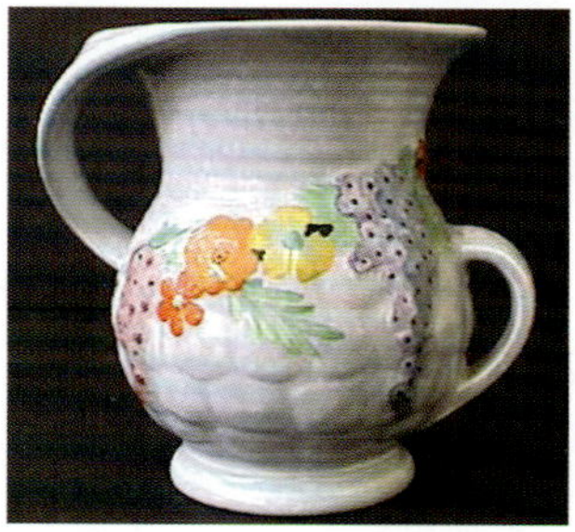

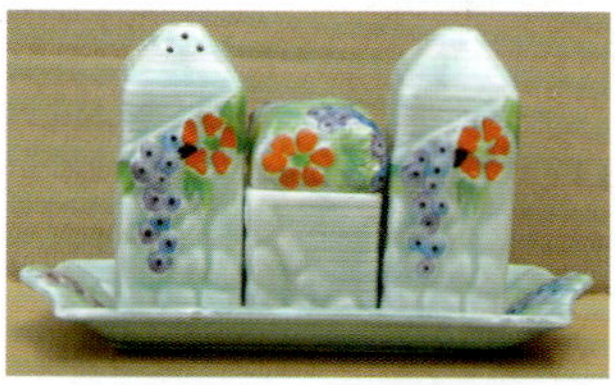

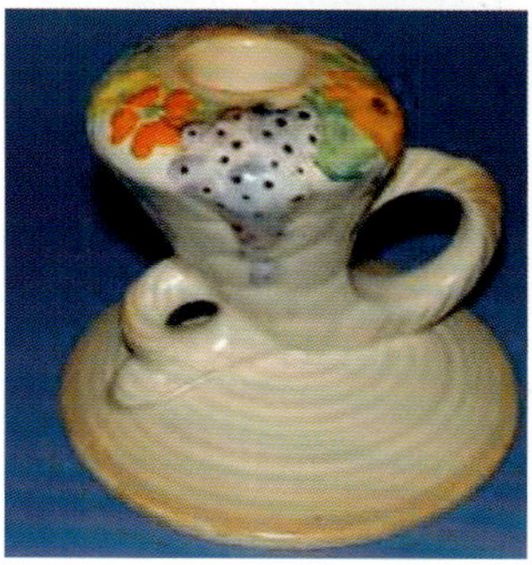

Carlton Ware introduced the embossed *Rock Garden* design in 1934/35, it was also commonly known as Garden Wall.

Rock Garden was produced during the time that Carlton Ware were developing some designs incorporating much bolder patterns such as *Oak Tree* and *Anemone.* But, in comparison *Rock Garden* seems quite tame, although the circular lines embossed within the design are similar to the ones in the *Oak Tree* design.

Rock Garden was produced in three colourways: green, peach and grey. The design has embossed circular or ribbed lines and a wall or brick effect etched into the pattern that gives it a definite feel of a garden. A variety of pretty and colourful garden flowers adorn the wall effect of the pattern to set the scene.

Some of the pieces, such as the Tray, Vase and the Two Handled Bowl, have handles which are more reminiscent of the Art Deco period. This is not mirrored in all of the styles.

1237 Tray, Elliptical £30 - £50
1238 Flower Jug, Tall £110 - £150
1239 Vase, two offset handles each side £40 - £60
1240 Float or Posy Bowl £45 - £55
1241, 1264 Leaf Butter, small handle, 2 sizes £20 - £35
1243 Cigarette Vase, unholed handles £30 - £40
1244 Vase, offset handle each side £50 - £80
1247 Soup Bowl, unholed handles £35 - £50
1248 Ashtray £20 - £40
1249 Flower Trough £30 - £45
1250 Jug or Pitcher, two handles on one side £40 - £55
1251 Candlestick £35 - £50
1252 Ashtray and Match or Cigarette Holder £45 - £60
1253 Vase, Bulbous, handles on one side £40 - £60
1254 Vase, offset handles each side £40 - £60
1262 Cruet Set £80 - £100
1265 Preserve with Lid £70 - £90
1287 Sauceboat and Stand £55 - £85
1336 Lamp ?
1336 Charger or Plaque ?
1353 Lamp, Unhandled ?

Blackberry/Raspberry

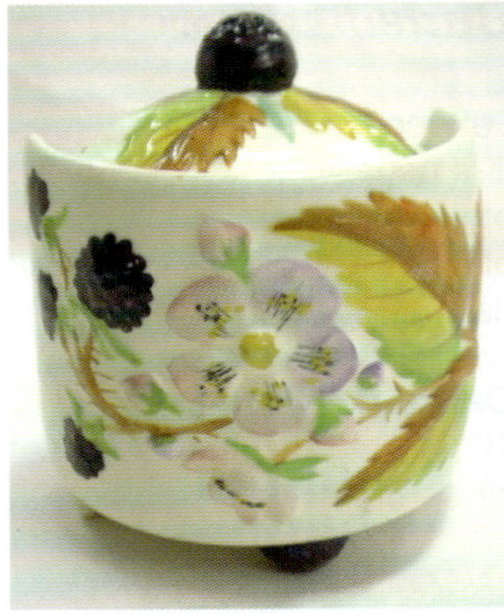

Blackberries and Raspberries are very much a part of the English Heritage and countryside. So, it is not surprising that this design was introduced as a very collectable range of tableware by Carlton Ware.

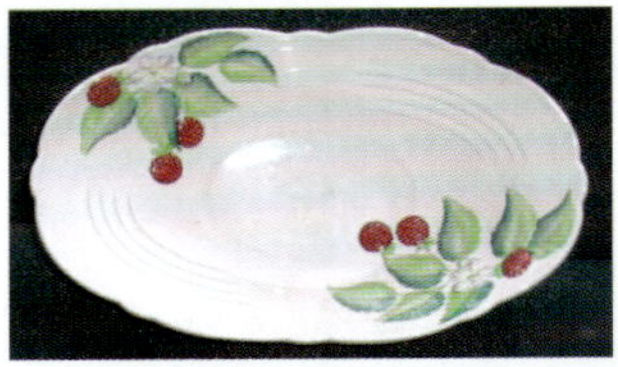

Carlton Ware introduced the *Blackberry* range in the mid 1930's, and about two-dozen different shape numbers were used. Given the similarities between the Raspberry and the Blackberry it isn't surprising that Carlton Ware introduced the *Raspberry* designs using the same moulds as the *Blackberry*. The difference was simply the colours used. The *Blackberry* range was generally on a green ground (with black berries) while the *Raspberry* range was generally on a pink ground (with red berries). The exception seems to have been the preserve pot, which was also produced in matt grey and white as well as the green and pink. It was made a lot earlier than all the other pieces, hence the large gap between the shape numbers.

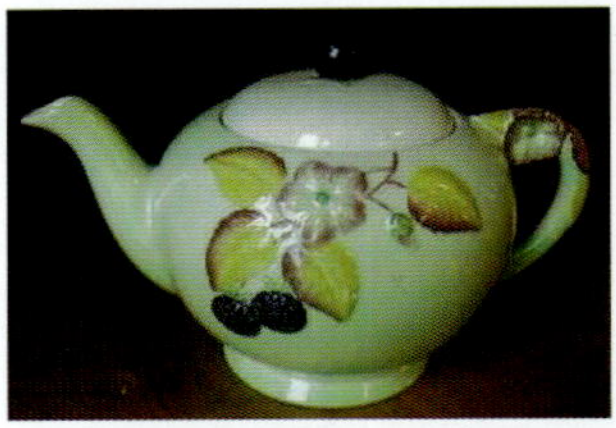

Some of the shapes of this beautiful embossed fruit design are quite angular, which could suggest a strong influence from Art Deco Period of the 1920's.

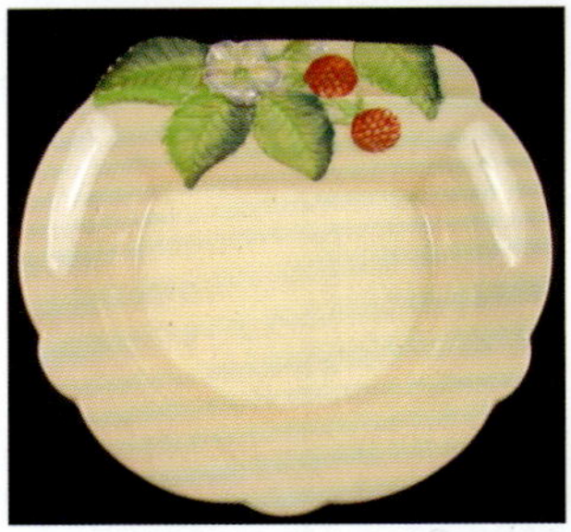

1266 Preserve £80 - £120
1473 Jam or Butter £30 - £45
1477 Spoon £20 - £40
1515 Crescent Tray £40 - £60
1516 Plate £30 - £45
1545 Sandwich Tray £40 - £60
1546 Diamond Tray £40 - £60
1547 Oblong Tray £40 - £60
1548 Covered Cheese £180 - £225
1559 Oval Tray £30 - £50
1560 Round Salad £30 - £50
1564 Salad Servers £40 - £60
1565 Biscuit Barrel £175 - £225
1570 Morning Tea Set (Tea for two) £330 - £450
Tea Pot £150 - £200, Cup & Saucer £50 - £80
Sugar £40 - £50, Cream £40 - £50
1580 Bon-bon dish £30 - £50
1581 Fruit £20 - £45
1584 Sauceboat and Stand £70 - £90
1586 Jug £60 - £90
1593 Sauce Container £25 - £45
1598 Cruet £100 - £150
1599 Butter Pat £20 - £35
1602 Jug with Lemon Squeezer £60 - £85
1662 Butter Pat Knife £20 - £40

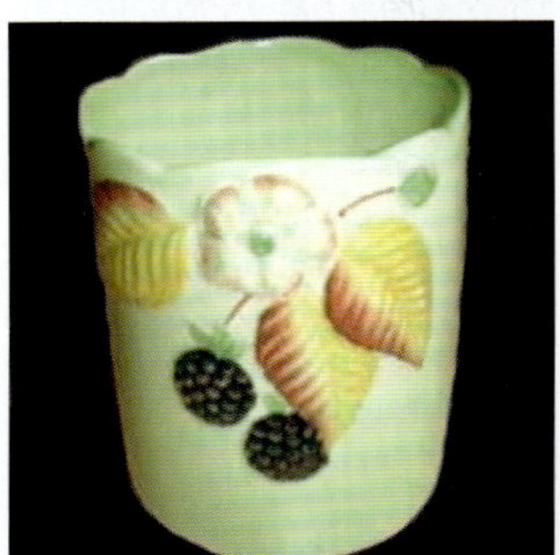

Curled Lettuce

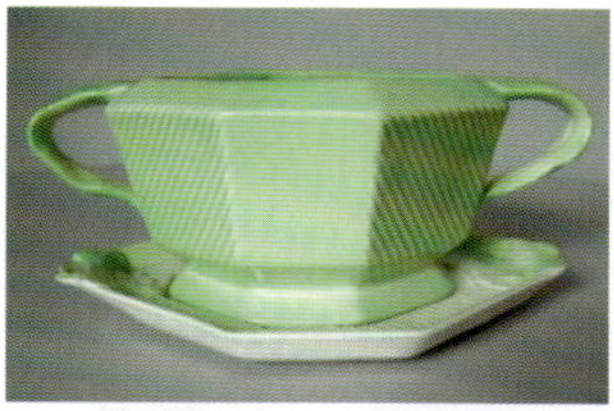

Lettuce is without doubt the world's most common salad plant. It is usually served whenever a "salad" is served, although our observation is that a lot of people end up leaving it on their plate. The word "lettuce" probably comes from the old French "laitues" meaning "milky".

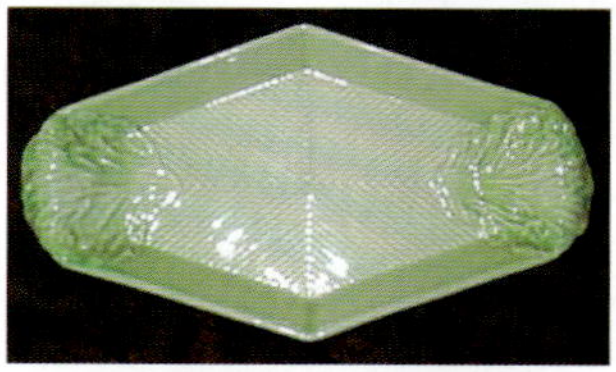

Carlton Ware introduced the *Curled Lettuce* Salad Ware in 1935. An old catalogue lists the following shapes and wholesale prices.

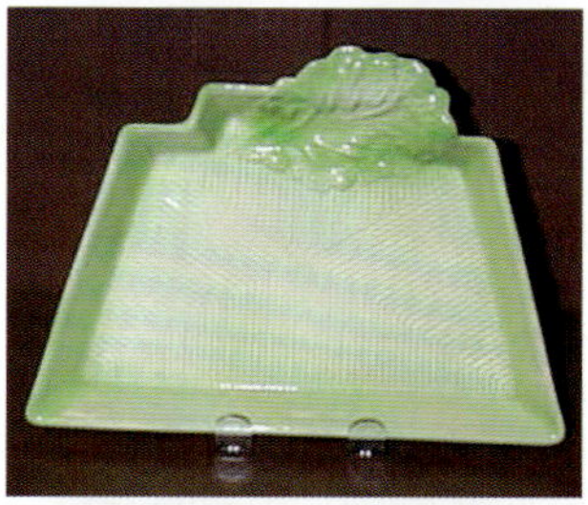

Crescent Dish,	L/s	30/-	Doz
	M/s	22/-	Doz
	S/s	14/6	Doz
Leaf Butter,	L/s	5/6	Doz
	S/s	3/6	Doz
Diamond Dish,	L/s	19/-	Doz
	S/s	12/-	Doz
Sauce Boat & Stand	L/s	19/-	Doz
	S/s	11/-	Doz
Mayonnaise Ladle		7/3	Doz
Triple Tray		22/-	Doz
Butter Knife		4/9	Doz
Square Plate,	6"	7/3	Doz
	7"	12/-	Doz
	8"	16/-	Doz
	9"	22/-	Doz
Oblong Dish		22/-	Doz
Salad Bowl & Servers		5/3	Set
Leaf Butter	L/s	5/6	Doz
	S/s	3/6	Doz

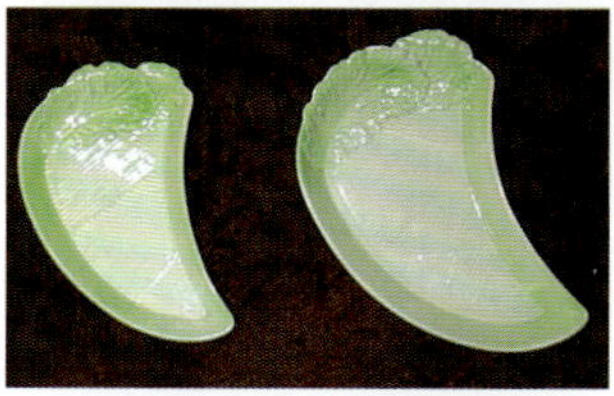

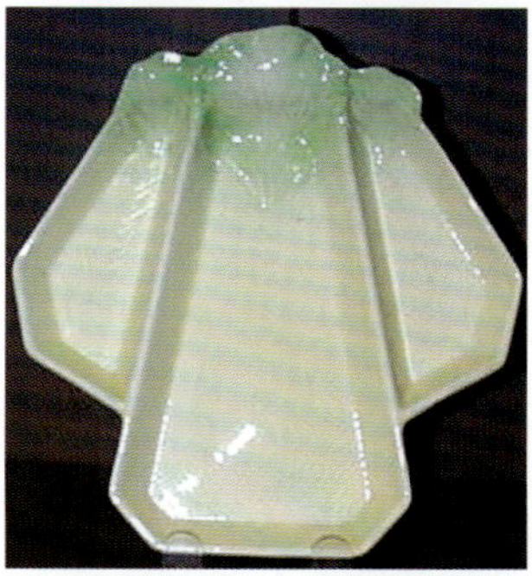

1367 Diamond Dish £10 - £20
1372 Sauce Boat and Tray £30 - £40
1374 Butter £10 - £20
1375 Oblong Tray £10 - £20
1380 Knife £10 - £20
1382 Crescent Dish £10 - £20
1383 Salad Bowl £30 - £40
1385 Square Plate, 4 sizes £10 - £20
1386 Triple Tray £15 - £25
1389 Sauce Boat and Tray £30 - £40
1390 Diamond Tray (less elongated than 1367) £10 - £20
1391 Salad Servers £15 - £30
1392 Mayonnaise Bowl & Stand £30 - £40
1412 Cress Drainer & Tray £30 - £50
1542 Cheese Plate £20 - £40

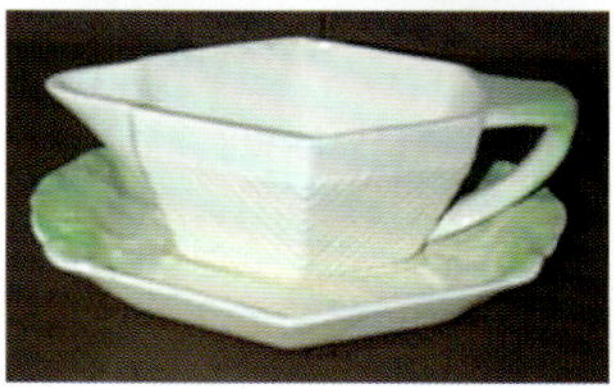

Buttercup

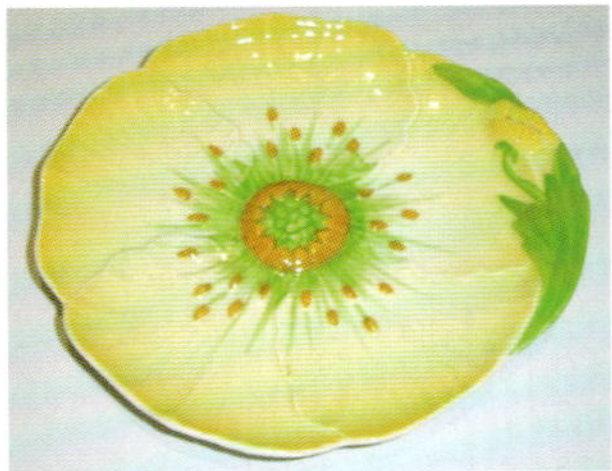

The *Buttercup* pattern is a very popular and very collectable design. Why did Carlton Ware use such a common plant which most consider a weed? This could have been due to the influence of 17th century rococo designs. During this period Josiah Wedgwood was also producing tea pots using the naturalistic designs of fruit and vegetables. Many other potteries followed this trend in the 1830's, the 1930s and 40's.

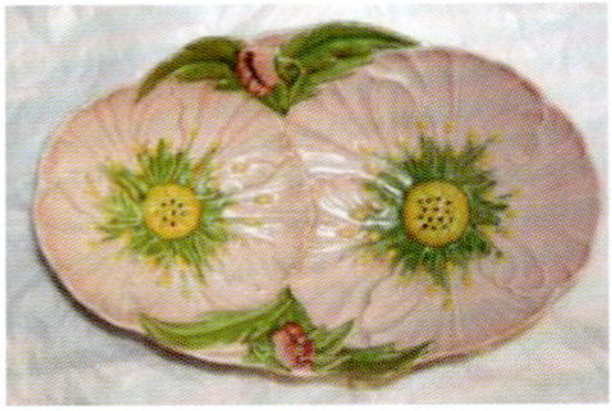

The pattern was introduced by Carlton Ware in about 1936 and continued until the 1940's and maybe a bit later. It was produced in two colourways: pattern number 3993 in yellow and 3994 in the much rarer pink.

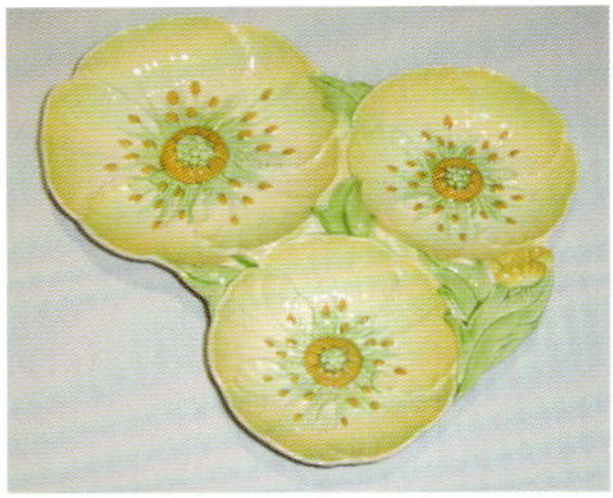

The *Buttercup* pattern is a very pleasing and aesthetic design. The buttercup itself is not used just as a painted decorative design on the outside of the piece, it is also used within the shape of each design. Many pieces with handles or spouts had aspects of the flower incorporated into this feature in a very decorative way.

The pattern was often sold as boxed sets, many of which can still be found today in excellent condition.

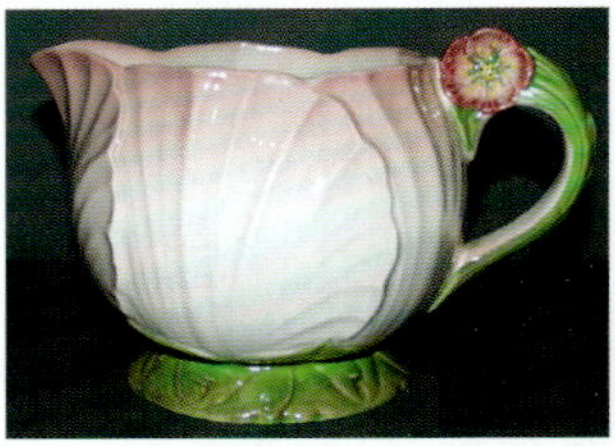

The pink colourway is probably more sought after, being rarer. It was not originally as popular in pink (perhaps appearing less natural than yellow) and consequently smaller quantities were made. Prices tend to be much higher for the pink range. You should add about 40% - 50% to the prices below.

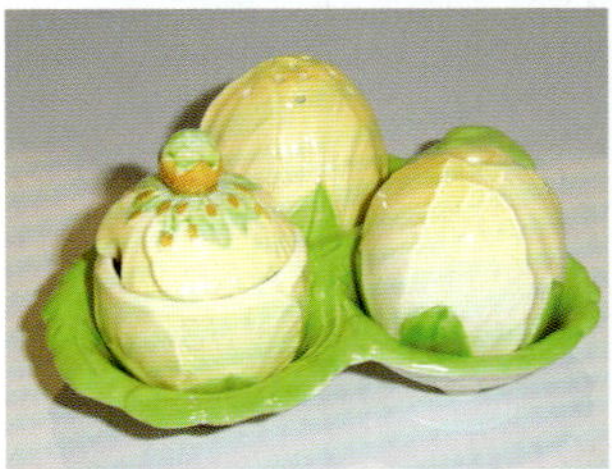

1395 & 1402 Butter & Knife £40 - £70
1478 & 1479 Salad Bowl & Servers £90 - £150
1482 Plate, 6", 7", 8", 9" £30 - £75
1483 Bowl, Oval, 3 sizes £30 - £75
1486 Preserve & Stand £90 - £155
1501 Cruet (on a Tomato Cruet Frame) £120 - £180
1510 Triple Tray £100 - £150
1511 Bon-Bon Dish £35 - £70
1512 Cress Dish and Tray £70 - £110
1513 Sauce Boat and Tray £50 - £70
1514 Comport £50 - £80
1522 Morning Tea Set (Tea for two) £400 - £600
Tea Pot, 3 sizes £180 - £300, Cup & Saucer £60 - £100
Sugar £70 - £100, Cream £50 - £80, Plate £25 - £40

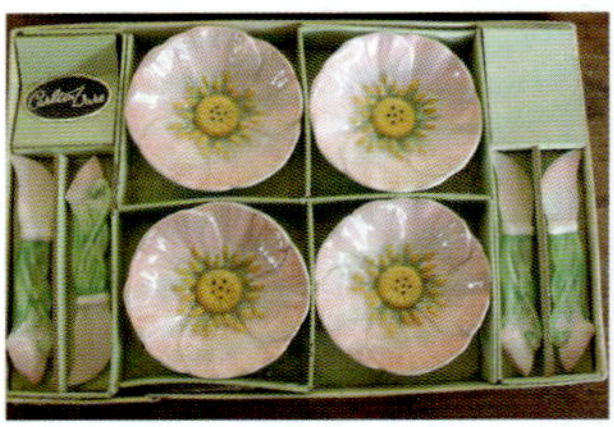

1523 Footed Bowl £50 - £80
1524 Jug, 2 sizes £70 - £110
1525 Reamer £100 - £150
1526 Toast Rack, Combination £120 - £170

1528 *Sauce Container £50 - £80*
1529 *Crescent Plate, 2 sizes £40 - £70*
1530 *Covered Butter or Cheese £200 - £400*
1531 & 1558 *Cheese Tray & Cheese Knife £80 - £150*
1532 *Toast Rack, 5 Bar £80 - £120*
1533 *Toast Rack, 3 Bar £70 - £100*
1534 *Round Butter £30 - £50*
1574 *Juicer and Jug £60 - £90*
1583 *Sugar Shaker £100 - £150*
1585 *Covered Mug £150 - £200*
1587 *Open Jam (also called Grapefruit) £90 - £120*
1595 *Egg Cruet £190 - £260*
1597 *Butter Pat £30 - £50*
1597 & 1661 *Butter Pat & Knife (Set of 4) £180 - £200*
1613 *Bulb Bowl, 10" £50 - £80*
1709 *Napkin Ring £100 - £160*

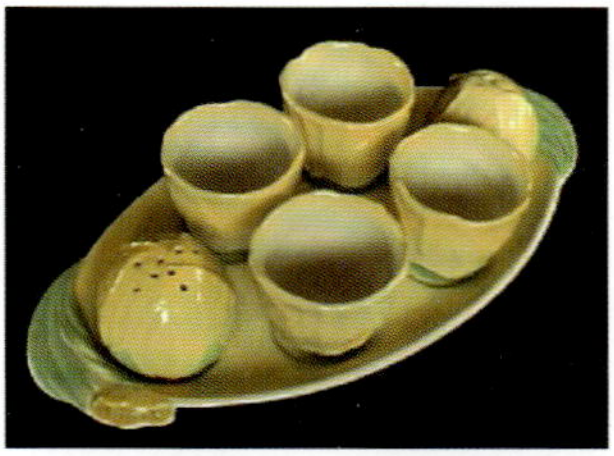

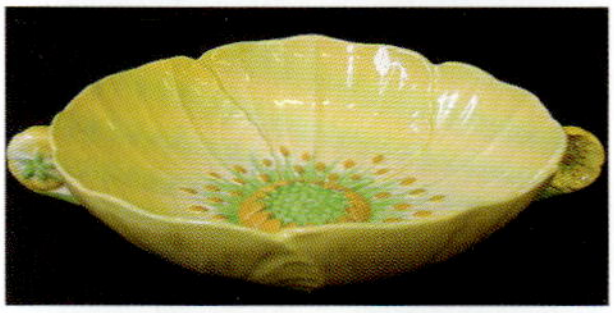

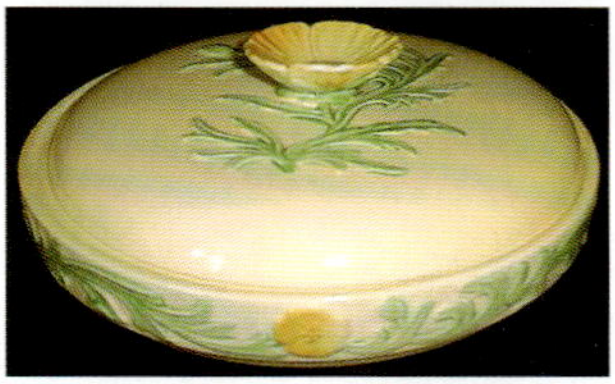

Late Buttercup or Buttercup Garland

In 1947 another version of the *Buttercup* pattern was introduced. This pattern was in some ways more simplistic than the earlier version and used the Buttercup flower as a decorative feature only.

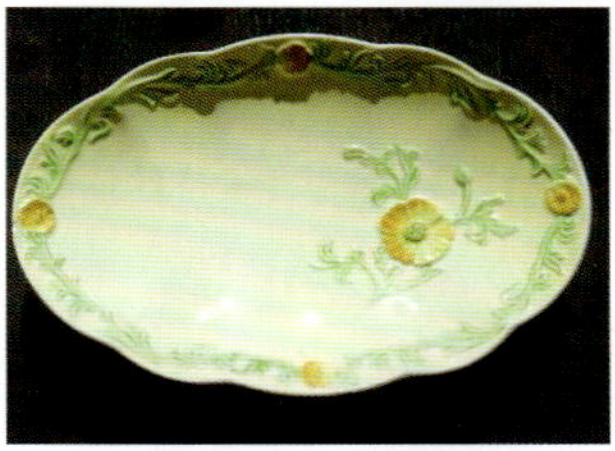

2030 *Powder Bowl, Covered Bowl £40 - £60*
2046 *Oval Tray £30 - £40*
2047 *Morning Tea Set (Tea Pot, Sugar, etc) £175 - £250*
Tea Pot £60 - £90, Cup & Saucer £25 - £35
Sugar £20 - £30, Cream £20 - £30 Plate £20 - £30
2055 *Tray £30 - £50*
2061 *Jug, 2 sizes £40 - £60*
2062 *Bon-bon dish £20 - £30*
2063 *Comport £40 - £60*
2064 *Salad Bowl £40 - £60*
2065 *Bread & Butter Plate £20 - £30*
2066 *Sauceboat and Stand £40 - £60*
2068 *Bowl £40 - £60*
2069 *Butter and Knife £30 - £45*
2074 *Cruet Set £60 - £90*

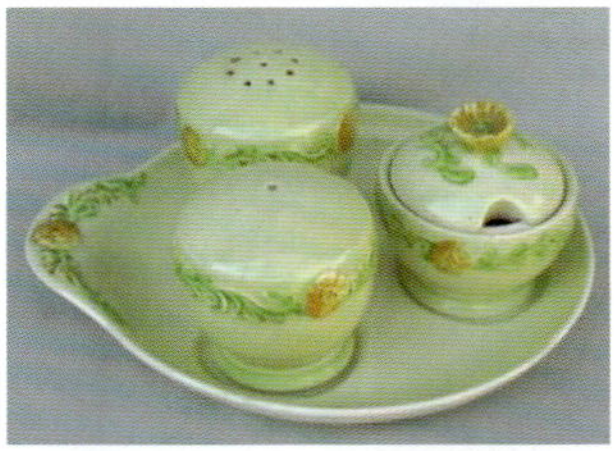

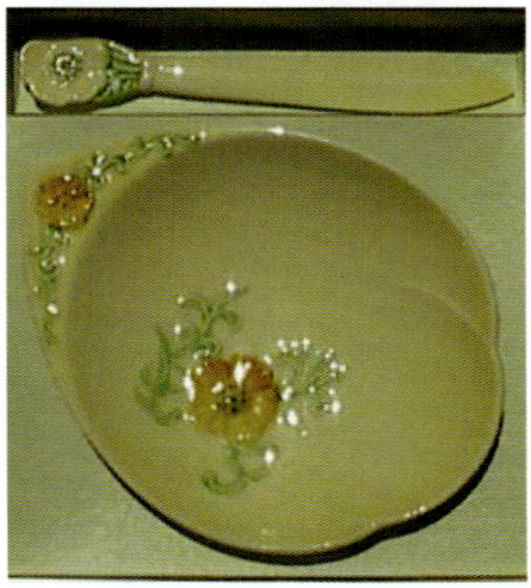

New Buttercup and Somerset

In the 1970's yet another version of the *Buttercup* pattern was introduced. This is commonly called *New Buttercup*, although Carlton Ware also used the name *Somerset*. Their advertising material (overleaf) stated that *Somerset* was a range with coloured flowers on a shaded earth brown background; whilst

New Buttercup was available with yellow buttercups and green leaves on a shaded spring green background.

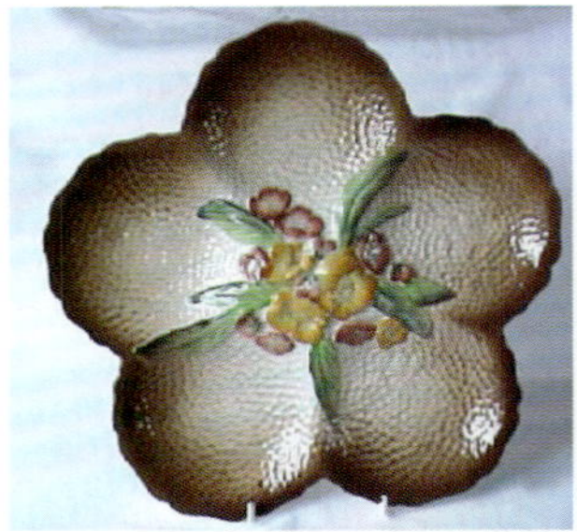

3021 Five way Tray £35 - £55
3024 Preserve £20 - £30
3025 Two way Tray £30 - £50
3026 Butter £10 - £20
3027 Coffee Set (Coffee for two) £90 - £150
Coffee £40 - £60, Cup & Saucer £15 - £25
Sugar £10 - £20, Cream £10 - £20
3028 Salt & Pepper £10 - £20
3029 Covered Butter £20 - £40
3030 Jug £20 - £40
3031 Sauceboat and Stand £25 - £45
3032 Plate, 5" £15 - £30
3033 Tea Pot £40 - £60
3035, 3036 Tray or Oval Dish, 2 sizes £15 - £25
3037 Beaker £15 - £30
3038 Cheese & Cover with Stand £30 - £50

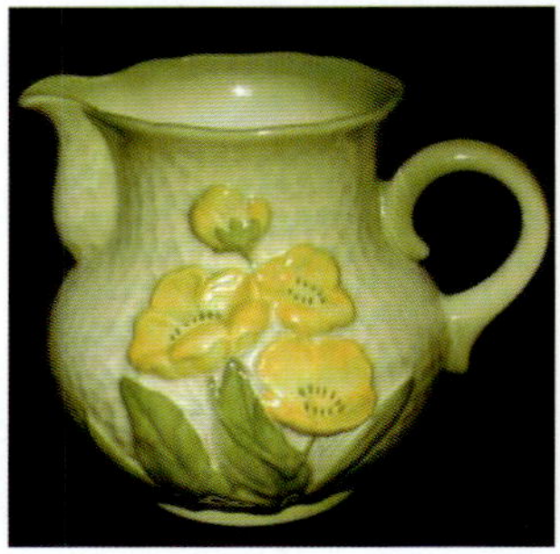

CARLTON WARE
Somerset

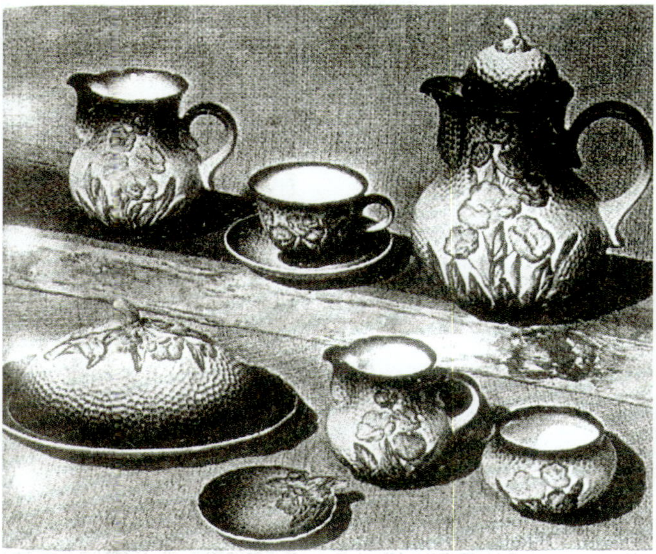

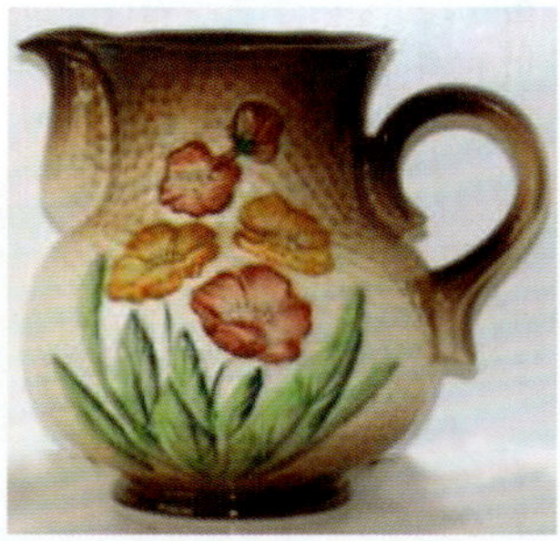

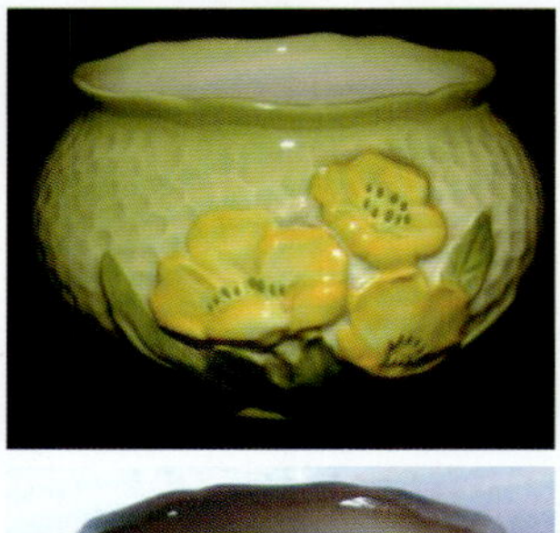

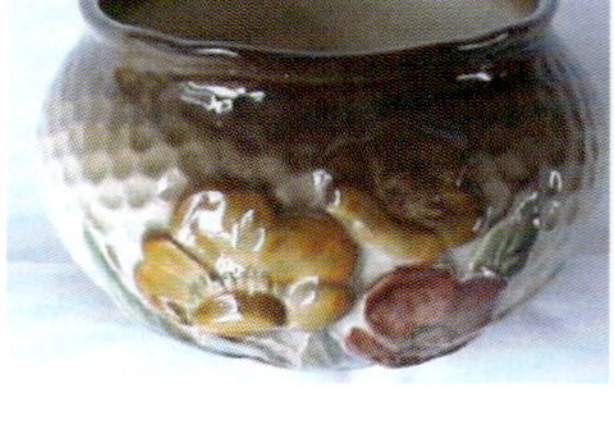

A range of hand-painted Tableware accessories and Gift Items, including Coffee Sets, Peppers and Salts, Covered Butters, Cheese Dishes and Trays with coloured flowers on a shaded earth brown background.

Also available in Buttercup decoration, i.e. Hand-painted Yellow Buttercups and Green Leaves on a shaded Spring Green background

Tulip

Tulips were first introduced into England from Holland in the 16th century when they were classed as a luxury item, especially the more unusual varieties. The Carlton Ware Embossed *Tulip* Range was first produced in 1937. This was a time when Carlton Ware and other producers were creating more freehand painted designs in response to the modern Art Deco era of the late 1920's to 1930's. This simplistic futuristic design with its angular shapes certainly fits in with the new minimalist modern designs. The designer of this pattern was probably Violet Elmer who created many designs for Carlton Ware around this period.

The *Tulip* range was produced in only one ground colour of matt off-white but had three choices. Each set usually had the flower heads painted either purple, orange or pink. But there were some exceptions for example the cruet set was a combination of all three colours, comprising purple flower on the mustard pot, pink on the pepper pot and orange on the salt pot. Also the biscuit barrel had more than one colour of flower heads. The stems and leaves of the tulips are painted in soft hues of green and the glaze was finished in a silky sheen.

Many of the shapes, such as the Jugs were made in a variety of sizes. For example, the Jug, shape 1416, came in six sizes marked /6 to /1 on the base. The plates were made in three sizes.

1403 Spoon £15 - £25
1404 Jam or Butter, 2 sizes £25 - £40
1416 Jug, 6 sizes £40 - £90
1417 Oval Dish £30 - £40
1418 Preserve £45 - £75
1419 Plate, 3 sizes £25 - £55
1420 Square Jug, 2 sizes £50 - £70
1421 Handled Crescent Plate, 3 sizes £40 - £80
1422 Sugar Sifter £60 - £95
1439 Morning Tea Set (Tea for two) £200 - £300
Tea Pot £70 - £100, Cup & Saucer £40 - £50
Sugar £25 - £40, Cream £25 - £40, Plate £25 - £45
1453 Salad £45 - £75
1457 Servers £30 - £50
1459 Cruet £60 - £95
1461 Biscuit £60 - £95
1736 Posy Holder £35 - £55
1811 Candlestick £25 - £40

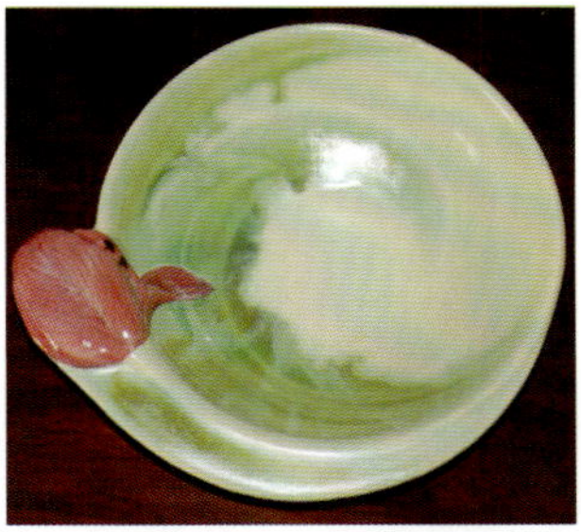
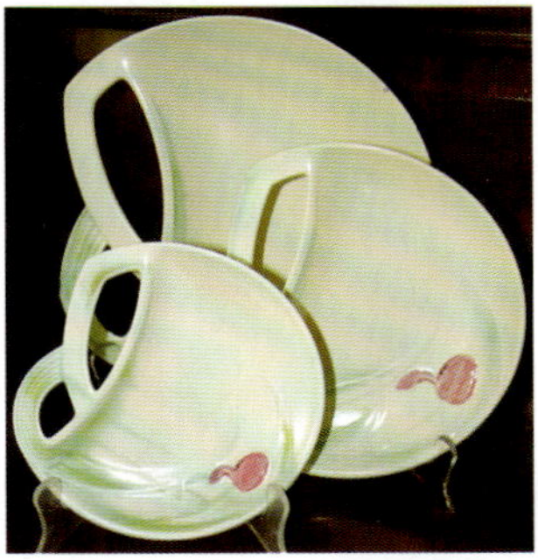
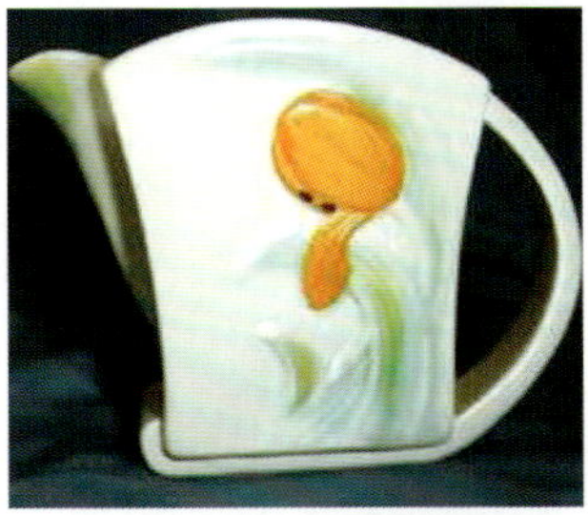
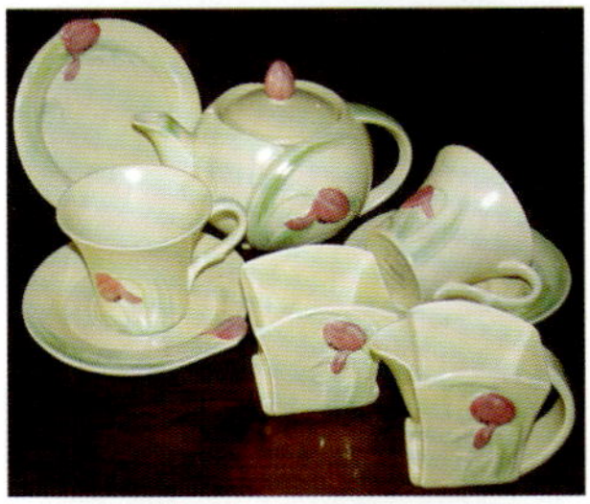
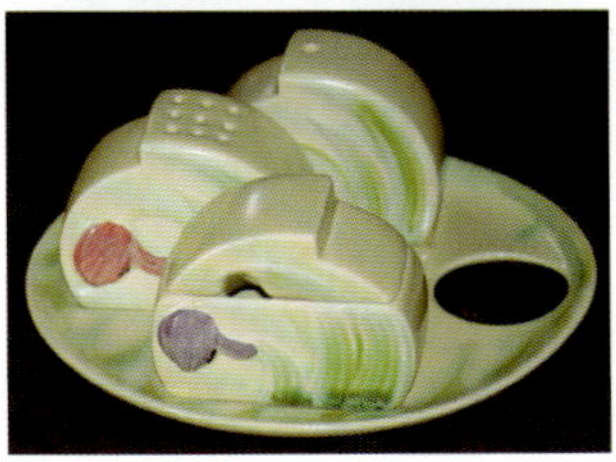

Daisy

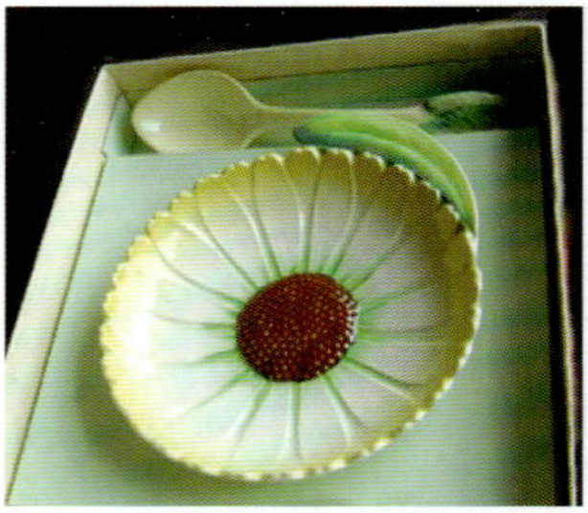

Introduced in 1936. The shape represents the flower head of a Daisy and has the occasional leaf.

Colours include pink with a bright yellow centre and yellow with a bright dark honey coloured centre.

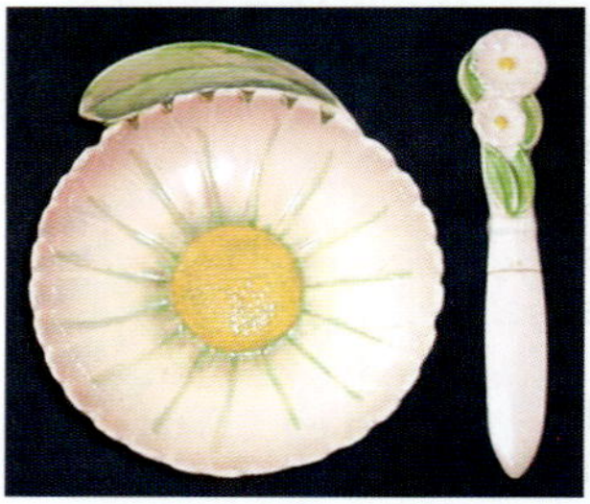

1472 Jam or Butter £30 - £50
with Knife or Spoon £45 - £70
1947 Dish, 9" £40 - £70
1951 Bowl, 6" £40 - £70

Pear

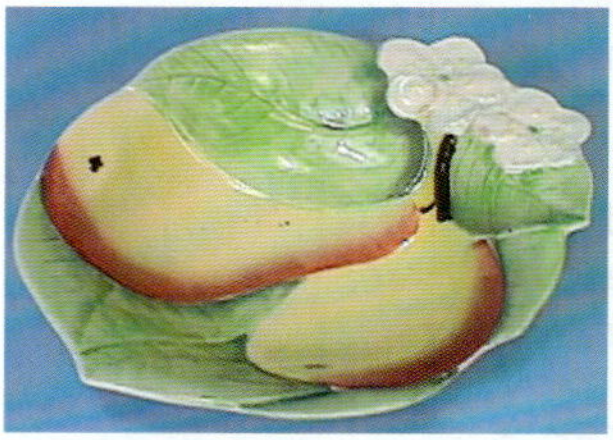

This piece occasionally appears in antique shops and antique fairs. It was made in about 1936 and does not appear to fit into any range. It has been suggested that this is part of the Fruit Ware range that was introduced much later on in the 1950's.

1474 Butter £20 - £40

Thistle

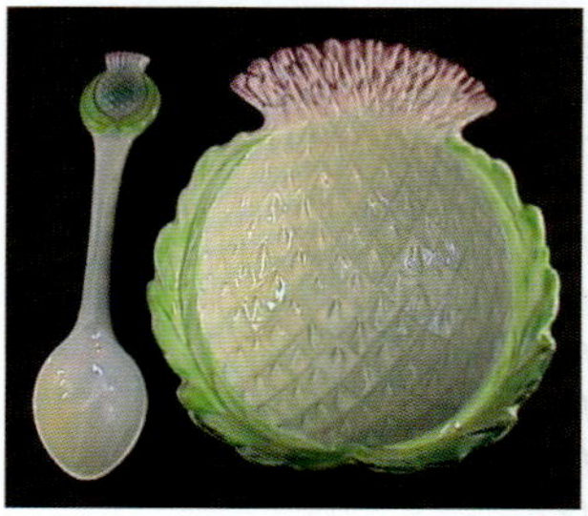

Another piece that does not fit into any particular range.

1576 & 1577 Butter & Knife £35 - £60
1576 & 1578 Jam & Spoon £35 - £60
1579 Ashtray £25 - £50

Lily

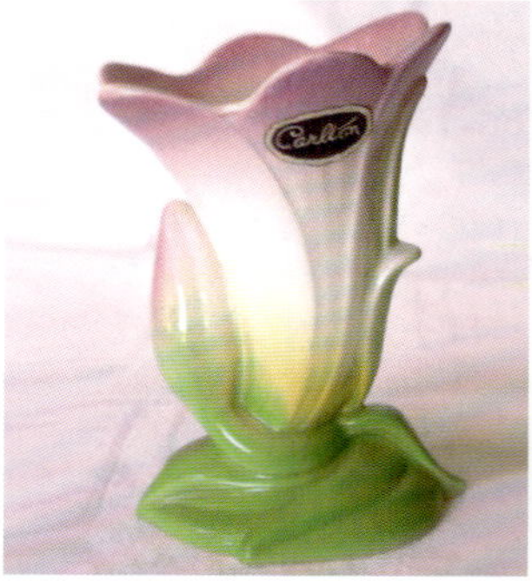

This Flower Vase was first made in 1940 and was available in pink, yellow and mauve. Occasionally you may come across one in white; this is because of war-time restrictions on decorated products.

1868 Flower Vase £25 - £40

Red Currant

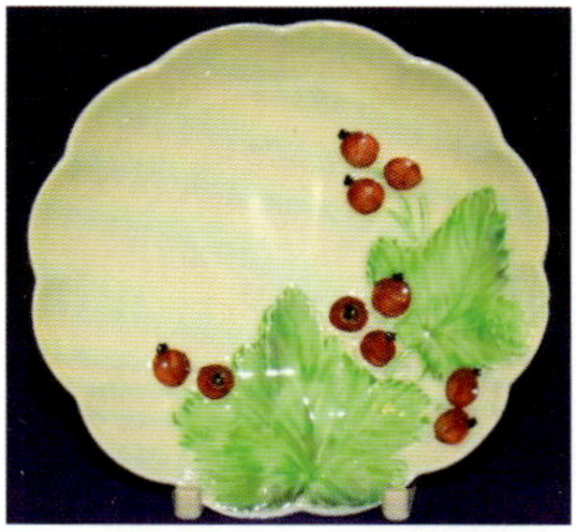

Carlton Ware introduced the *Red Currant* embossed range in the late 1930's, around 1937/38. It was produced in the popular colourways of pale green and creamy yellow. These colours were often used in the Fruit and Floral embossed ranges, perhaps for economic prudence but also because they do show the floral and fruit designs to great effect, which is also very pleasing to the eye.

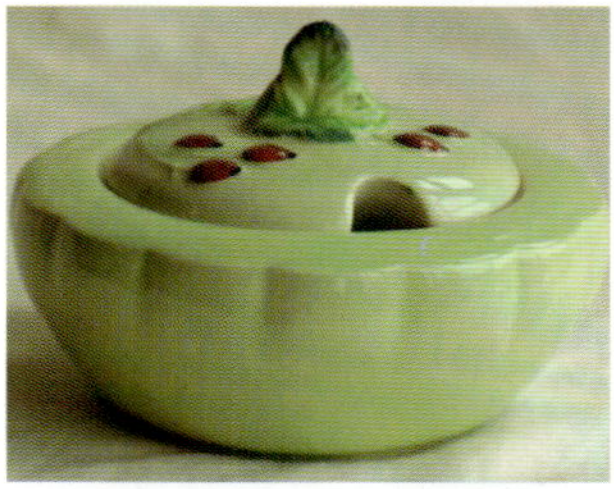

This design is a realistic depiction of red currant and has beautiful bright red berries. The leaves are a very realistic shape and are painted in a blend of green with intricate brush stokes. Some of the pieces such as trays, butter dish and stand for sauceboat are also shaped like a leaf with serrated edges.

This was another variation of fruit that was added to the famous Carlton Ware Fruit and Floral embossed range. These bright and cheerful designs were very popular with the public at that time, and still are very sought after.

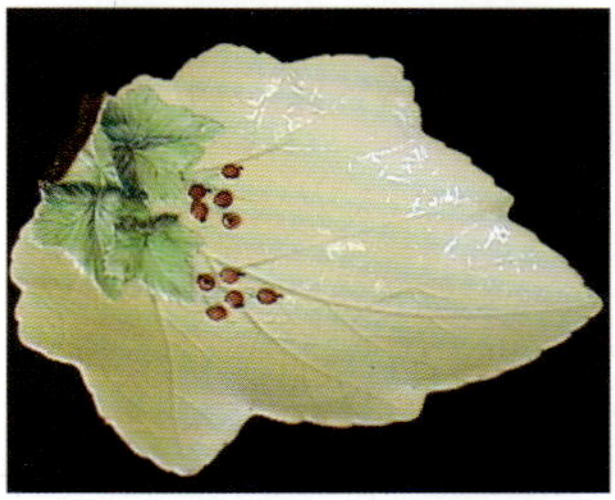

The trade press of the day were always interested in any new designs and often sung the praises of Carlton Ware. In addition Carlton Ware advertised their new designs in the trade press.

These ranges were introduced to add variety and to create a greater interest in their utility wares. They were of course in total contrast to the Lustre wares which although popular were perhaps not accessible and affordable to all.

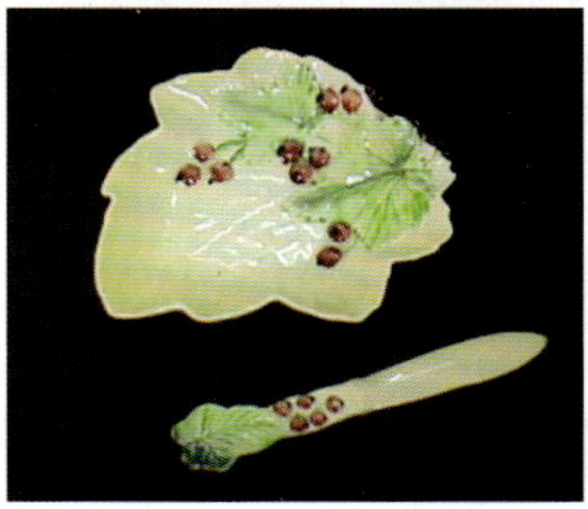

1603 Butter or Jam £20 - £30
1603 & 1605 Butter & Knife £30 - £50
1603 & 1606 Jam & Spoon £30 - £50
1607 Preserve £50 - £80
1637 Leaf Tray £30 - £50
1656 Leaf Jam £20 - £30
1657 Preserve, with leaves on side £40 - £60
1658 & 1659 Cheese Tray & Knife £30 - £60
1660 Sauceboat and Stand £30 - £50
1679 Double Butter £30 - £50
1708 Napkin Ring £40 - £80
1730 Jam Pot Holder £40 - £60

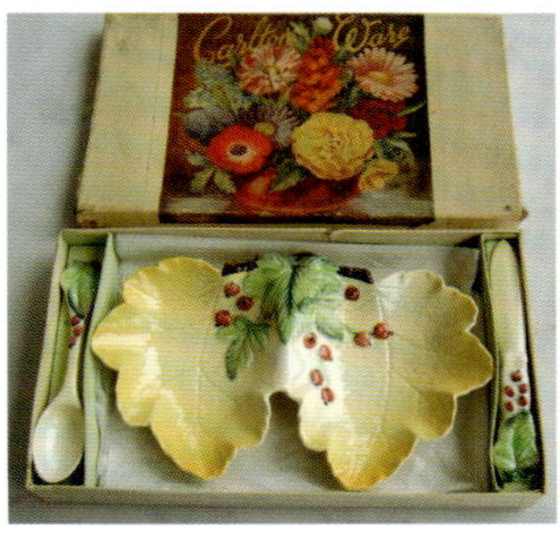

Apple Blossom

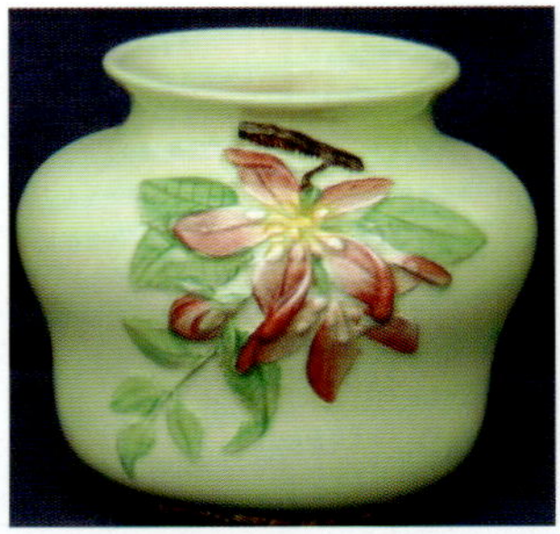

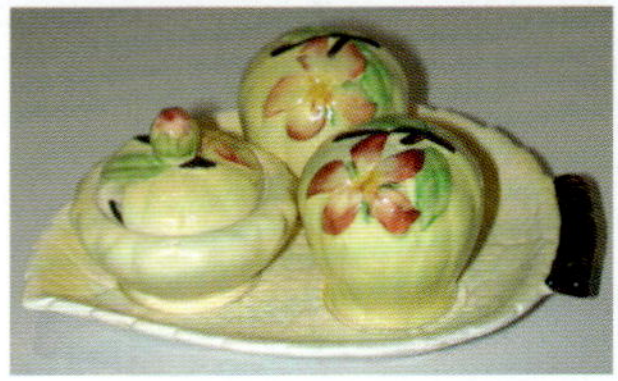

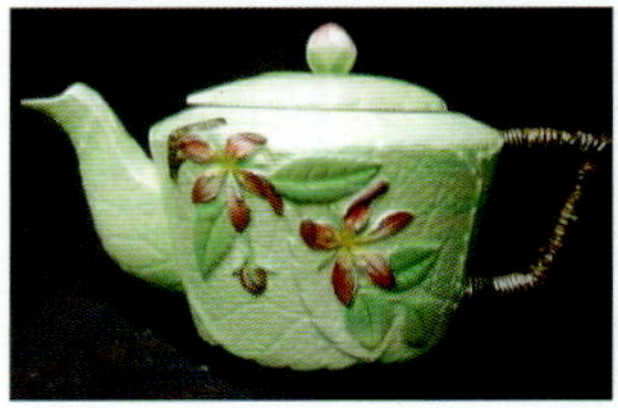

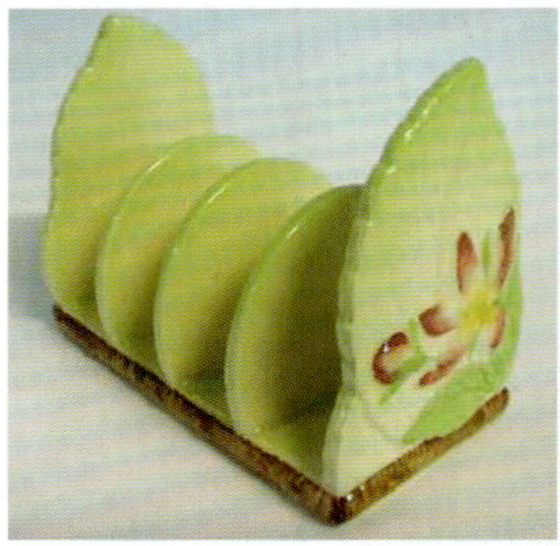

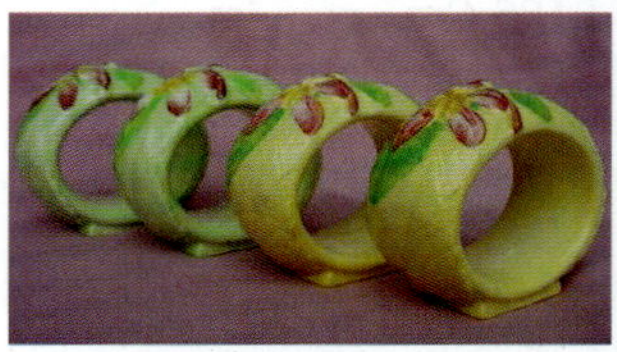

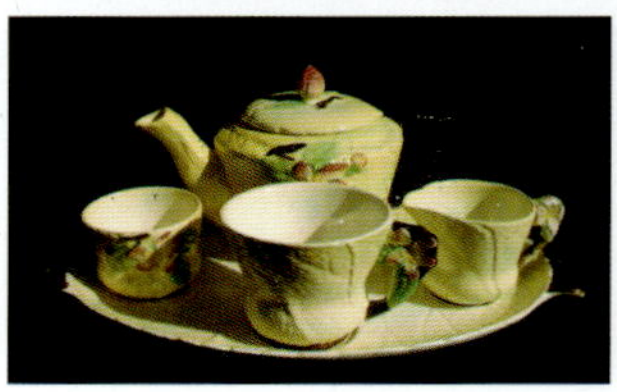

The *Apple Blossom* range was introduced in 1937 in two colourways, yellow and green. The flowers were hand painted in a deep pink colour, the stamens in yellow and the leaves in green. The branch was painted in a brown colour and often the handle or grip on the piece was a realistic looking branch.

During the war years there were restrictions to the pottery industry which prohibited the use of hand decorating of pieces for the home market. As a result you may come across some pieces in a plain colour such as pale yellow, pale green or pink.

An advertisement from 1940 advertised *Apple Blossom* as *"A Breath of Fresh Air. The latest designs of Carlton Ware will add freshness to your display and your customers will appreciate the air of Summer time and Apple Blossom which has inspired this product of the Craftsman's Art".*

The *Apple Blossom* range was huge, very popular and continued to be produced over a very large number of years.

1614 Leaf Tray £30 - £50
1617 Triangular Tray 4", 6", 9" £30 - £50
1618 Preserve £65 - £95
1621 Butter £30 - £50
1621 & 1655 Butter & Knife £50 - £80
1638 Vase 3 sizes £70 - £100
1648 Vase Bulbous, 3 sizes £70 - £100
1649 Vase 3 sizes £70 - £100
1650 Cheese Plate £35 - £55
1651 Cheese Knife £20 - £30
1652 Sauceboat and Stand £55 - £80
1653 Cruet Set £80 - £100
1654 Spoon £20 - £30
1655 Butter Knife £20 - £30
1663 Salad Servers £50 - £70
1664 Bon-bon dish £35 - £50
1665 Oval Bowl, 3 sizes £40 - £70
1668 Cress Dish £55 - £80
1669 Footed Bowl £45 - £70
1670 Morning Tea Set (Tea for two) £250 - £400
Tea Pot £120 - £160, Cup & Saucer £35 - £70
Sugar £30 - £50, Cream £30 - £50, Plate £15 - £25
1671 Salad £75 - £100
1680 Double Butter £40 - £60
1686 Jug, 2 sizes £70 - £100
1687 Beaker and Cover £95 - £135

1688 *Triple Tray* £35 - £60
1689 *Mayonnaise Bowl, Stand and Ladle* £85 - £120
1696 *Toast Rack* £80 - £110
1697 *Jug, Tall* £250 - £320
1700 *Jug, double handle, 3 sizes* £175 - £250
1701 *Egg Frame and 4 Egg Cups* £110 - £140
1704 *Covered Cheese* £175 - £225
1707 *Serviette Holder* £40 - £70
1710 *Vase* £70 - £90
1714 *Toy Teaware* £250 - £500
1720 *Morning Set on Tray* £250 - £500
1723 *Sugar - Toy Set size* £30 - £50
1728 *Mayonnaise Bowl, unhandled* £40 - £60
1729 *Pickle Dish* £20 - £30
1756 *Cream, Tall* £35 - £55
1799 *Toyware* £250 - £500
2008 *Lamp* £180 - £250

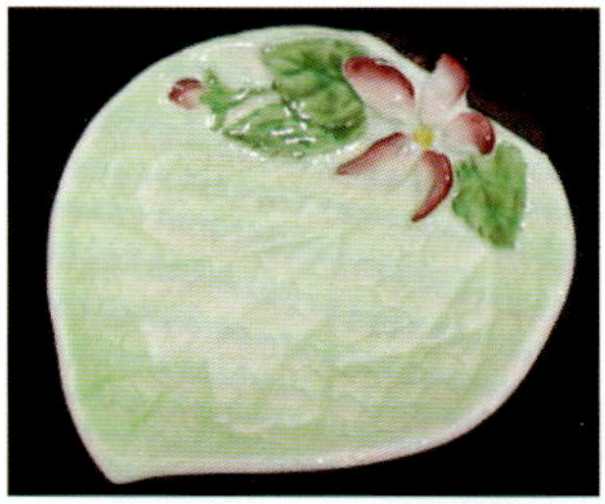

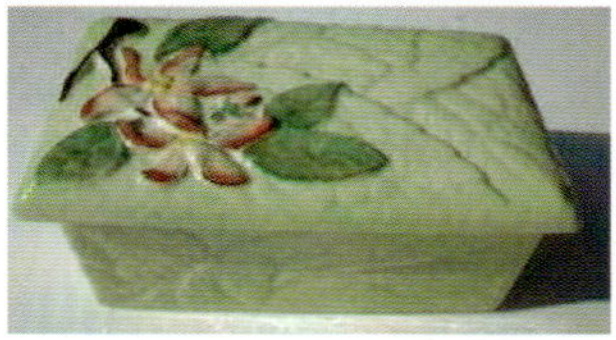

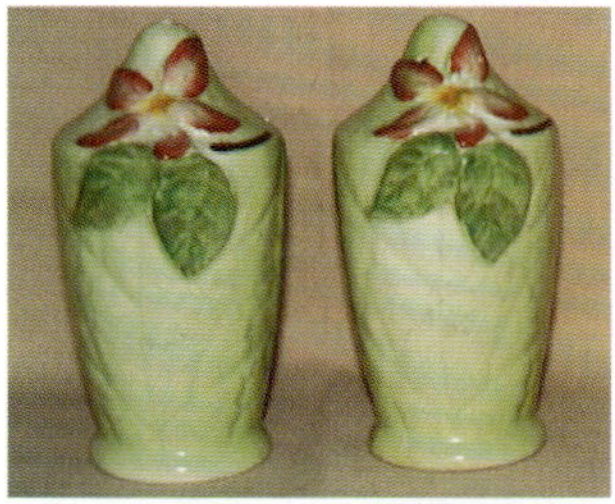

Apple Blossom - AW

In 1975 Arthur Wood & Son reintroduced the *Apple Blossom* range with a dozen new shapes. The back stamp for these pieces was the curved rubber stamp rather than the Australian. Many collectors consider these to be not as "sharp or delicate" as the earlier versions. The moulds were possibly less crisp resulting in thicker potting.

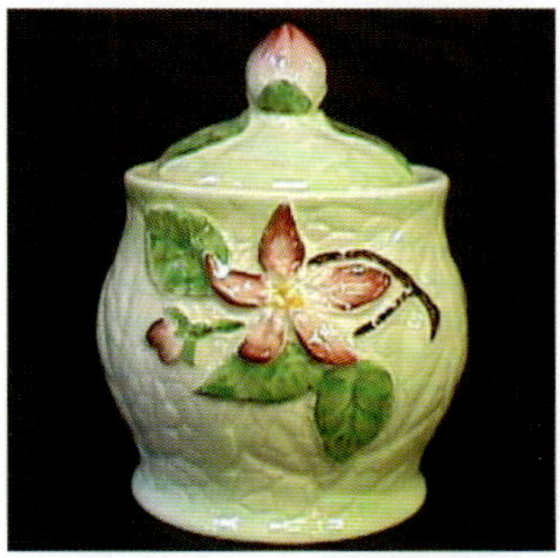

3175 *Sauceboat and Stand* £40 - £60
3176 *Individual Butter* £20 - £30
3178 *Long Tray* £30 - £50
3179 *Covered Butter* £50 - £75
3180 *Jug - 1 pint* £40 - £70
3182 *Pepper and Salt* £25 - £40
3183 *Preserve* £50 - £80
3185 *Cheese and Stand* £75 - £125
3186 *Crescent Tray* £25 - £40
3188 *Salad Bowl* £30 - £50
3189 *Leaf Tray* £25 - £35
3192 *Toast Rack* £40 - £70

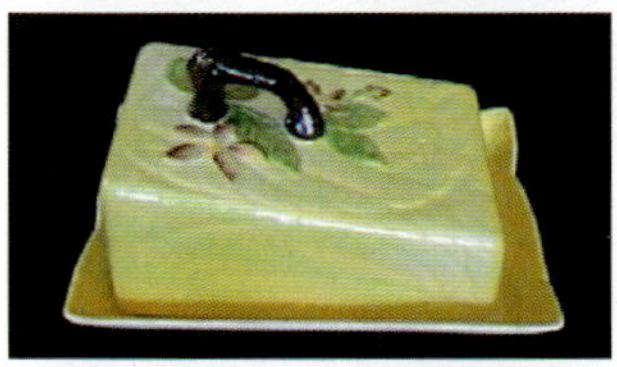

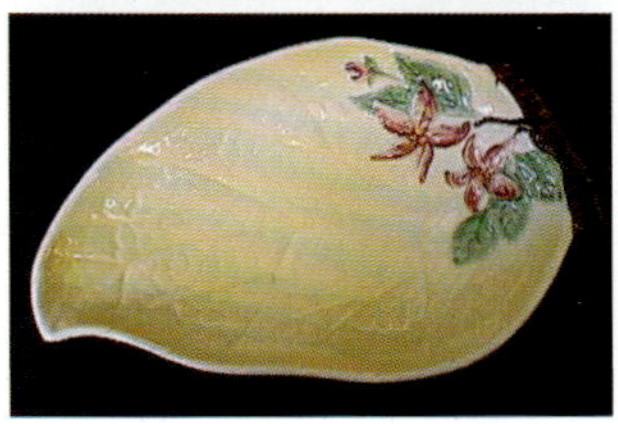

Water Lily

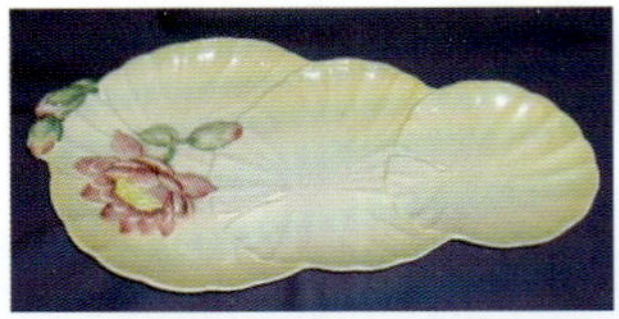

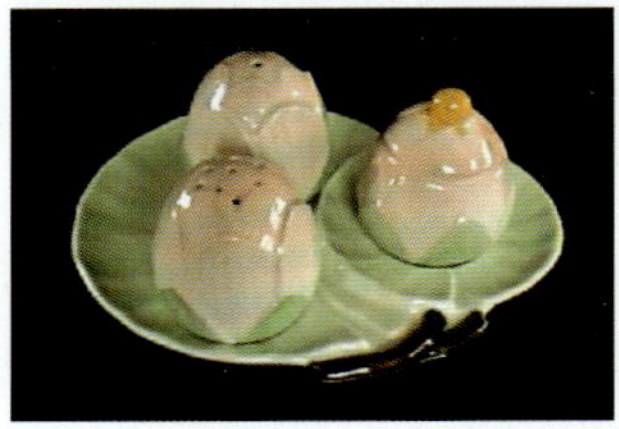

The embossed *Water Lily* range depicts a realistic Water Lily or part thereof. The first piece was introduced around 1937 but most of the pieces were made in 1939 onwards. The range was very popular and continued for a number of years.

Water Lily was produced in two colourways, yellow and green. The yellow background was usually decorated with a pink water lily and the green background generally was decorated with a yellow water lily. There seem to be some exceptions to this rule especially for the Cruet sets, candlesticks, tea pots, creamer, sugar bowl and the boxed sets. These appeared in the naturalistic or realistic shape of the water lily and often had green leaves and the petals of the flower in either yellow or pink. Some pieces can be found in an undecorated condition or just plain green or yellow ground. This was not an oversight but could be attributed to some wartime pieces that were created for the home market. The production of expensive and luxury goods was restricted during this period, which included hand painted decorations in colours and gilts with glazing being rationed.

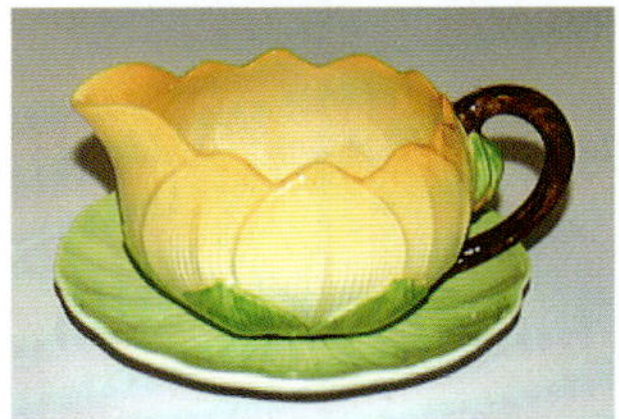

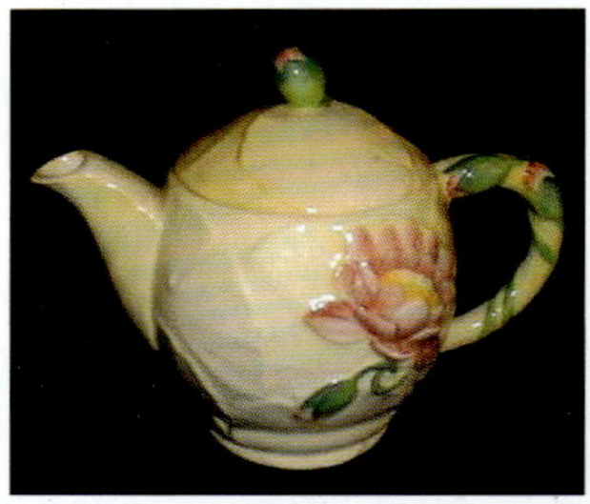

1718 Posy Holder £40 - £60
1738 Cruet Set £100 - £160
1741 Twin Lobed Plate £50 - £70
1750 Serving Bowl, Oval Bowl £50 - £70
1773 Cheese Tray & Knife £60 - £90
1774 Cress Dish and Tray £70 - £100
1776 Sauce Boat and Tray £50 - £80
1777 Handled Basket £90 - £120
1778 & 1782 Salad Bowl & Servers £80 - £120
1779 Candlestick £30 - £50
1781 3 Lobed Tray £60 - £90
1783 Plate, 9", 6" £30 - £50
1784 Jam & Spoon or Butter & Knife £35 - £65 each set
1786 Morning Tea Set (Tea for two) £350 - £500
Tea Pot £120 - £170, Cup & Saucer £55 - £80
Sugar £50 - £70, Cream £50 - £70, Plate £30 - £50
1787 Covered Beaker £90 - £150
1788 Jug, 3 sizes £60 - £80
1789 Bon Bon £40 - £70
1798 3 Way Tray £80 - £100
1801 Toast Rack, 5 bar £60 - £100
1804 Preserve Pot £50 - £90
1805 Biscuit Barrel £150 - £220
1806 Jug, Juicer & Tray £50 - £80
1820 Covered Cheese £150 - £200

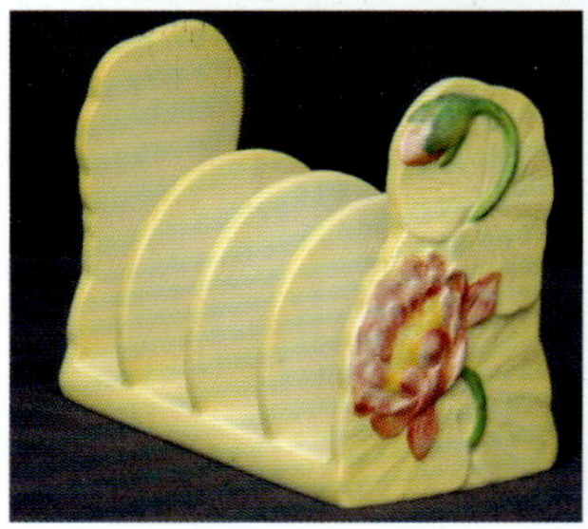

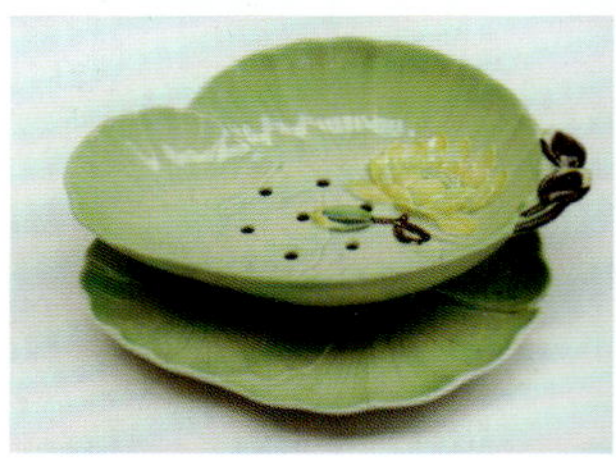

Carlton Ware produced a number of Posy Holders, often in a pattern which had no other shape except possibly a Candle Holder. If other pieces have been made in a range then often the posy holder looks very different. Some of the Posy Holders are shown on this page.

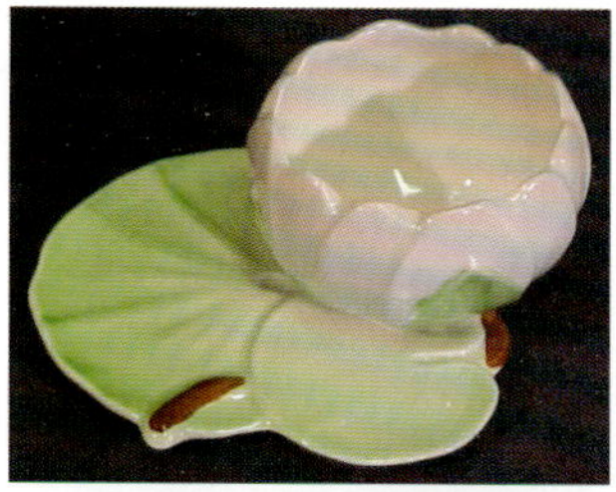

Water Lily

1718 Posy Holder £40 - £60
1779 Candlestick £30 - £50

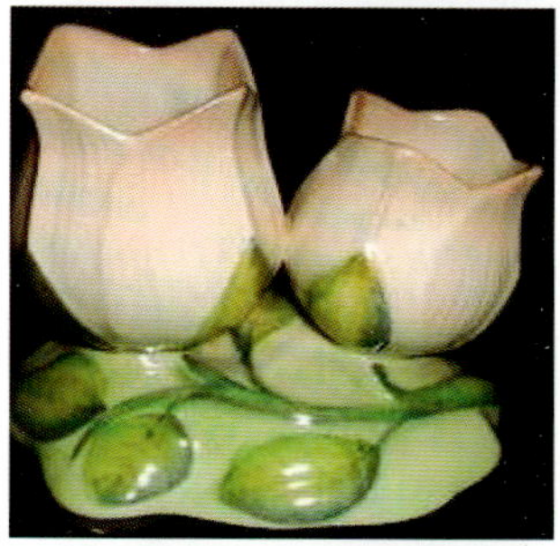

Bell

Only a double posy holder was produced in this pattern.

1715 Posy Holder £30 - £40

Daffodil

This is available in a variety of colours, including plain white, white with green and yellow with green. The white version was because of war-time restrictions on decorated products.

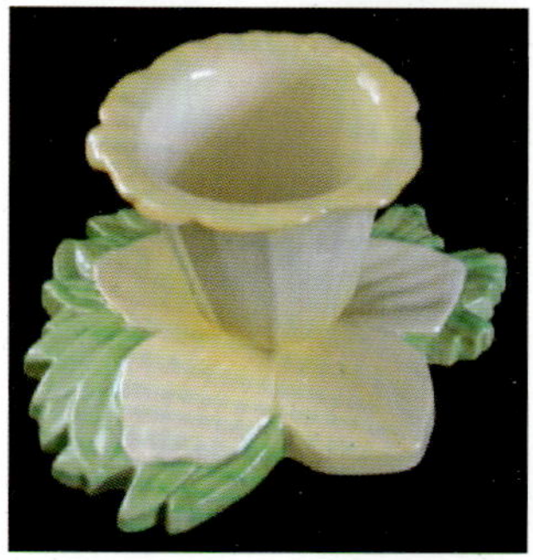

1732 Posy Holder £50 - £70
1780 Candle Holder £45 - £60

Tulip

1736 Posy Holder £35 - £55
1811 Candle Holder £25 - £40

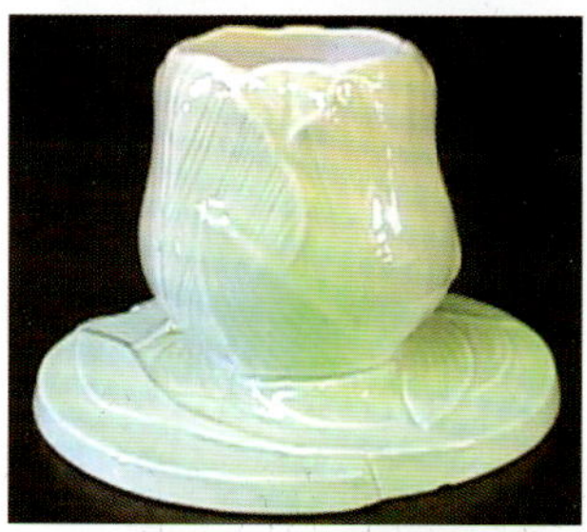

Arum Lily

A very popular posy holder which displays beautifully. It was available in pink, yellow and mauve.

1740 Posy Holder £40 - £65
1855 Candle Holder £35 - £55

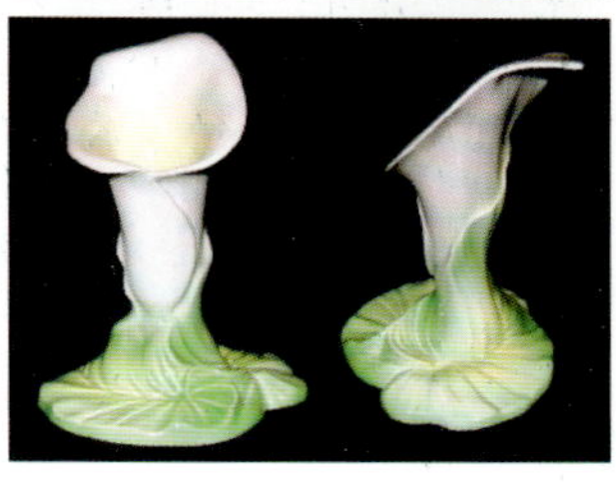

Crocus

A sketch of this piece appears on the next page. It was available in pink, yellow and mauve.

1832 Posy Holder £60 - £80

Crocus

Carlton Ware introduced the embossed *Crocus* range in the late 1930's. This was another addition to a long sequence of flower and fruit designs that are very popular with Carlton Ware collectors.

This design was produced in two colourways of light green and pale yellow. The design of pretty spring flowers is very fetching and pleasing to the eye in these subtle colourways. As usual the Carlton Ware paintresses paid a lot of attention to all the finer details. It is finished with a nice glossy glaze.

This design is a realistic representation of spring flowers sprouting through the grass. The combination of mauve and red Crocus flowers and yellow and pink Primula flowers shown in full bloom is very pretty. The accompanying Crocus leaves are very realistic and what you would expect to see in the wild. The primula leaves are tinged with yellow to authenticate the look.

To complete the picture the flowers and leaves appear to be sprouting from soil at the base of the design. The jugs in this design have a Crocus flower embossed into the shape of the handle, which adds another dimension to the design.

1747 Serving Dish, 2 sizes £30 - £70
1759 Comport £45 - £70
1760 Bon Bon Dish £50 - £80
1765 Flower Jug, Pitcher, 2 sizes £200 - £250
1766 Bulb Bowl £60 - £100
1808 Mug with Cover £140 - £190
1809 Preserve Jar with Lid £80 - £120
1832 Posy Holder £60 - £80
Cruet £85 - £125
Egg Set £95 - £130

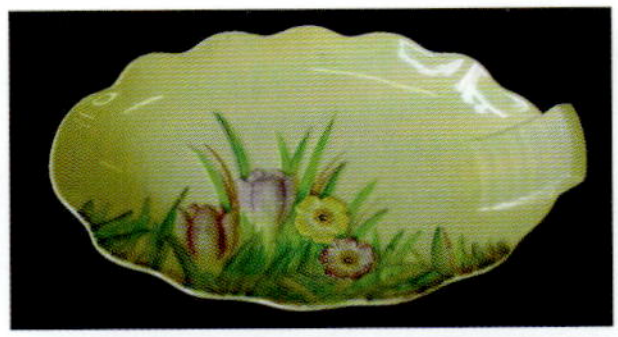

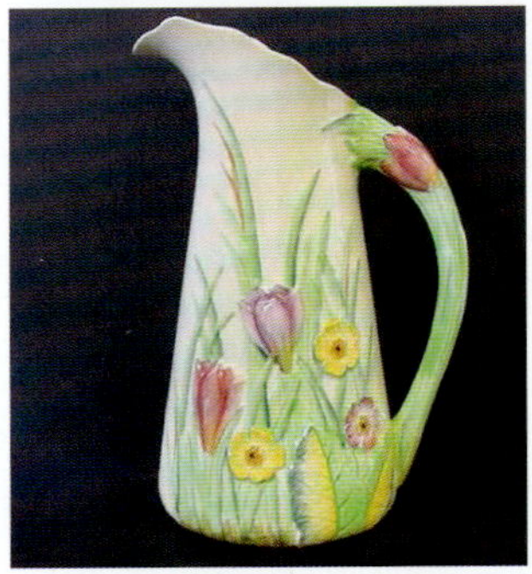

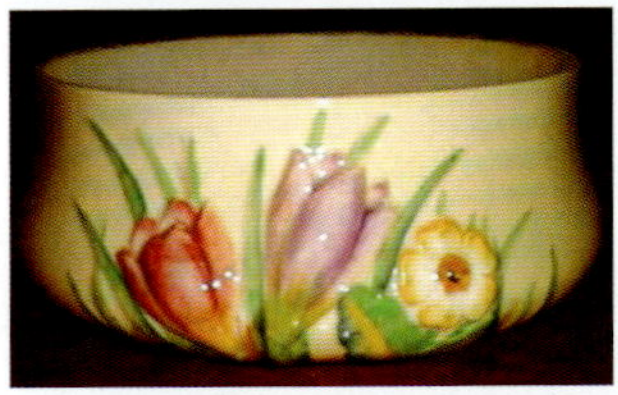

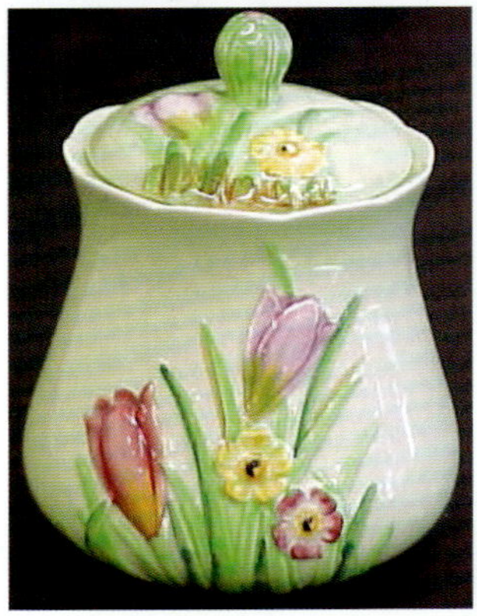

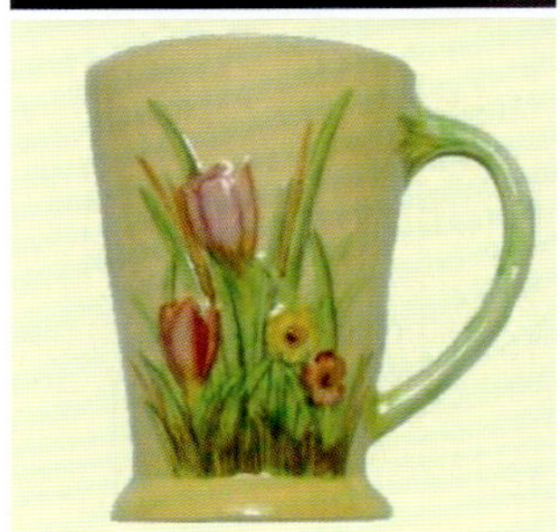

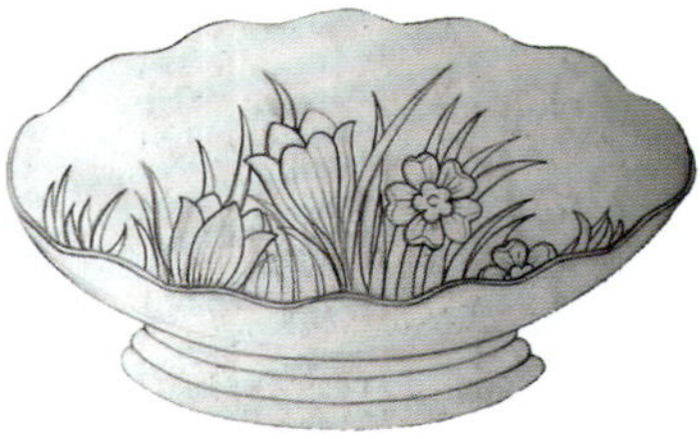

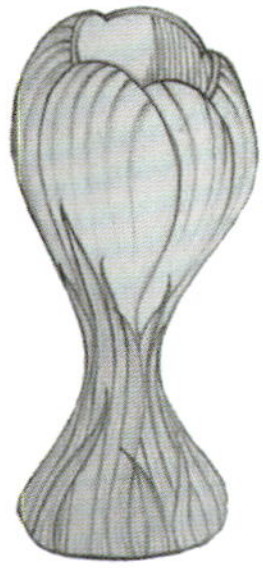

Gladioli

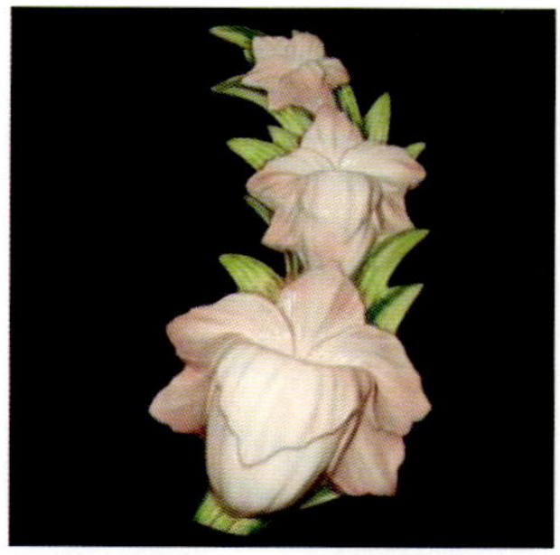

Another one-off pattern. It displays beautifully on a wall.

1744 Bracket £200 - £300

Poppy

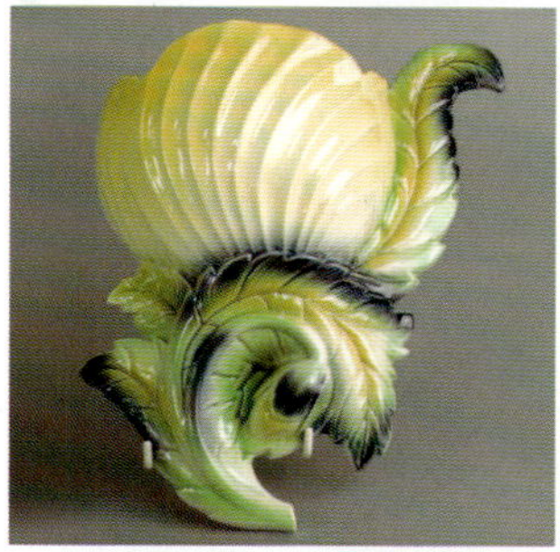

The wall bracket is a very decorative large Poppy flower head rising out of fern like leaves and a poppy in bud. This design was introduced in 1939.

Carlton Ware described shape 1872 as a Flower Vase in their advertising literature, but it is probably closer to what is now known or described as a posy holder. This design was first introduced in the early 1940's. It was available in three colours, pink, yellow and mauve.

Please refer to page 50 for details of the *Poppy* range.

1746 Bracket £140 - £170
1872 Flower Vase £25 - £40

Pyrethrum

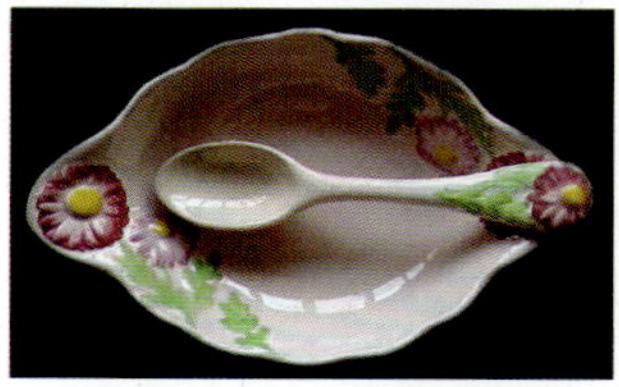

Another single item range. This Butter Dish is available in a number of colourways including green, pink and violet.

1751 & 1757 Jam & Spoon £45 - £80

Wallflower

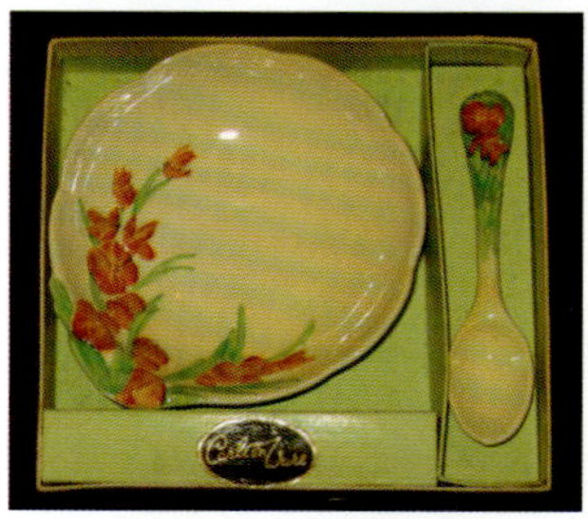

We're not sure why only one shape was produced in this naturalistic representation of a Wallflower. Examples can be found with their original boxes.

1752 & 1763 Jam & Spoon £45 - £60
1752 & 1758 Butter & Knife £45 - £60

Clover/Shamrock

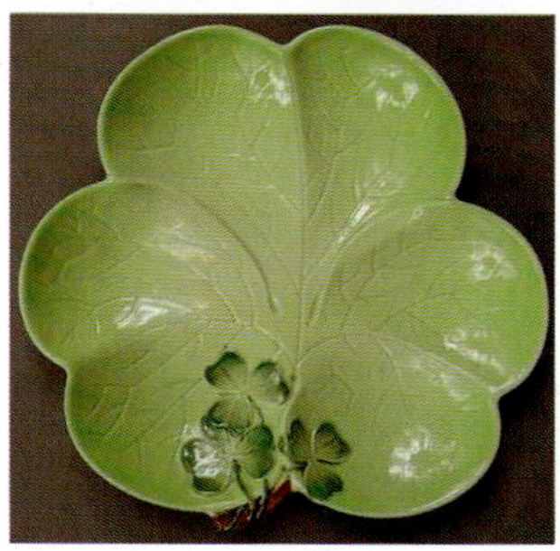

First introduced in 1939, very rarely seen.

1754 Clover Tray £20 - £40
1874 Shamrock Cress Dish & Stand £30 - £50

Narcissus

Introduced in 1939.

1767 Jug £70 - £120

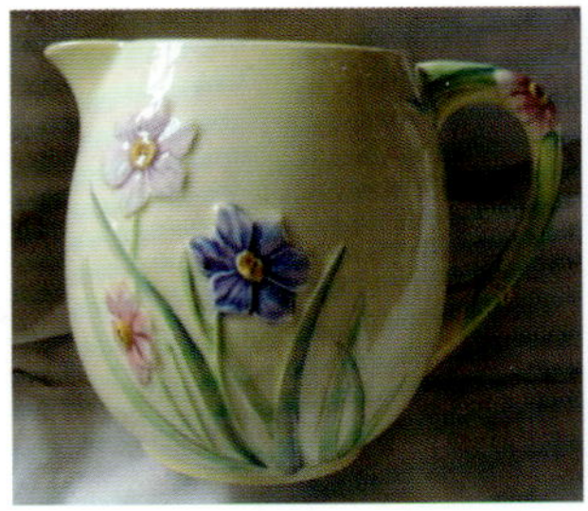

Begonia

Introduced in 1939. This is another of the single item ranges, often still available as a boxed set.

1768 Butter & Knife or Jam & Spoon £45 - £60 each set

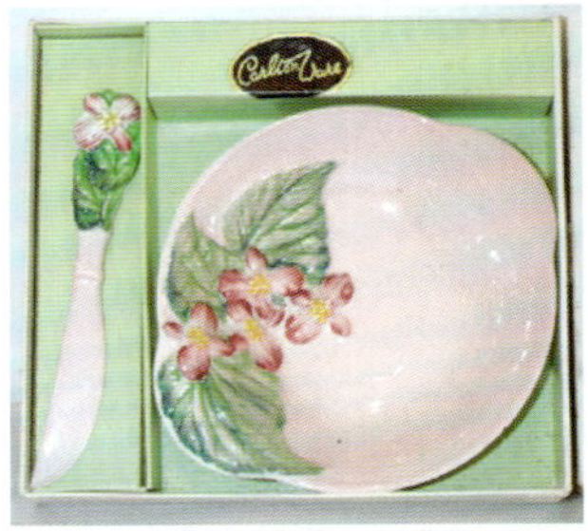

Forget-me-not

Introduced in 1939. Another of the single item ranges, often still available as a boxed set.

1769 Butter & Knife or Jam & Spoon £45 - £60 each set

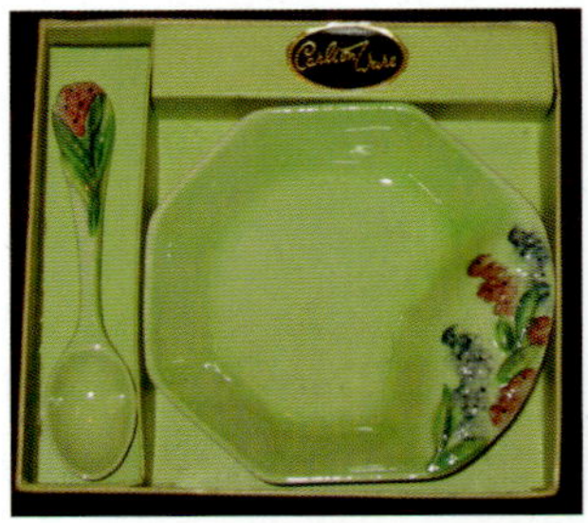

Campion

Introduced in 1939. The Butter Dish was mainly sent to Australia and New Zealand and is now rarely seen in the UK.

1771 Butter & Knife or Jam & Spoon £45 - £60 each set
1873 Flower Vase £40 - £60

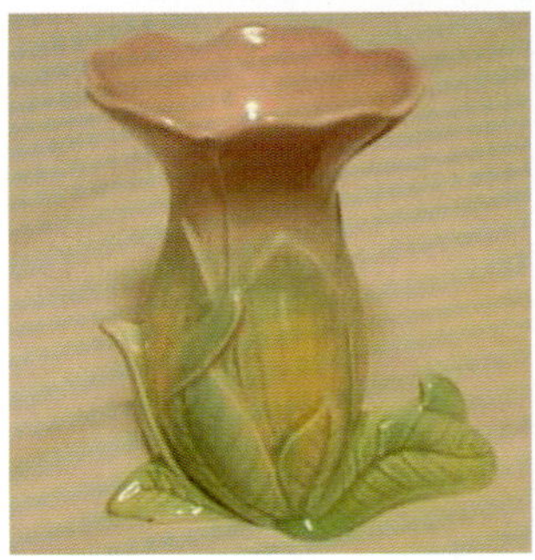

Margarite

Introduced in 1940.

1867 Flower Vase £40 - £60

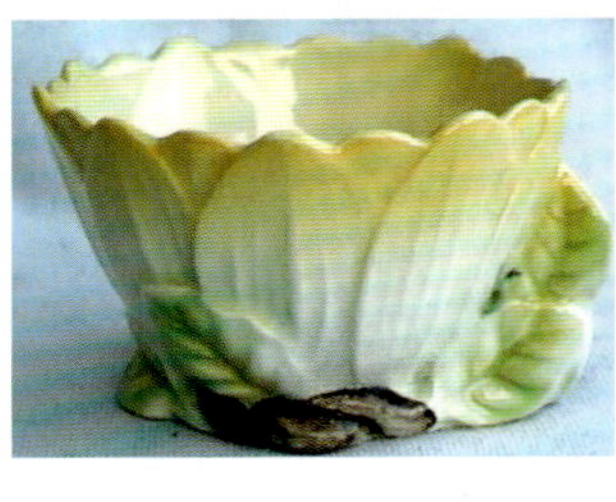

Basket

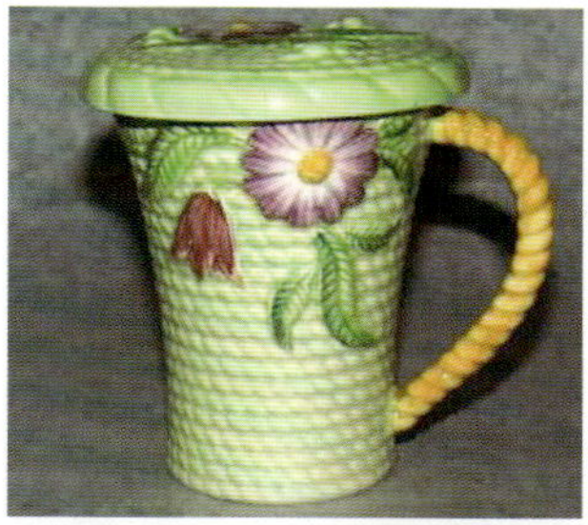

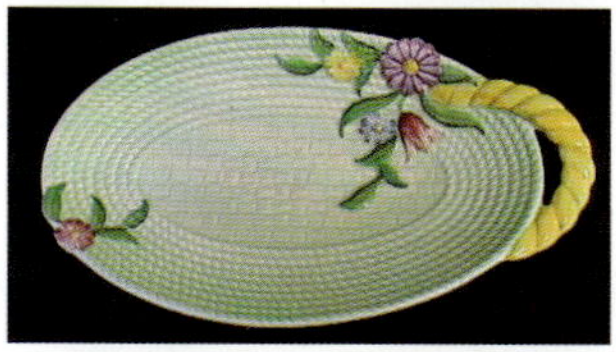

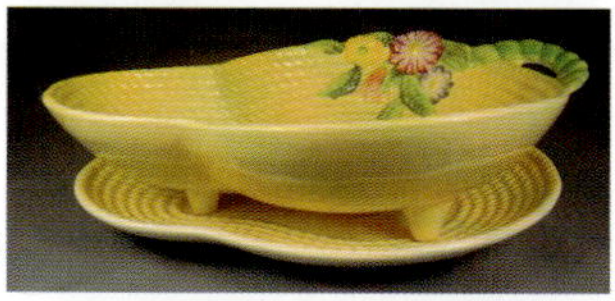

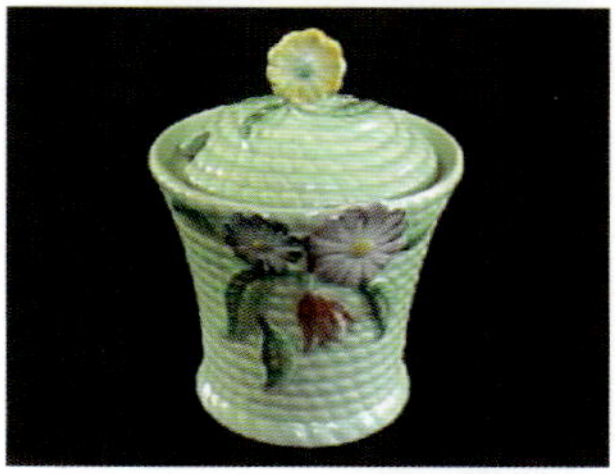

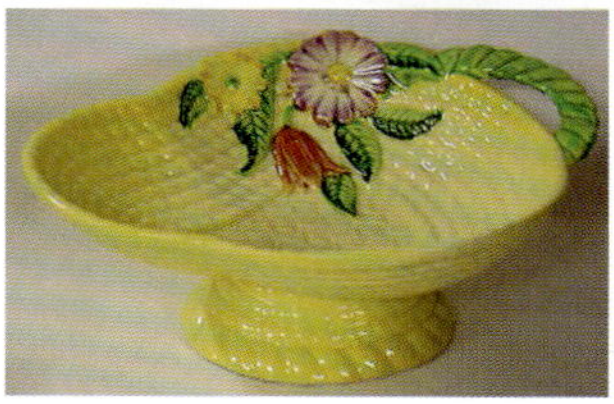

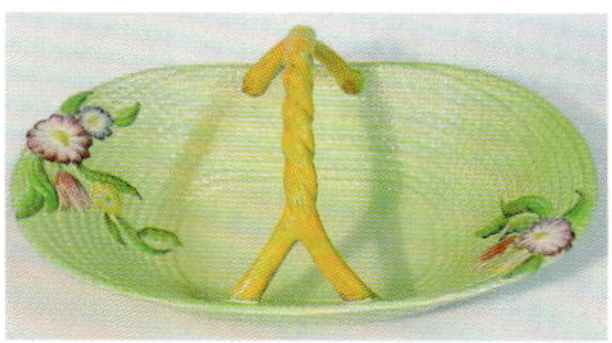

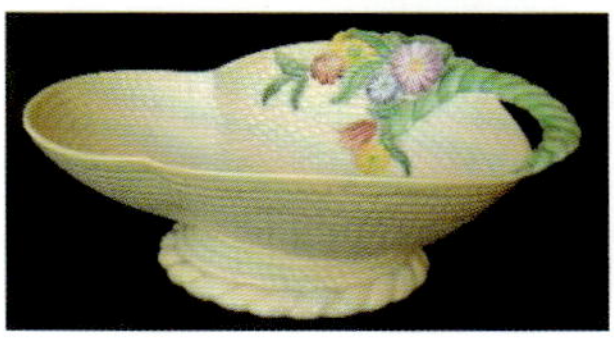

Carlton Ware introduced the embossed range of *Basket* in 1939. This range was produced in the popular colourways of green and yellow, which is replicated in many of Carlton Ware's embossed Floral and Fruit embossed ranges.

The design has pretty spring flowers that are very realistic in appearance. They resemble varieties of Primula flowers in full bloom. The leaves are also very realistic looking and are the shape that you would expect for a Primula leaf. A bell shaped flower that looks similar to a Fritillary usually accompanies the blooms.

The embossing on the design is a very unusual basket weave which resembles a twine or rope effect. This is replicated in the handles. Some pieces such as bowls and servers have a more traditional basket weave effect in the base of the design.

The green colourway pieces are decorated with yellow handles and similarly the yellow colourway has the contrasting green handles.

This design shouldn't be confused with other baskets with flowers in different Floral and Fruit embossed ranges. The detail on this design is finished with lovely hand painted detail that is synonymous with Carlton Ware.

This pattern is also known as *Springtime*.

1775 Handled Flower Basket £80 - £120
1803 Handled Vase/ Basket, 2 sizes £50 - £80
1810 Handled Vase, 2 sizes £50 - £80
1876 & 1944 Salad Bowl and Servers £80 - £120
1907 Covered Beaker £100 - £170
1908 Single Handled Sandwich Tray £40 - £60
1909 Bon Bon £30 - £50
1910 Lemon Squeezer £80 - £100
1911 Handled Basket £100 - £150
1912 Preserve Pot and Cover £90 - £120
1913 Cress Dish & Stand £50 - £100
1922 Serving Open Bowl £40 - £70

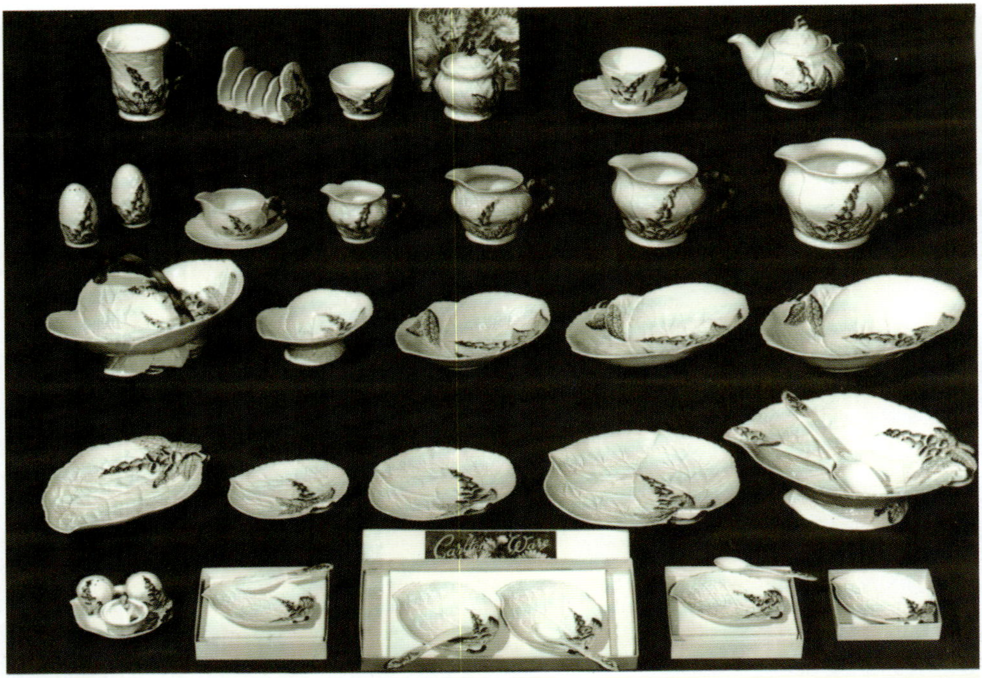

FOXGLOVE DESIGN

Carlton Ware

4285 YELLOW
4286 GREEN
4621 PEACH/CHARTREUSE

FOXGLOVE DESIGN

Prices—each

4285 Yellow
4286 Green
4621 Peach/Chartreuse

Beaker 3/7 Covered 4/9	Toastrack 4/1	Sugar 3/–	Preserve & Spoon boxed 5/7 {Preserve 3/7 {Spoon 1/3	Cup & Saucer 3/3	Teapot 2 cup 5/8
Pepper & Salt l/s 4/– {Pepper 2/– {Salt 2/–	Sauce Boat & Stand 3/2 {Sauce Boat 2/1 {Stand 1/1	Cream Jug 2/9	Jug ½ pint 3/7	Jug 1 pint 4/9	Jug 1½ pint 6/–
Handled Basket 11/8	Bon Bon 3/11	Oval Bowl s/s 3/11	Oval Bowl m/s 5/5	Oval Bowl l/s 6/10	
Leaf Tray 4/5	Dish 4″ 2/1	Dish 6″ 2/9	Dish 9″ 5/5	Salad Set 15/2 {Bowl 10/10 {Servers 4/4	
Cruet Set 5/5 {Pepper & Salt s/s boxed 2/10 {Pepper 1/2 {Salt 1/2	Butter & Knife boxed 3/3 {Butter 1/5 {Knife 1/3	Combined Butter & Knife and Jam & Spoon boxed 6/2	Jam & Spoon boxed 3/3 {Jam 1/5 {Spoon 1/3	Individual Boxed Butter 2/–	

Foxglove

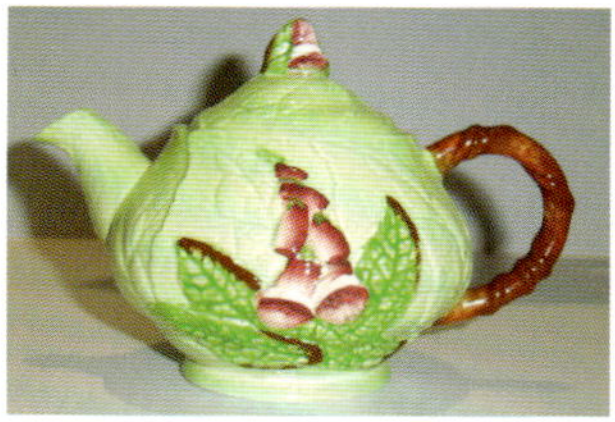

Foxglove is one of the better-known floral embossed wares that was produced by Carlton Ware; it was introduced in the early 1940's. *Foxglove* was a very popular pattern and still is loved and collected profusely by many collectors.

The embossed design is a very detailed and intricate depiction of the veins of a leaf including the ridged edges. The flower also is very realistically detailed along with its stem and leaves. The main colourways are green and yellow. They both have the Foxglove flowers painted in the colour of purple and the leaves are green but edged with a brownish tinge, perhaps suggesting that the flower has reached maturity or nearing the end of its long life.

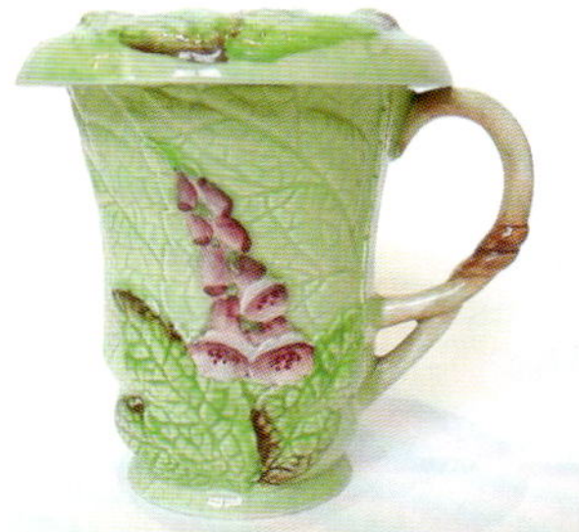

A leaflet advertising the *Foxglove* range states that the colourways are yellow and green as well as Peach/Chartreuse. The latter colour was probably added to the range about four years later on and is shown on the leaflet by being stamped on rather than printed. A pink colourway has also been seen with the usual purple flowers.

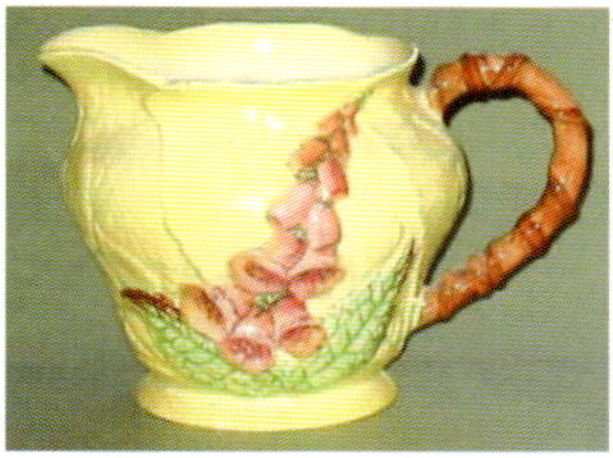

Another strange anomaly is that the saucers used for the *Foxglove* range seem to have been recycled from the *Apple Blossom* range, which would explain the different shape number of 1670 on the base of the saucer. This was probably due to economics and the fact that there weren't really any other distinguishing features on it.

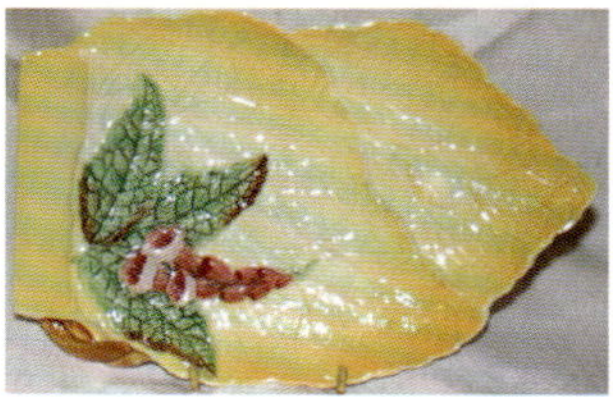

1870 Leaf Tray £25 - £35
1875 Butter Dish £25 - £35
1879 Salad Bowl £60 - £100 and Servers £90 - £150
1881 Preserve Pot and Cover £60 - £80
1882 Flower Jug, Pitcher £130 - £180
1883 Morning Tea Set (Tea for two) £300 - £400
Tea Pot £130 - £170, Cup & Saucer £40 - £60
Sugar £40 - £65, Cream £40 - £75 Plate £20 - £40
1884 Handled Basket £75 - £120
1885 Jug (3 sizes) £45 - £95
1886 Beaker and Cover £90 - £120
1887 Cheese Plate and Knife £45 - £75
1888 Bon-bon dish £40 - £60
1895 Toast Rack £70 - £90
1896 Cruet Set £70 - £100
Salt and Pepper, large size £45 - £75
1897 Sauceboat and Stand £50 - £80
1898 Butter & Knife or Jam & Spoon £40 - £60 each set
1903 Oval Bowl, 3 sizes £20 - £50
1904 Plate £20 - £40

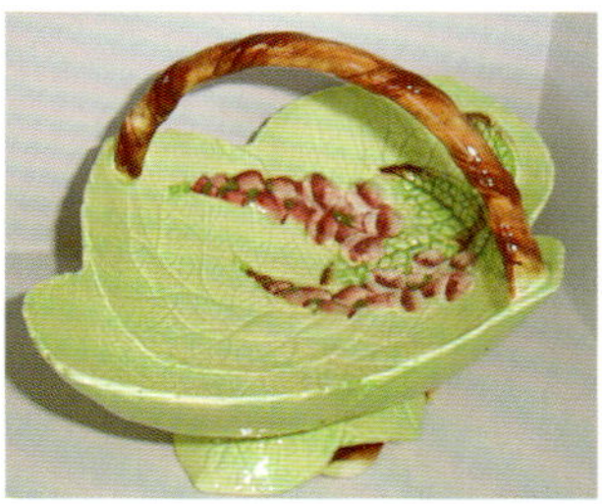

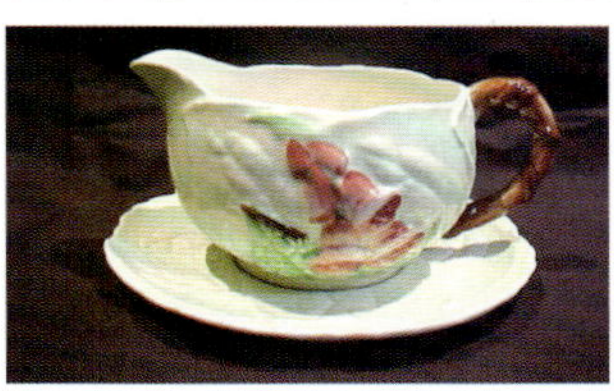

Clematis

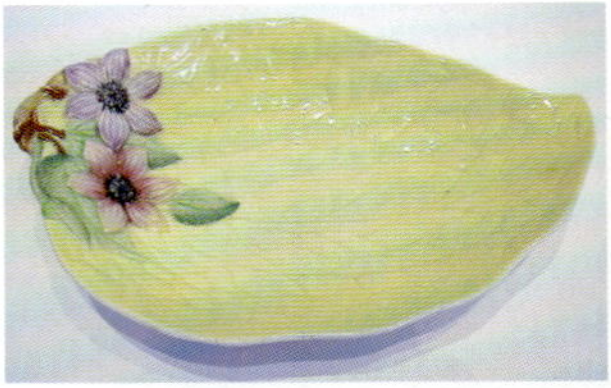

This is another of the beautiful designs that Carlton Ware produced in the Fruit and Floral embossed ranges. It was introduced some time during the war period around 1942 to 1945.

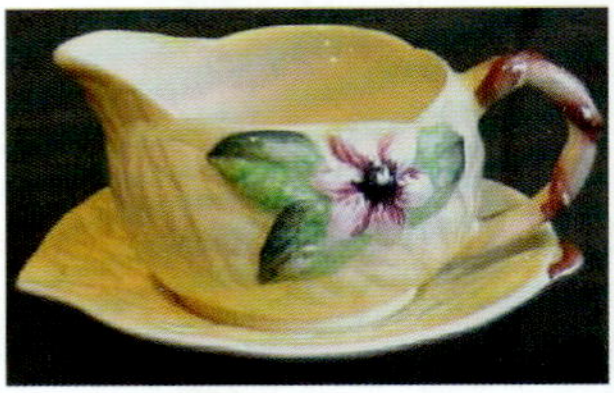

The colourways that this design was produced in were the usual green and yellow but with the addition of a blue colourway.

The flowers on the design are unmistakably varieties of Clematis with pretty pink and purple flower heads. The flower heads and green leaves are attached to a brown woody stem, which is also replicated in the handles of some pieces giving the appearance of a climbing plant.

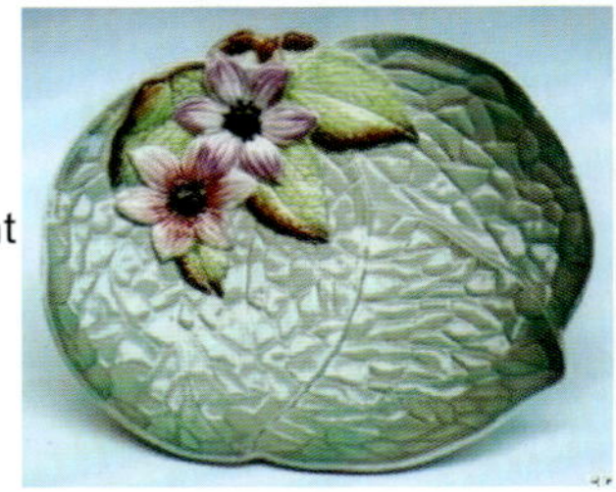

The leaf effect of veins is continued through into the embossing of the pattern and also dishes or trays complement the design by being shaped like a leaf as with many of the other Floral and Fruit embossed ranges. In this design some of the larger plates and trays have leaves overlapping one another to great effect.

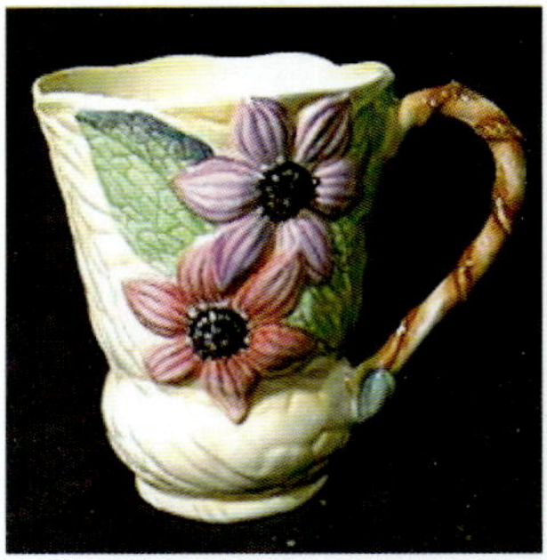

Once again Carlton Ware produced a very attractive design with very clear detailing on the whole design but especially on the flowers and leaves.

1953 Leaf Plate £30 - £50
1957 Beaker & Cover £90 - £120
1958 Oval Bowl, 3 sizes £35 - £65
1959 Sauceboat and Stand £65 - £90
1960 Tall Cream £30 - £50
1961 Supper Tray £30 - £50
1962 Cress Dish and Stand £70 - £95
1963 Plate, 2 sizes £30 - £50
1964 Butter £25 - £40
2275 Basket Tray, one hole £35 - £50
Egg Set £90 - £130

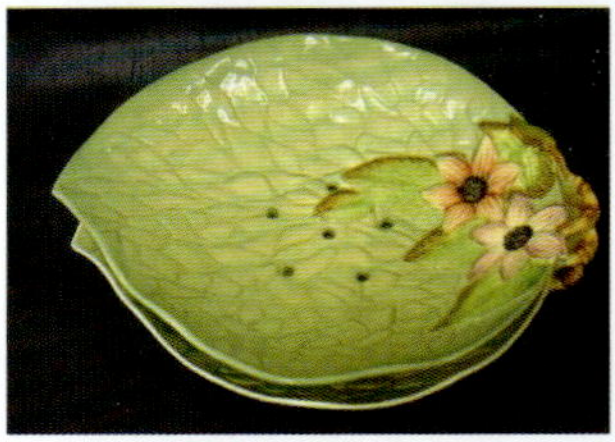

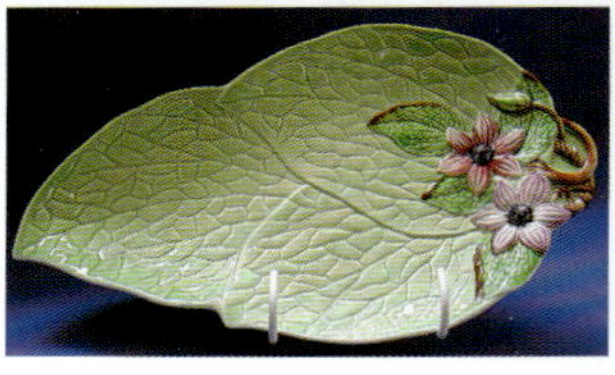

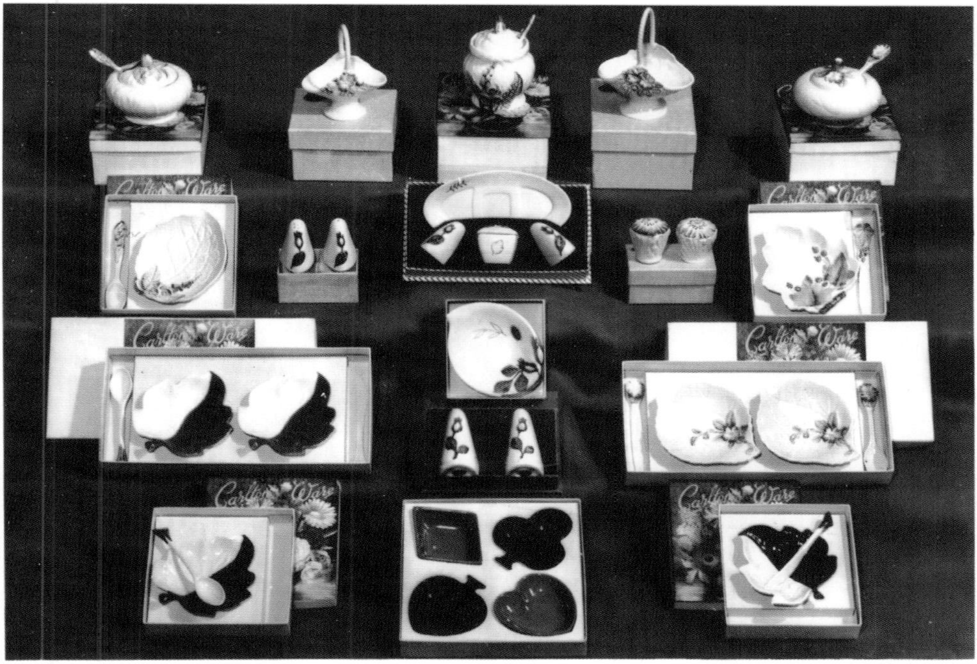

BOXED Carlton Ware ITEMS

Wild Rose (WR) Green & Yellow
Redcurrant (RC) Yellow
Flower Baskets—Green & Yellow
Foxglove (FG) Green, Yellow & Peach/Chartreuse
Pin Stripe (PS) Lime Green, Brown & Sand
Windswept Brown/Cream, Green/Blue & Pink/Blue

BOXED ITEMS

Prices—each

Hazelnut (HN) Green, Matt Cream & Blue
Leaf—4551 twin-tone Green
„ —4552 „ „ Grey
„ —4553 „ „ Brown/Cream
„ —4601 „ „ Chartreuse
Bridge Set Butters Black & Red

Preserve & Spoon .. AB (obsolete)

Flower Basket .. 1775/3 4/11

Preserve & Spoon .. FG 5/7

Flower Basket .. 1775/2 6/3

Preserve & Spoon WR 5/7

Jam & Spoon .. FG 3/3
Also in : WR, RC, HN PS, WS

s/s Pepper & Salt .. HN 2/10

Cruet Set .. HN 7/2

s/s Pepper & Salt .. NP (obsolete)
Also in : HN, FG, WR 2/10 Leaf 2/9

Butter & Knife RC 3/3
Also in : FG, WR, HN, PS, WS

Combined Butter & Knife and Jam & Spoon Leaf 5/8

Single Butter HN 2/–
Also in : RC, FG, WR, Leaf, PS, WS

Combined Butter & Knife and Jam & Spoon WR 6/2
Also in : FG, HN, RC, PS, WS

l/s Pepper & Salt HN 5/6

Jam & Spoon Leaf 3/–

Bridge Set Butters 7/8

Butter & Knife Leaf 3/–

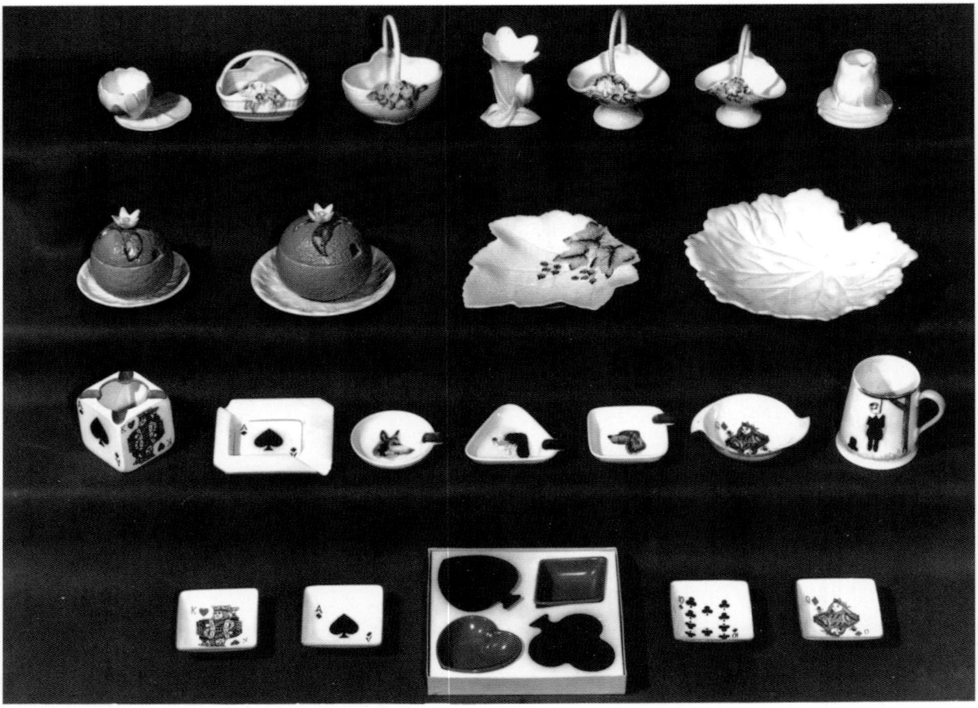

Posy Holders—Pink & Yellow
Flower Baskets—Green & Yellow
Jaffa Preserve—Orange, Stand—Green
RC Leaf Tray—Yellow
Vine Leaf Dish—Green & Yellow

Card Series—Straw Glaze
Dogshead—Straw Glaze
Hangsman Mug—White
Bridge Set Butters—Black & Red

SUNDRIES

Prices—each

Waterlily Posy Holder 2/9	Flower Basket 1810/3 4/1	Flower Basket 1803/2 5/5	Lily Posy Holder 2/5	Flower Basket 1775/2 5/5	Flower Basket 1775/3 4/1
	Boxed 4/11	Boxed 6/3		Boxed 6/3	Boxed 4/11

Jaffa Preserve & Stand s/s 5/5	Jaffa Preserve & Stand l/s 6/9	Redcurrant Leaf Tray 4/5	Vine Leaf Dish 4/9
{Preserve 4/4 Stand 1/1	{Preserve 5/5 Stand 1/4		

Card Series Ashbowl 2256 4/8	Card Series Ashtray 899 3/4 Sets of 4—13/4	Dogshead Ashtray 1914 2/6	Dogshead Ashtray 1915 2/6	Dogshead Ashtray 1917 2/6	Card Series Butter 1387 3/2 Sets of 4—12/8	Hangsman Mug 3/2

Card Series Butter 2266 2/6	Card Series Butter 2266 2/6	Bridge Set Butter boxed 7/8	Card Series Butter 2266 2/6	Card Series Butter 2266 2/6
		{Not boxed—per set of 4—6/–		

Card Series

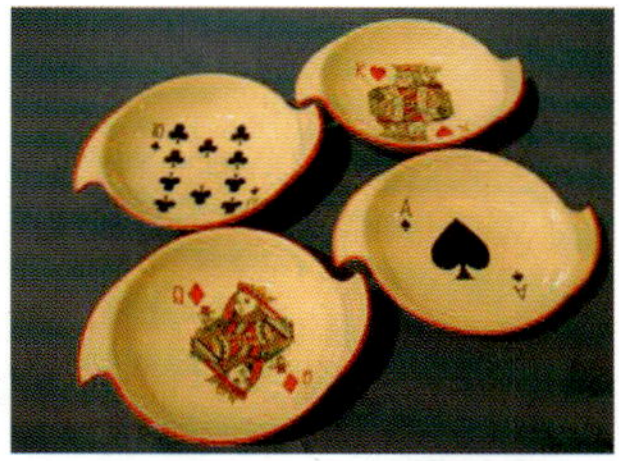

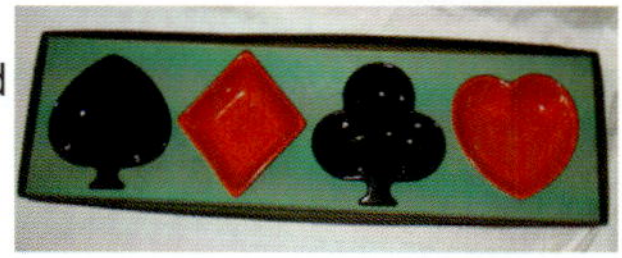

A variety of *Card Series* items were made by Carlton Ware. The earliest was an Ashtray from the early 1930's. This was square in shape and had a playing card as the pattern. This particular shape was still being sold in 1959/60 and later. The circular butter dishes were first sold in the mid 1930's. The set of Bridge butter pats, each shaped in one of a spade, diamond, club and heart, were introduced in the early 1950's. The Ashbowl and square butter pat were introduced in the mid 1950's.

899 Square Ashtray £20 - £40
1387 Circular Butter, 2 ears £10 - £20
2146 Bridge Butter Pat or Ashtray Set £40 - £80
2215 Ashbowl, Cube, with Dice indents £25 - £40
2256 Ashbowl, Cube £25 - £40
2266 Square Butter £10 - £20

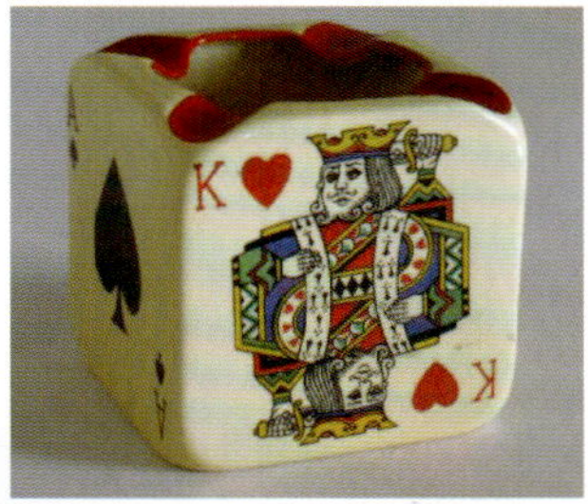

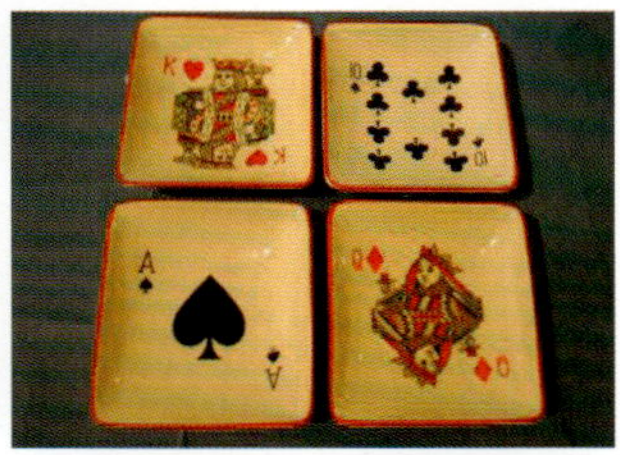

Ashtray

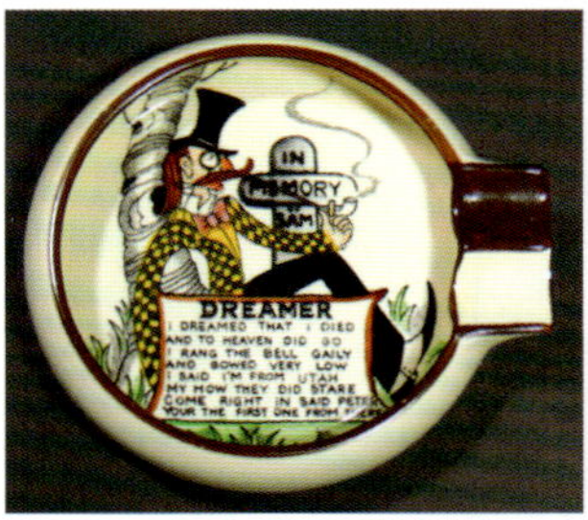

Some ashtrays were produced with a transfer-printed illustration and verse. One such verse reads *In memory of Sam* with a poem entitled *Dreamer*. Different city names were inserted into the poem. Also, *you're* was miss-spelt as *your*! Occasionally you'll find an ashtray with a picture of a town or scene instead; these were sold as a souvenir and are probably of a lower value.

1230 Ashtray, single cigarette rest on each side £15 - £20
1755 Ashtray, double cigarette rest on one side £15 - £20

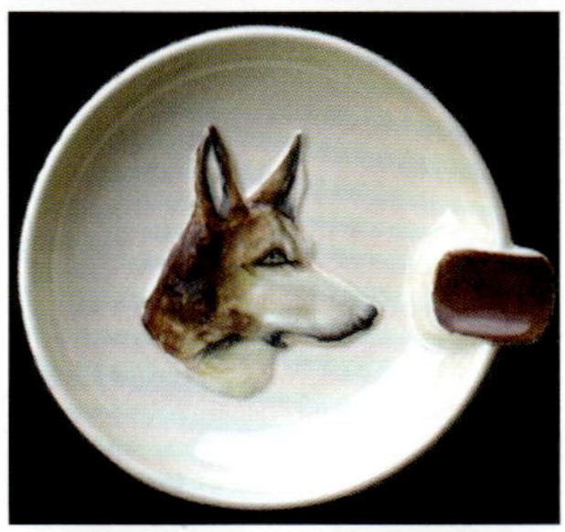

Dogshead

The *Dogshead* range of ashtrays were introduced in about 1940 and as can be seen from the Black & White catalogue page opposite, continued to be sold into at least the 1960's.

1866 Ashtray with Foxhound £5 - £10
1914 Ashtray with Alsatian £5 - £10
1915 Ashtray with Spaniel £5 - £10
1916 Ashtray with Terrier £5 - £10
1917 Ashtray with Setter £5 - £10
1918 Ashtray with Bull Dog £5 - £10

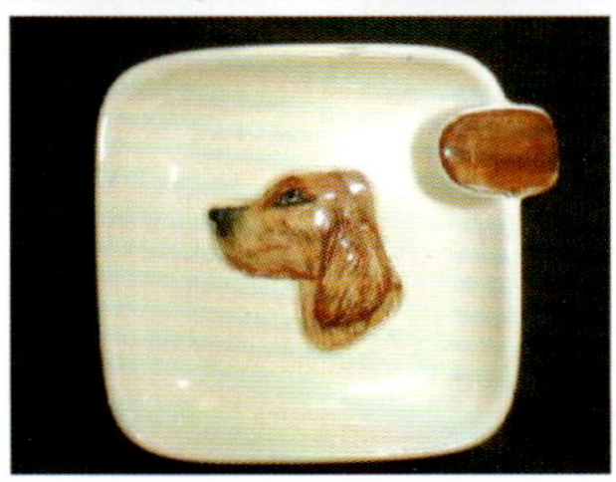

Primula

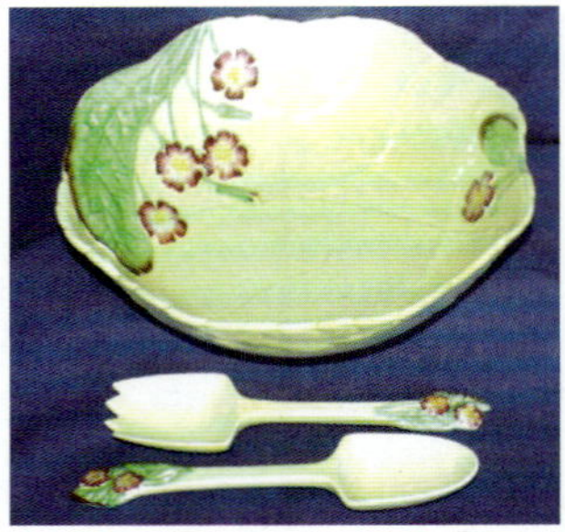

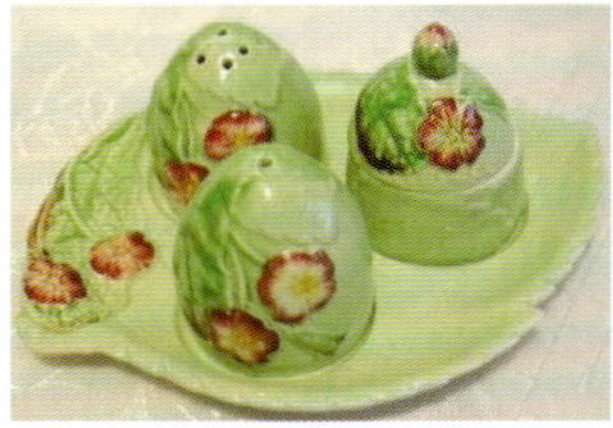

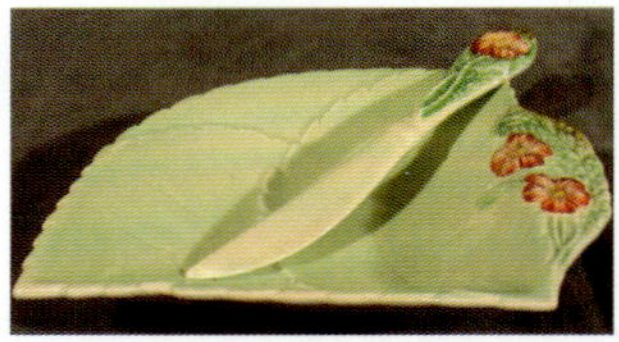

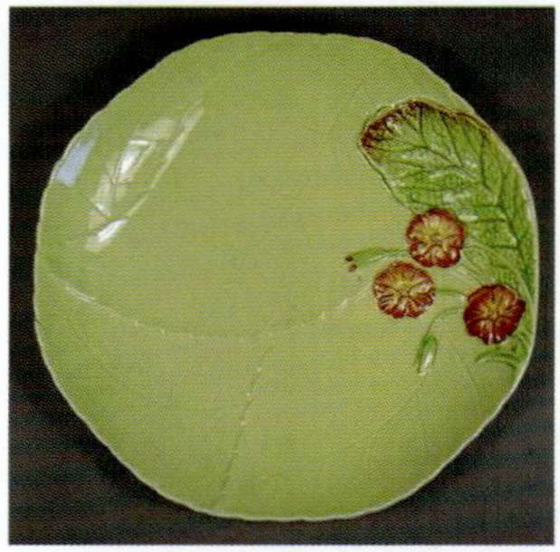

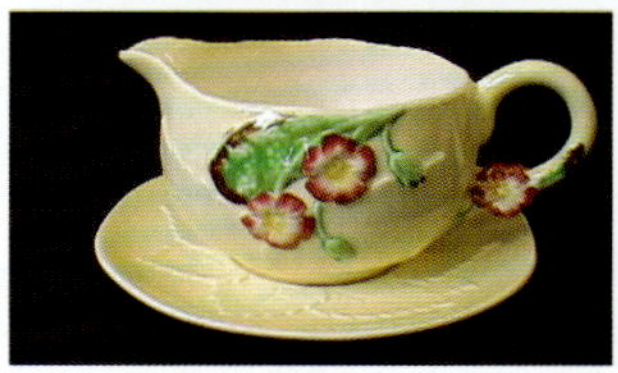

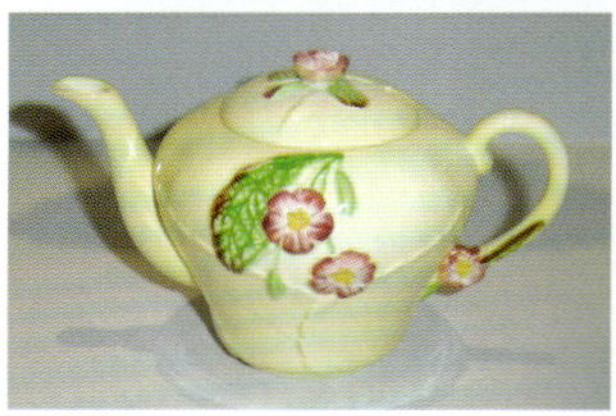

The Primula flower family are a large and very spectacular group of plants that include the primrose and cowslip. These can be found growing profusely in many English gardens and hedgerows. So not surprisingly another well known flower design to add to the lovely range of Carlton Ware embossed fruit and floral wares.

Carlton Ware introduced the *Primula* range in about 1945. It was produced in the very popular colourways of creamy yellow and light green. The flowers were painted in a light reddish purple with yellow and white stamens. This was replicated on both colourways.

The patterns numbers of this design are 4368 and 4369 respectively for the two colourways.

These colourways do seem to have been a good way of presenting the flowers to great effect in a naturalistic way. And after all, these colours had sold well for Carlton Ware on previous designs so why change it now.

As usual Carlton Ware managed to capture all the details of this pretty flower and leaves in a very realistic way. This was complemented by shaping some of the pieces in the style of a leaf complete with embossed veins and serrated edges. Well, after all what could be more lovely than nature itself.

1975 Leaf Tray £20 - £40
1982 & 2052 Butter & Knife £30 - £50
1982 & 2052 Jam & Spoon £30 - £50
2005 Salad Bowl, Fork and Spoon £100 - £150
2012 Cruet £100 - £150
2036 Butter, Triangular £20 - £35
2038 Morning Tea Set (Tea for two) £250 - £400
Tea Pot £130 - £170, Cup & Saucer £40 - £60
Sugar £30 - £50, Cream £30 - £50, Plate £20 - £40
2039 Dish, 4 sizes £20 - £40
2040 Long Dish £25 - £50
2041 Preserve and Lid £50 - £80
2048 Bon-bon dish £30 - £50
2049 Sauceboat and Stand £40 - £60
2052 Jam Spoon & Butter Knife £20 - £40
Candle Stick £30 - £50
Toast Rack £40 - £60

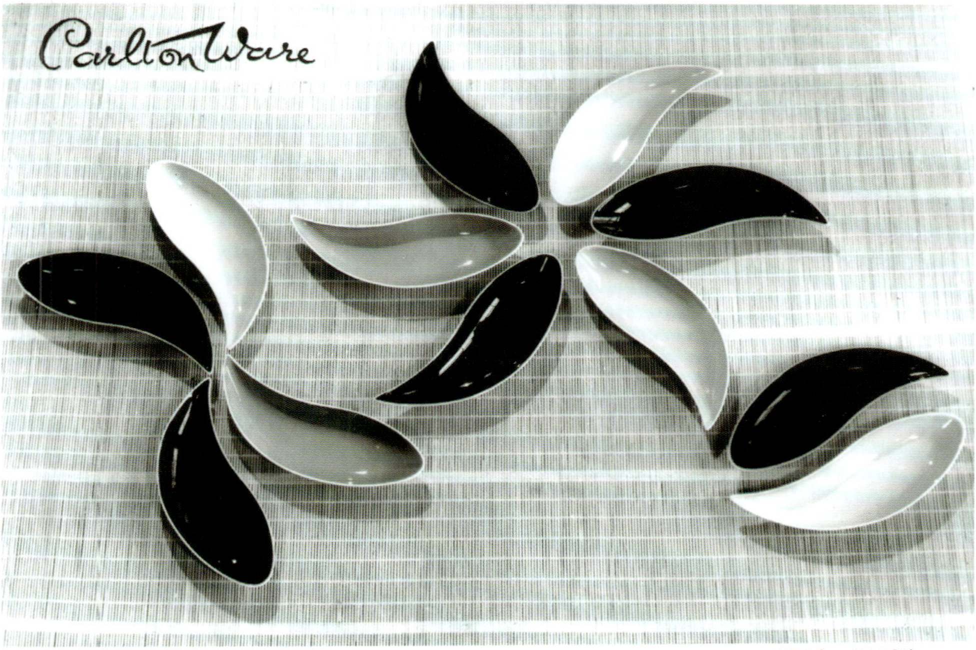

4623 LEAF GREEN
4624 BLUE
4625 LEAF BROWN

HORS D'ŒUVRES DISHES

4626 BLACK
4627 CHARTREUSE
4628 LAVENDER

4623 Leaf Green
4624 Blue
4625 Leaf Brown
4626 Black
4627 Chartreuse
4628 Lavender

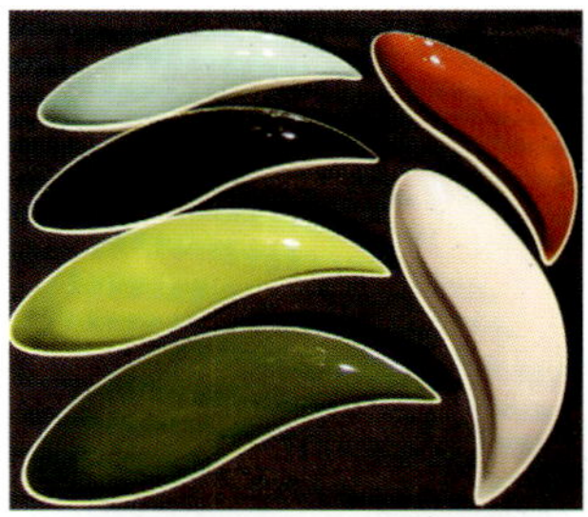

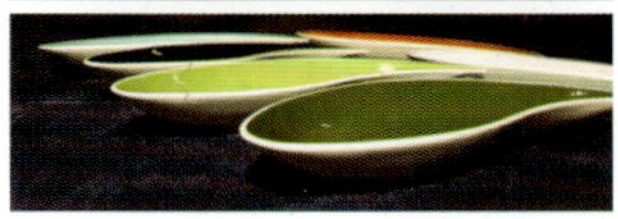

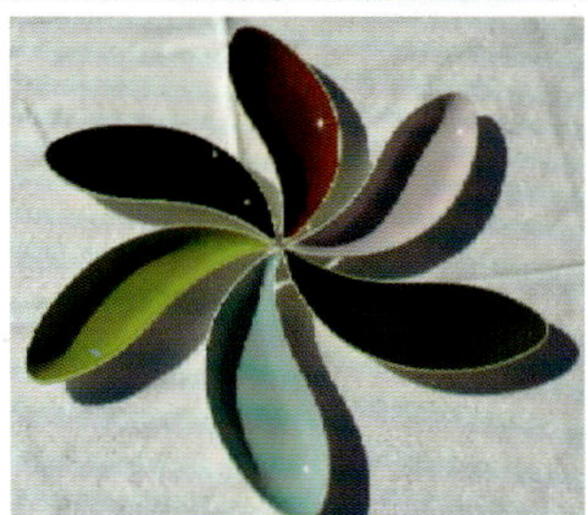

HORS D'ŒUVRES DISHES.

Each Dish	3/3
Per Set of Six Dishes	19/6

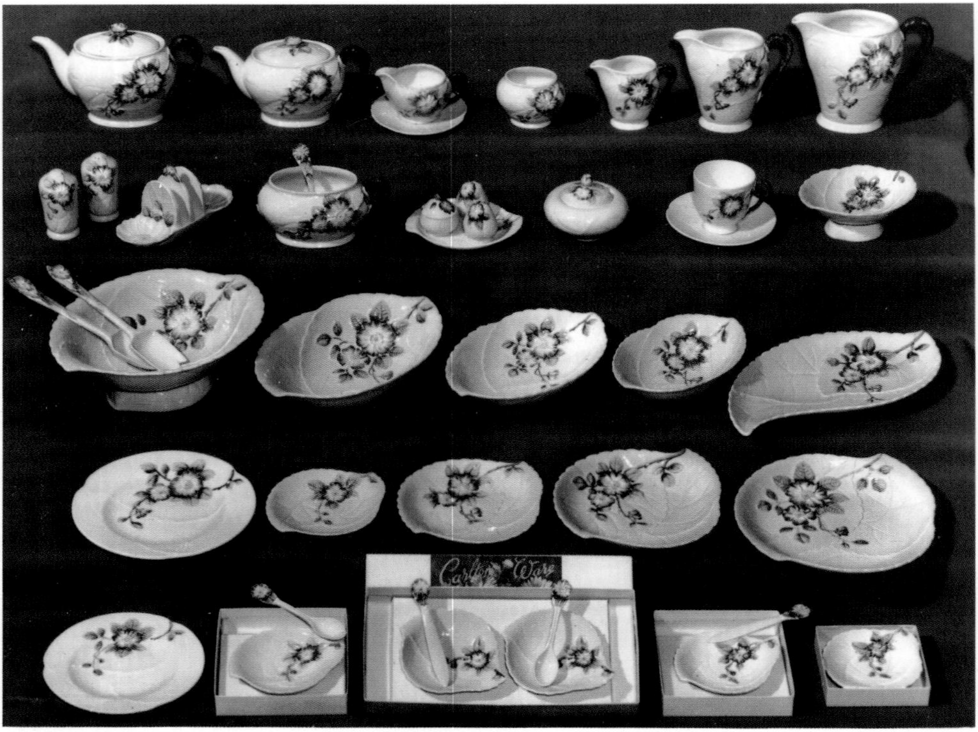

WILD ROSE DESIGN

Carlton Ware

4427 YELLOW
4428 GREEN

WILD ROSE DESIGN

4427 Yellow
4428 Green

Prices—each

Teapot 4 cup 7/9 .. Teapot 2 cup 5/11 .. Sauce Boat & Stand 3/7 .. Sugar 2/9 .. Cream 3/– .. Jug s/s ½ pint 4/6 .. Jug l/s 1 pint 5/8

{Sauce Boat 2/5
{Stand 1/2

Pepper & Salt l/s 4/– .. Combined Toastrack 4/11 .. Mayonnaise Bowl & Ladle 6/11 .. Cruet Set 5/5 .. Preserve 3/7 .. Cup & Saucer 3/8 .. Bon Bon 3/11

{Pepper 2/–
{Salt 2/–

{Bowl 4/8
{Ladle 2/3

{Pepper & Salt s/s boxed 2/10

{Pepper & Salt s/s not boxed 2/4 pr.

{Preserve & Stand 4/7

{Preserve & Spoon 4/9

{Preserve, Spoon & Stand 5/9

{Preserve & Spoon boxed 5/7

Salad Bowl & Servers 15/2 .. Oval Bowl l/s 6/10 .. Oval Bowl m/s 5/5 .. Oval Bowl s/s 3/11 .. Supper Tray 5/8

{Bowl 10/10
{Servers 4/4

Plate 8″ 4/5 .. Dish 4″ 2/1 .. Dish 6″ 2/9 .. Dish 8″ 4/5 .. Dish 9″ 5/5

Plate 5″ 2/4 .. Boxed Jam & Spoon 3/3 .. Comb. Butter & Knife and Jam & Spoon Boxed 6/2 .. Boxed Butter & Knife 3/3 .. Individual Butter Boxed 2/–

{Jam 1/6
{Spoon 1/2

{Butter 1/6
{Knife 1/2

Wild Rose

This hugely popular range was first introduced in the late 1930's but the majority of the pieces were made in 1950's.

2108 Oval Dish 4", 6", 8", 9" £30 - £60
2114 Butter & Knife or Jam & Spoon £20 - £40 each set
2115 Morning Tea Set (Tea Pot, Sugar, etc) £250 - £450
Tea Pot £100 - £150, Cup & Saucer £45 - £80
Sugar £40 - £70, Cream £40 - £70 Plate £20 - £50
Round Plate 5", 8" £20 - £50
2116 Oval Bowl, 3 sizes £40 - £60
2117 Cruet Set £70 - £100
Salt & Pepper, large size £30 - £50
2118 Toast Rack £60 - £90
2119 Supper Tray (Long Tray) £20 - £50
2120 Preserve with cover £50 - £80
2121 Sauceboat and Stand £50 - £80
2122 Bon Bon £45 - £70
2123 Salad Bowl and Servers £70 - £90
2124 Jug, 2 sizes £60 - £100
2132 Mayonnaise Bowl & Ladle £70 - £100

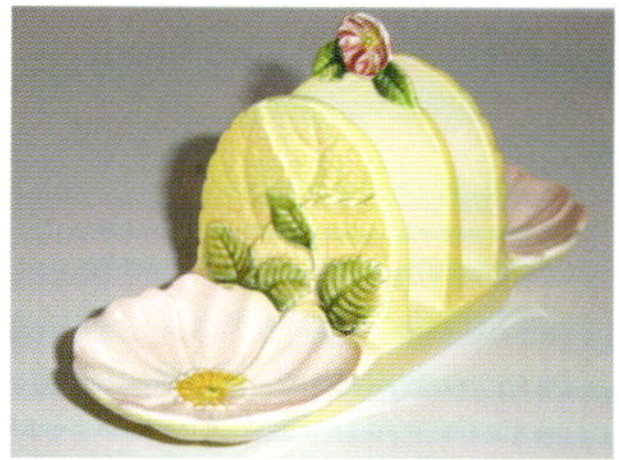

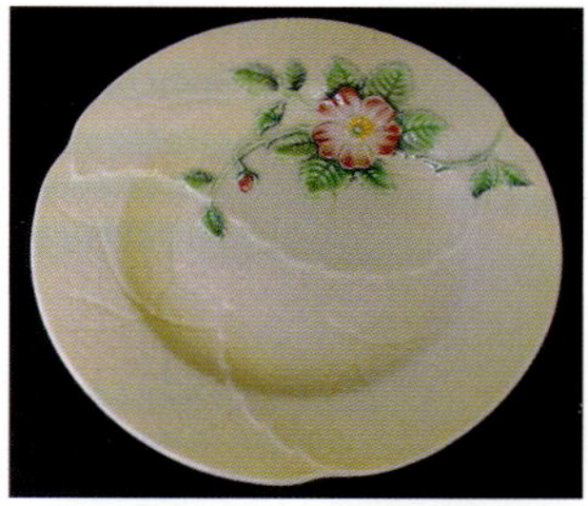

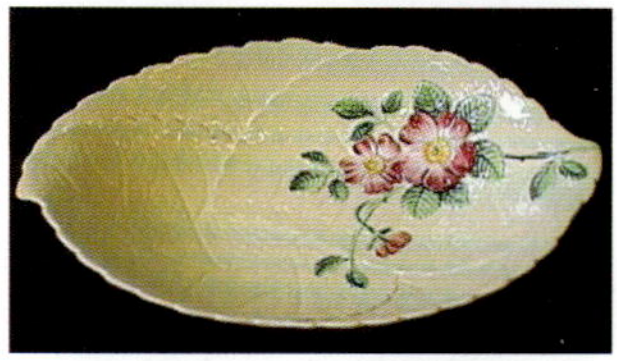

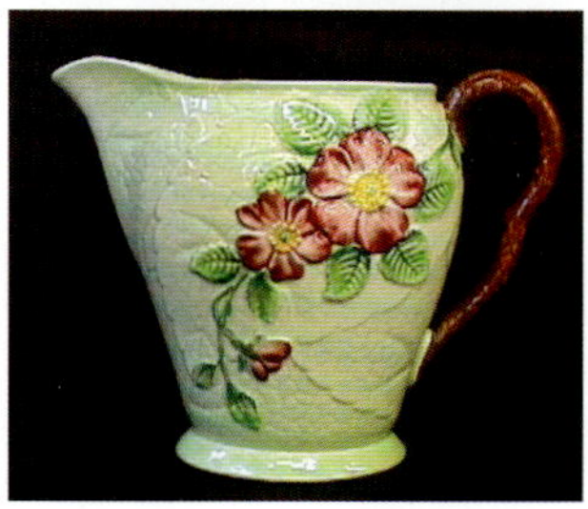

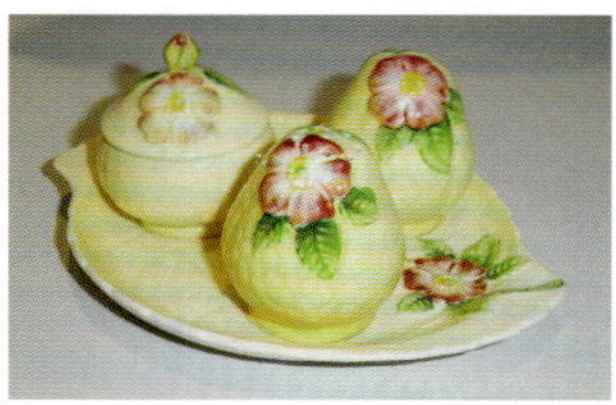

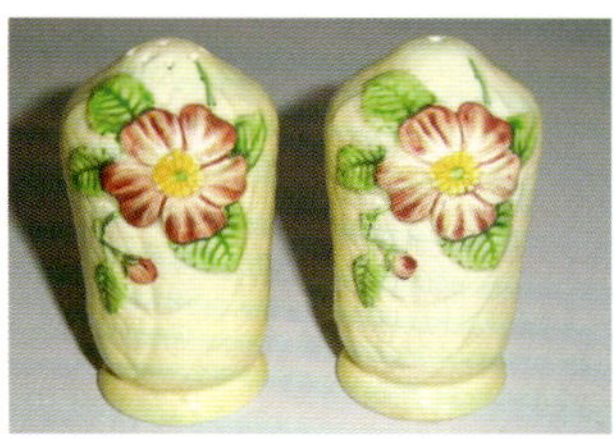

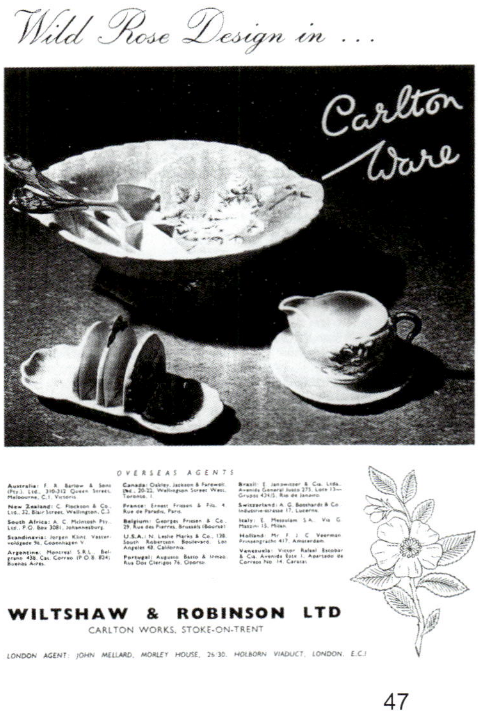

Poppy and Daisy

Carlton Ware introduced the embossed *Poppy & Daisy* range in the late 1940's in pink, pale green and a turquoise/blue colourway.

This beautiful design has lovely embossed flowers that are very pronounced and detailed. The design mainly consists of a profusion of realistic Daisy flower heads with yellow stamens. These are usually arranged in a circle around the edge or perimeter of a piece. The Daisies are interspersed with larger Poppy flower heads that have the unmistakable paper like petals of a Poppy and the black stamens in the centre.

2010 Round Bowl £60 - £90
2033 Oval Tray £50 - £80
2034 Vase, 3 sizes £80 - £180
2042 Bowl, 3 dips, 3 sizes £50 - £140
2051 Bowl/Plate, 2 sizes £50 - £80
2053 Bon-bon dish £40 - £70
2054 Large Footed Bowl, Fluted £70 - £100
2057 Round Vase, 3 sizes £60 - £160
2079 Lamp Base £90 - £120

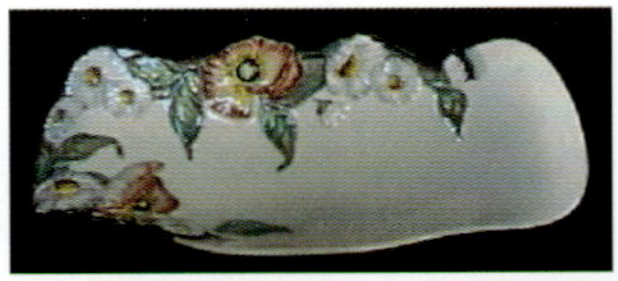

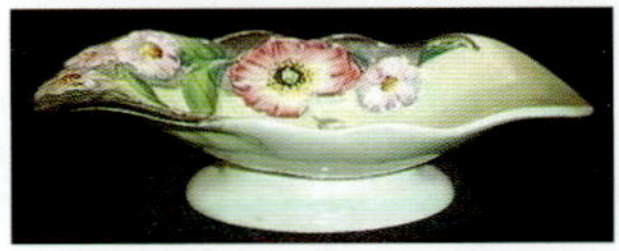

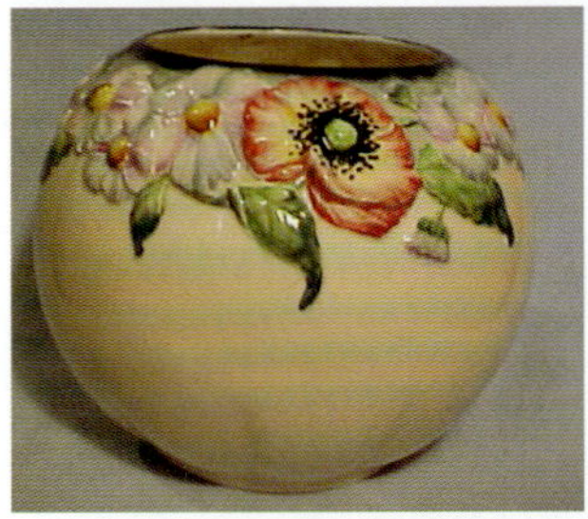

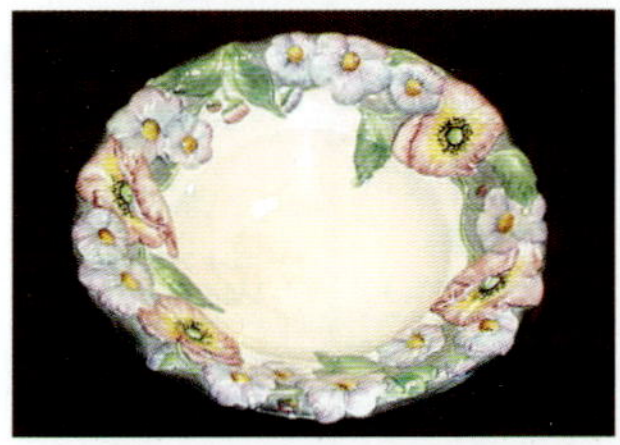

New Daisy

New Daisy embossed was probably introduced in 1948/49 according to the shape numbers allocated to them. It was produced in the pink, pale green and turquoise colourways that are the same as *Poppy and Daisy*. The design has a garland of realistic Daisy flower heads with yellow stamens. These are interspersed with green leaves much the same as *Poppy and Daisy* but without the unmistakable poppies.

The patterns *Poppy & Daisy* and *New Daisy* are obviously similar in many ways and often confusion arises between these two patterns. The best way of identifying the *Poppy & Daisy* pattern is to find a flower head that has many black stamens clustered in the centre and looks like a poppy.

2043 Vase, 2 sizes £60 - £90
2044 Oval Tray £60 - £80
2045 Sugar and Cream £50 - £70 each
2056 Preserve £60 - £90
2402 Lamp (2043 upside down) £60 - £90

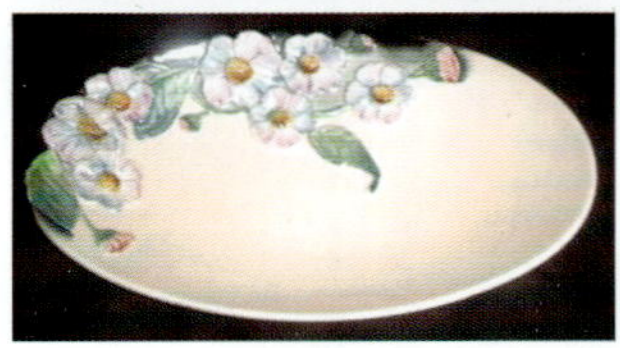

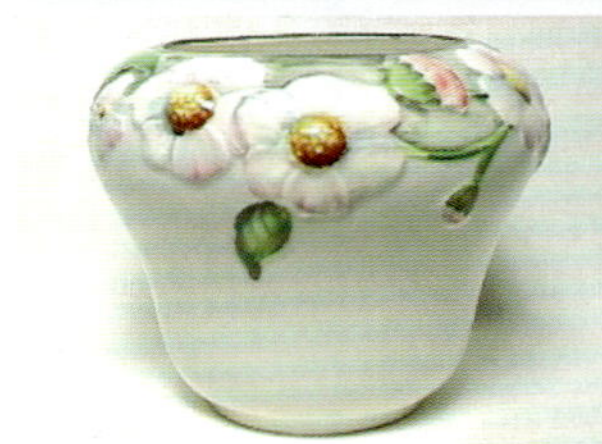

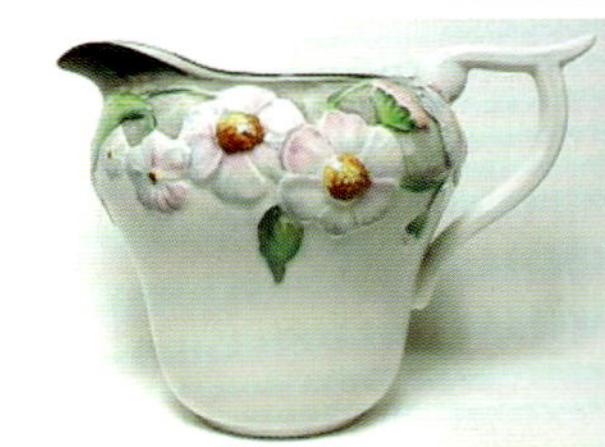

Cherry

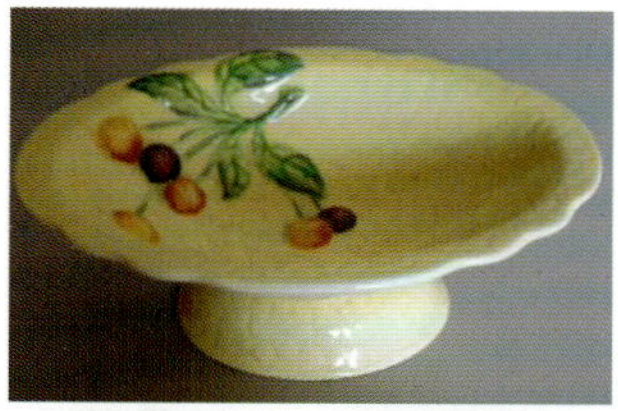

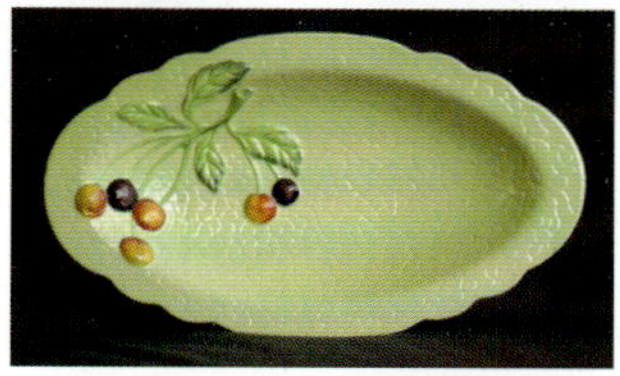

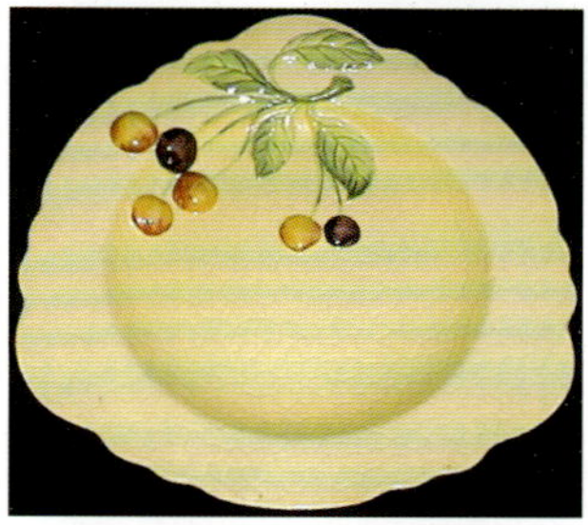

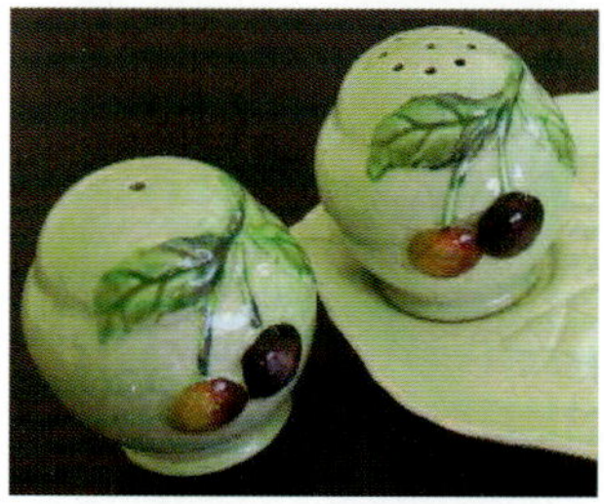

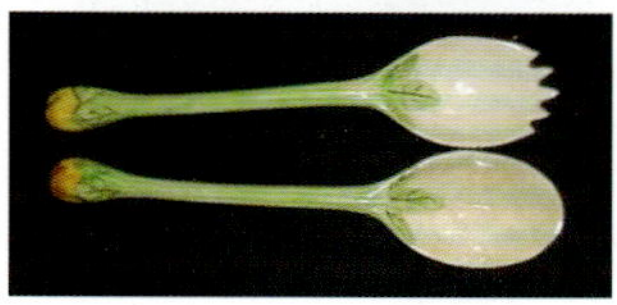

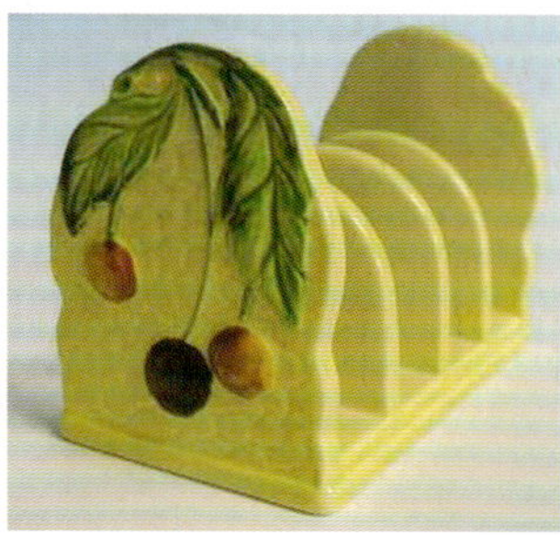

This is another of the beautiful designs that Carlton Ware produced in the Fruit and Floral embossed range. It was introduced some time during the war period from 1940 to 1945.

This design was produced in the popular colourways of green and yellow; these were a favourite for the embossed ranges.

The fruit that appears on the design are unmistakably Cherries. They are beautifully hand painted and the contrast between the ripe purple cherry and the yellowish ripening cherry make a very fetching design. The sprigs of cherries are attached to stems and leaves in a realistic detailed style.

The embossing finish in the design could be described as having the same mottled effect and look of crazy paving. Many of the pieces in this range have a lovely fluted edge to the rim; this is an added feature that adds greatly to the style of the design.

2109 Oval Plate, 3 sizes £20 - £40
2126 Oval Bowl, 3 sizes £30 - £50
2127 Preserve Jar, Lid & Ladle £50 - £80
2128 Tall Cream £30 - £60
2129 Sugar £30 - £60
2130 Cream £30 - £60
2133 Plate, 3 sizes £20 - £40
2134 Butter & Knife or Jam & Spoon £40 - £70 each set
2135 Cruet Set £70 - £100
2136 Salad Bowl & Servers £80 - £120
2137 Bon Bon £30 - £50
2153 Mug £30 - £60
2155 Jug, 2 sizes £30 - £60
2158 Toast Rack £50 - £80
Comport, twin handled £30 - £60

Poppy

This beautiful embossed Carlton Ware design was introduced in the late 1940's and continued into the early 1950's. It was made in the colourways of pink, yellow and green.

The *Poppy* pattern is very different from the *Poppy and Daisy* range and cannot be confused. This is because the *Poppy* design is formed in to the shape and the finish of the pieces; thus creating the detail of many flower heads that overlap each other with many folds and details on the petals within the embossed design of the pieces.

The brightly painted Poppy head has black and pink stamens that surround the heavily embossed yellow, pink or green centre. All pieces, with the exception of the bon bon dish show a fern-like leaf similar to that of an oriental poppy which often curves around the edge of the piece, similar to the *Tulip* design.

This really is a fabulous addition to the famous embossed flower ranges. And, as usual Carlton Ware did not scrimp on the lovely realistic details to the finished design of all the pieces in this range.

2257 Plate, 3 sizes £40 - £70
2263 Jug £60 - £90
2276 3 Way Tray £60 - £90
2278 5 Way Tray £100 - £150
2281 Oval Bowl, double poppy, 3 sizes £50 - £80
2284 Butter & Knife or Jam & Spoon £50 - £80 each set
2285 Preserve with lid & spoon £70 - £110
2287 Bon Bon £40 - £60
2288 Sugar and Cream £40 - £70 each
2289 & 2291 Salad Bowl & Servers £90 - £130
2290 Toast Rack, combination £80 - £120
2292 Tea Pot £140 - £200
2293 Cruet £100 - £150
Salt & Pepper, Tall £40 - £70
2294 Sauceboat & Stand £60 - £80

Carlton Ware also produced some other embossed pieces called *Poppy* but these were much earlier and do differ from the *Poppy* range described above. See page 35.

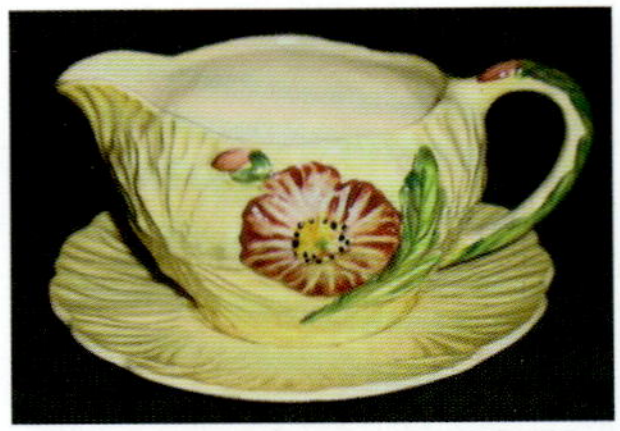
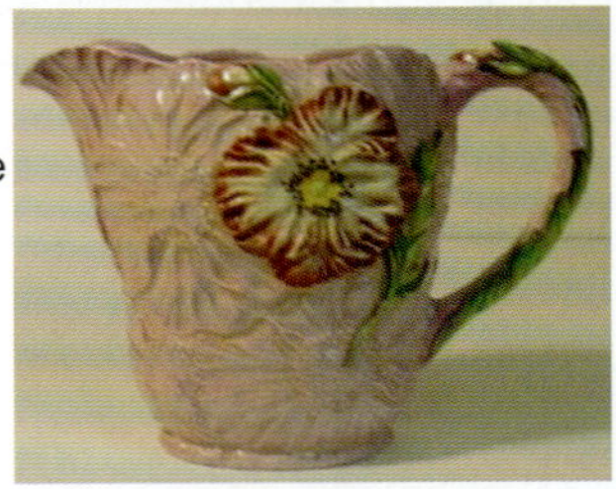
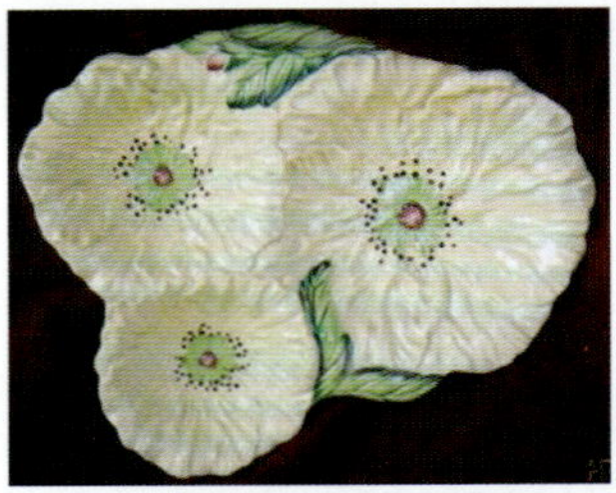
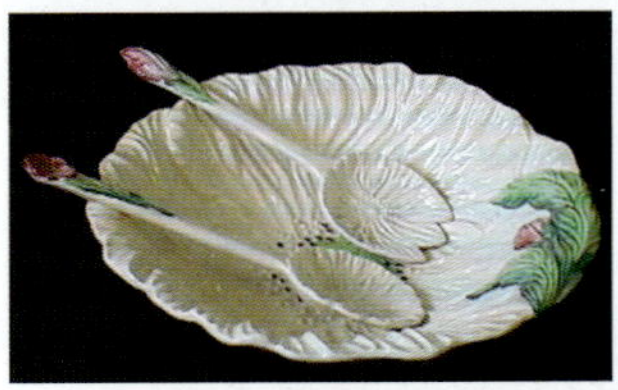
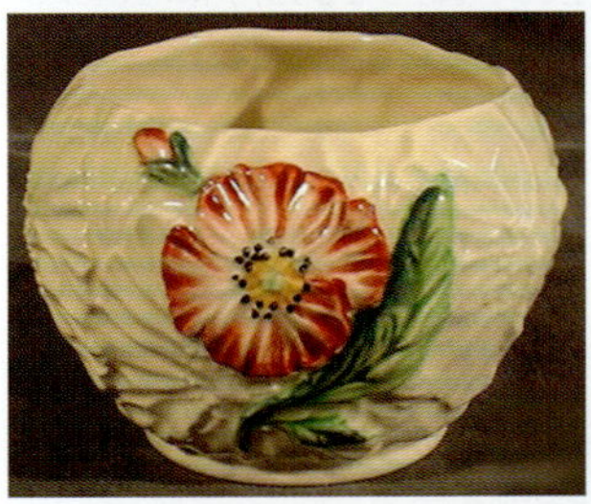
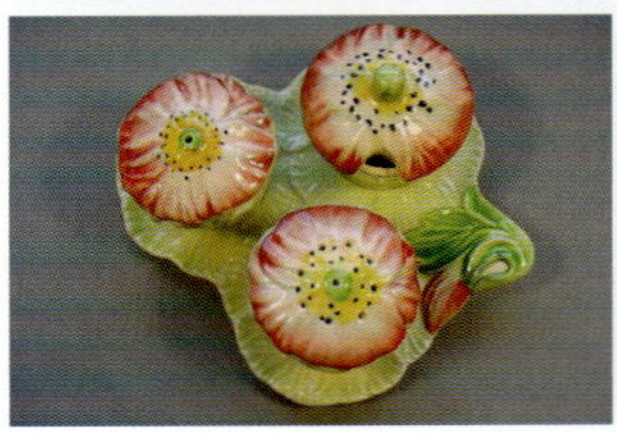

Hydrangea

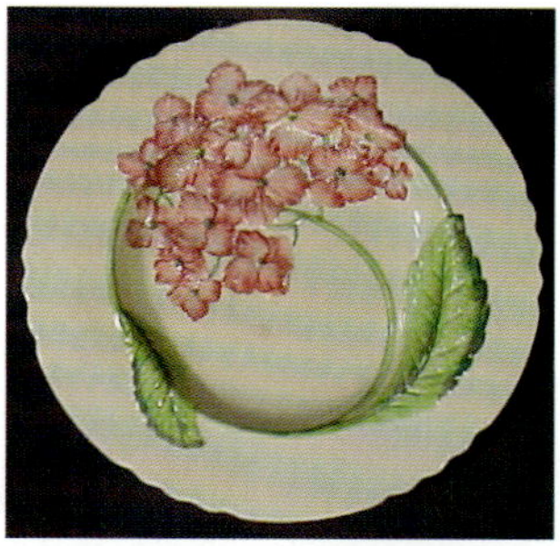

Most of us are familiar with the Hydrangea plant with its pink or blue flowers. In acid soil the blooms are blue, in alkaline soil the flowers are pink whilst in neutral soil they will be white.

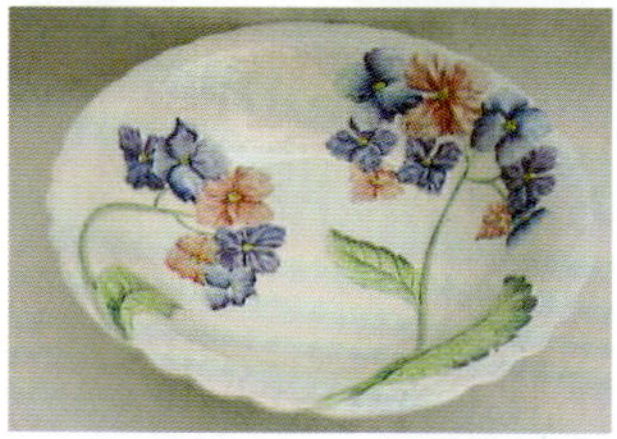

Carlton Ware introduced the *Hydrangea* range in the early 1950's. The flower heads were coloured in pink or blue and sometimes a mixture of the two. The background colours were pale blue (pattern 4449) and pale green (pattern 4448).

Counterfeit copies are circulating and one should be careful. Many of these fakes are easy to spot because the four-petal flower heads have a mixture of pink and blue petals. For details take a look at the chapter on Fakes.

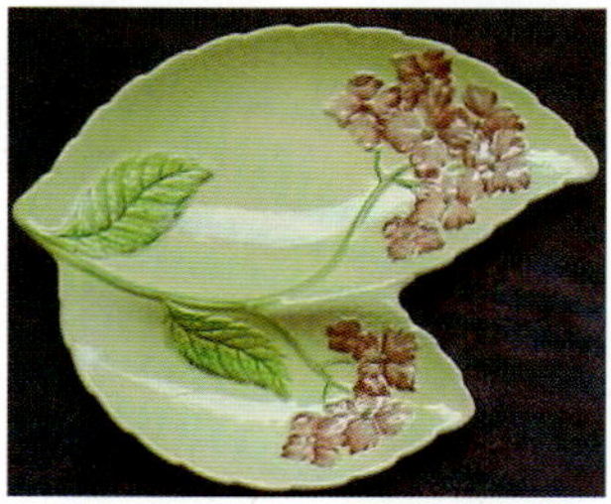

2086 Vase £70 - £90
2154 Vase, Tall, 3 sizes £100 - £160
2161 Tray, 3 sizes £60 - £120
2165 Flat Bowl, 2 sizes £70 - £110
2167 Vase £70 - £90
2169 Bon-bon dish £50 - £80
2170 Round Bowl £110 - £170
2171 Wall Vase £70 - £110
2172 Preserve with Cover £80 - £120
2173 Sugar & Cream £60 - £80 each
2174 Oval Bowl, 2 sizes £80 - £130
2176 Footed Bowl £100 - £140
2209 Two way Tray £90 - £110
2210 Five way Tray £120 - £170
2219 Three way Tray £100 - £130
2261 Wall Vase, Flat Back, 2 sizes £80 - £120
2264 Flat Back Lamp Base £90 - £130

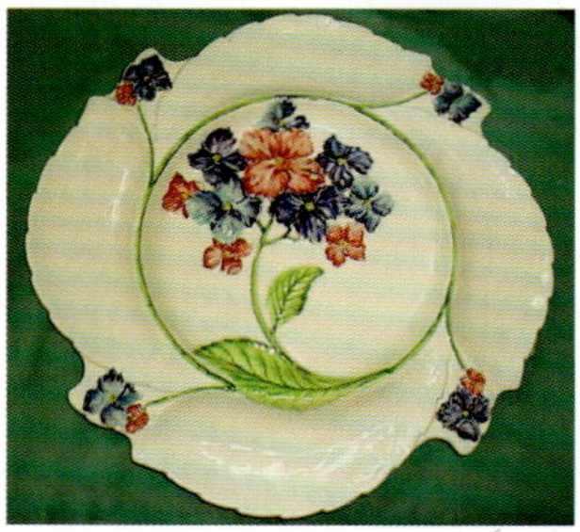

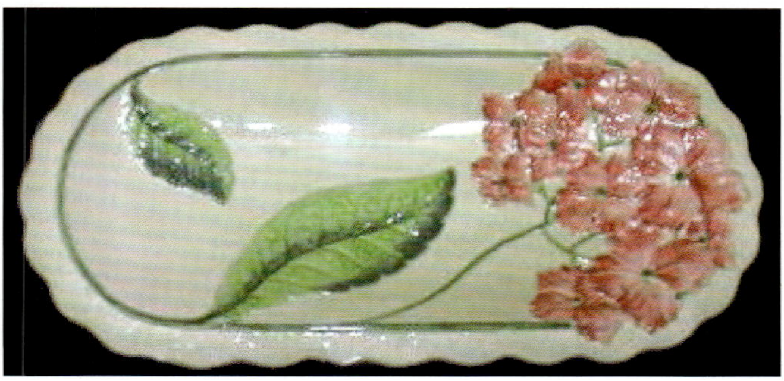

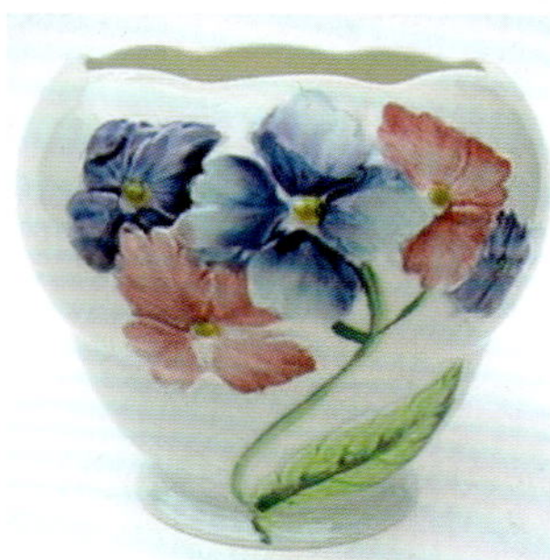

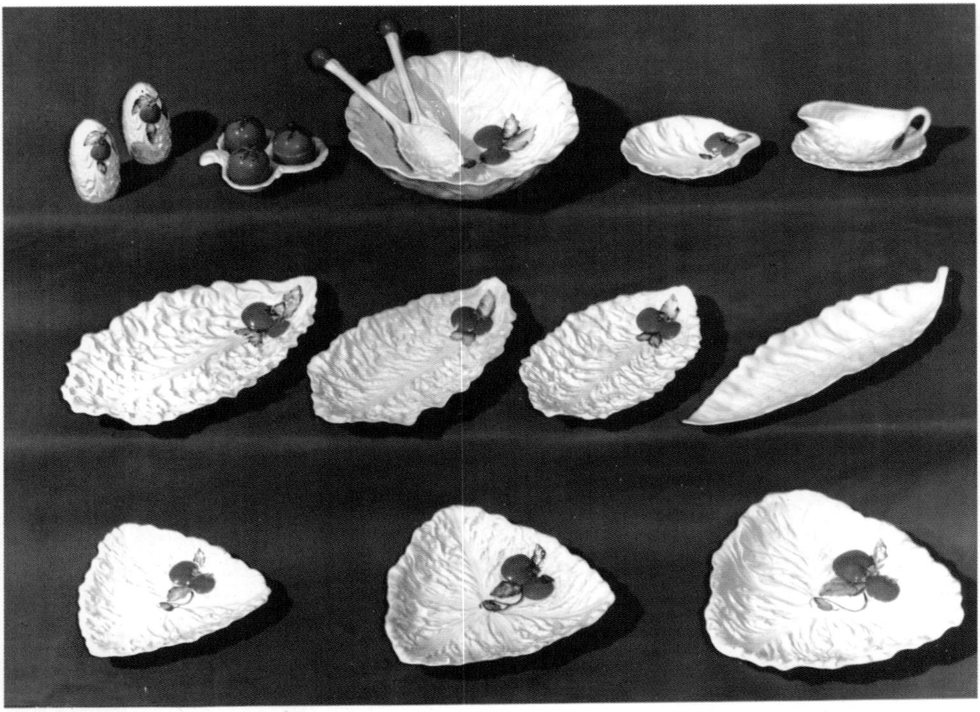

LETTUCE & TOMATO DESIGN Carlton Ware GREEN

LETTUCE & TOMATO DESIGN

Green

Prices—each

Pepper & Salt l/s	..	Cruet Set	..	Salad Set	..	Butter	..	Sauce Boat & Stand
4/–		5/5		13/9		1/6		3/3
Pepper 2/–		Pepper & Salt s/s boxed 2/10		Bowl 9/3				Sauce Boat 2/2
Salt 2/–		Pepper 1/2		Servers 4/6				Stand 1/1
		Salt 1/2						

Tray l/s	..	Tray m/s	..	Tray s/s	..	Cucumber Tray
5/11		4/8		2/11		3/8

Triangular Plate 6″	..	Triangular Plate 8″	..	Triangular Plate 9″
2/9		4/5		5/5

Salad Ware

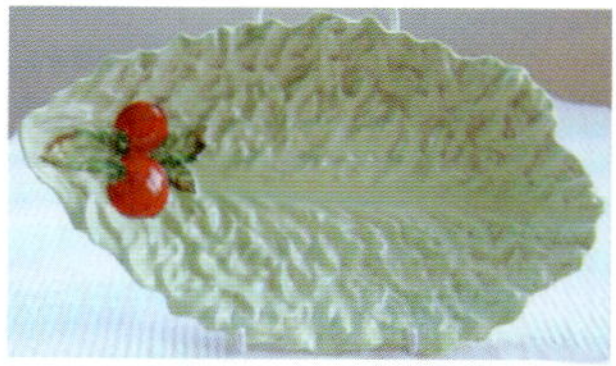

Carlton Ware produced *Lettuce and Tomato Salad Ware* at various stages in their existence. This probably means that it was very popular with the public of the day.

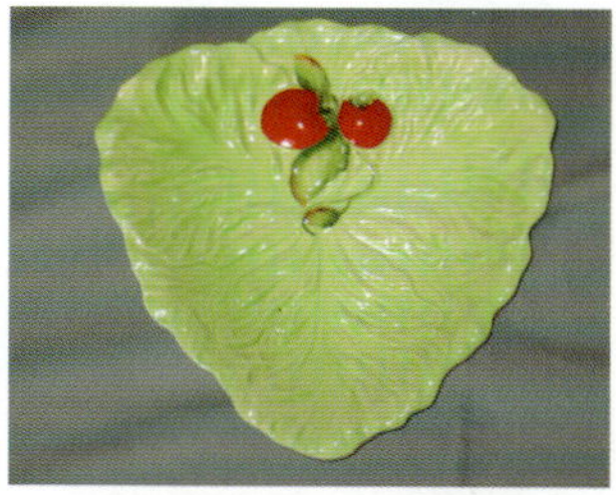

Most people profess to have seen or owned some of this range, which may have been inherited from their granny's attic. It does look rather fetching when it is displayed in full sets which include the salad bowl and servers.

We don't have records of the earlier versions except that they had very prominently raised tomatoes on a yellowish ground colour although some pieces were made on a white ground. The early pieces had a "heavy" appearance.

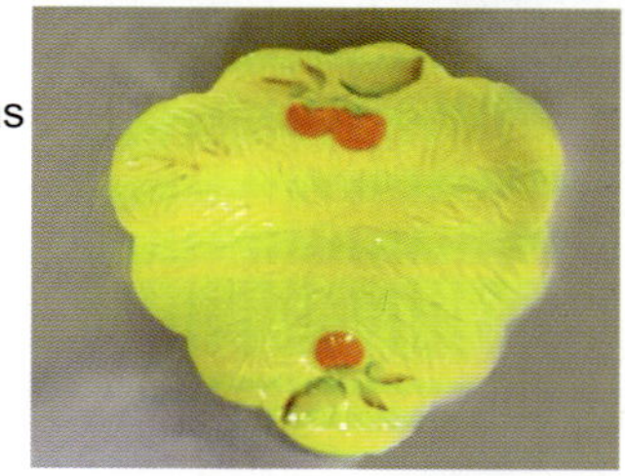

The range listed below is probably the third range produced and was first made in the early 1950's. The ground colour was green with was adorned by a bright red cherry tomato.

The embossing in this range obviously replicates crinkly lettuce with many grooves and intricate veins. This was probably not very practical for using but would have brightened up a serving of salad.

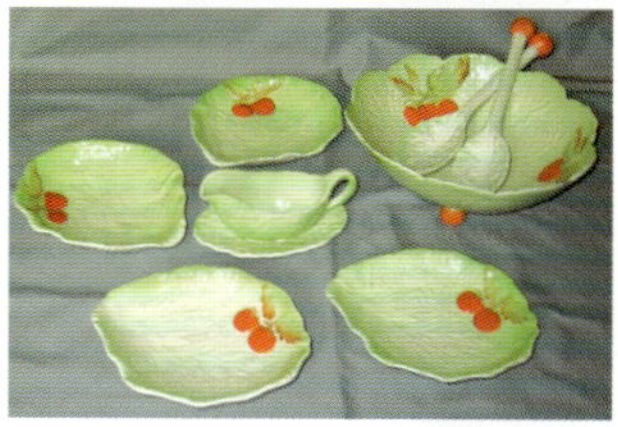

The range was discontinued in about 1976 because the red paint was based on lead and this was deemed as a health risk.

2092 Butter £10 - £20
2093 Triangular Plate, 3 sizes £20 - £40
2094 Salad Bowl & Servers £50 - £70
2095 Tray, 3 sizes £10 - £30
2096 Sauceboat and Stand £20 - £40
2099 Cucumber Tray £30 - £40
2131 Cruet £40 - £60
Basket £40 - £60
Cress £50 - £75
Footed Bowl £30 - £50
Salt & Pepper, large £35 - £55
Toast Rack, 2 slice £30 - £40

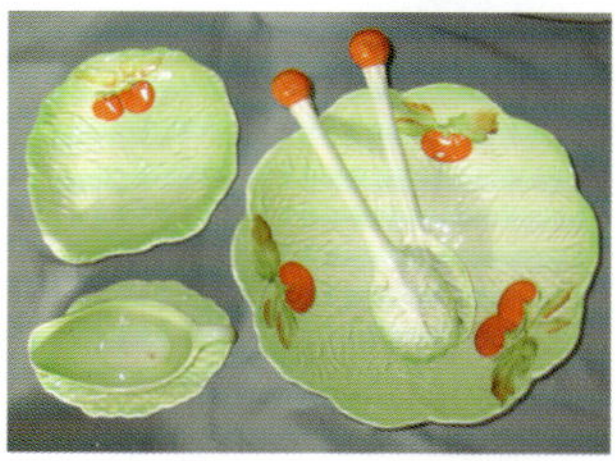

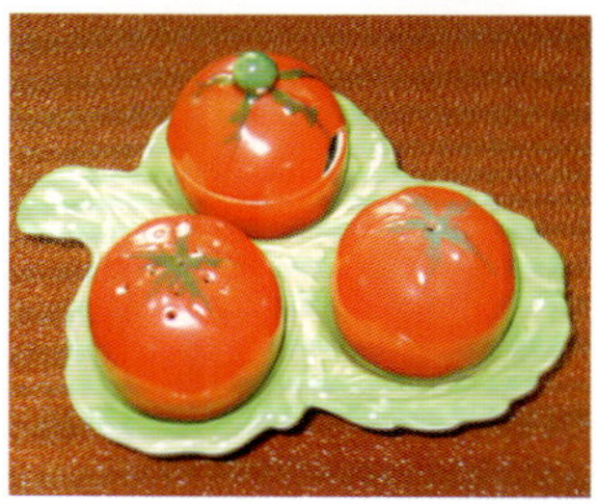

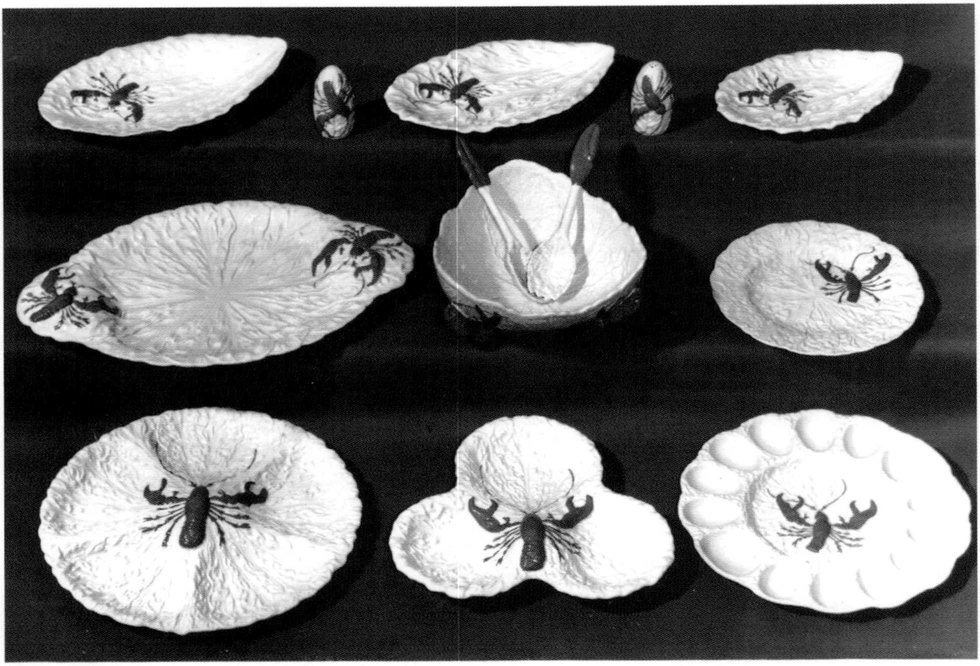

LOBSTER DESIGN Carlton Ware GREEN

LOBSTER DESIGN

Green

Prices—each

Tray l/s 5/11	..	Salt 2/–	..	Tray m/s 4/8	..	Pepper 2/–	..	Tray s/s 2/11

Serving Tray 16/11	..	Salad Set 24/3	..	Plate 9″ 4/8
		{ Salad Bowl 19/5 { Servers 4/10		

Five-Way Tray 14/8	..	Three-Way Tray 10/2	..	Egg Dish 11/5

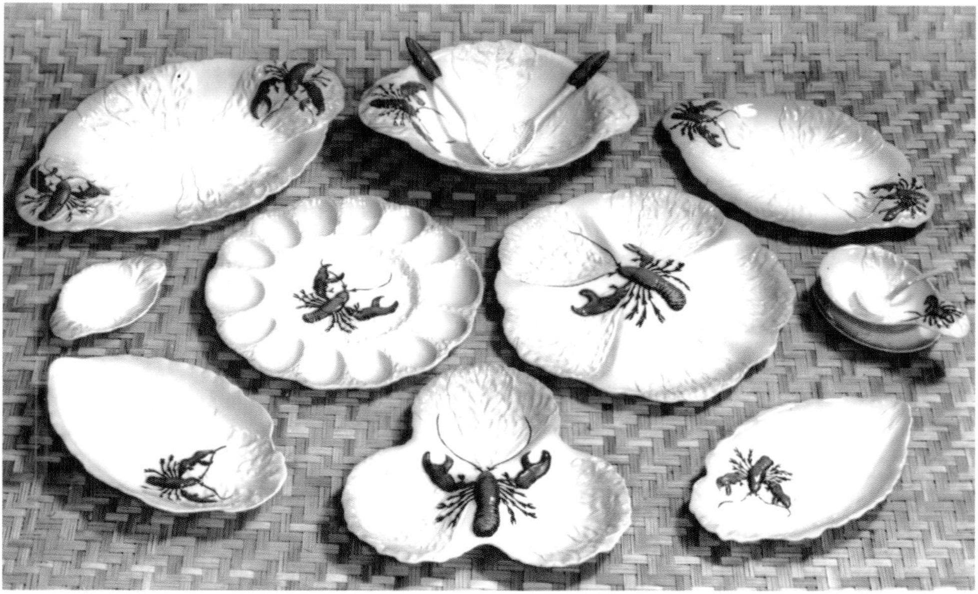

LANGOUSTE Carlton Ware RANGE

LANGOUSTE DESIGN

4634 Chartreuse
4633 CREAM

Prices—each

Serving Tray l/s 16/11	..	Salad Set 17/6 Bowl 12/6 Servers 5/–	..	Serving Tray s/s 9/3

Butter 1/5	..	Egg Dish 11/5	..	5-way Tray 14/8	..	Mayonnaise Set 7/6 Bowl 5/2 Ladle 1/– Stand 1/4

Tray l/s 5/11	..	3-way Tray 10/2	..	Tray s/s 4/8

PEPPER + SALT L/S 4/-PR.
PLATE 9". .. 4/8.

Lobster & Langouste

The *Lobster* design was first introduced in the mid 1920's. It was very popular and remained in production until the 1970's.

It was originally available in one colour - green. In the 1950's Carlton Ware renamed *Lobster* to *Langouste* and introduced two colours, Cream and Chartreuse (a variety of green). The colour of the Lobsters was also a bit more realistic. At the same time Carlton Ware also introduced a few new shapes.

The Black & White photographs from the Sales Literature of 1959, early 1960's shows that both names, *Lobster* and *Langouste*, were used. *Lobster* for the original green colour and *Langouste* for the newer cream and chartreuse colours.

We are often amused to see some people describe the Egg Tray as an Oyster Tray.

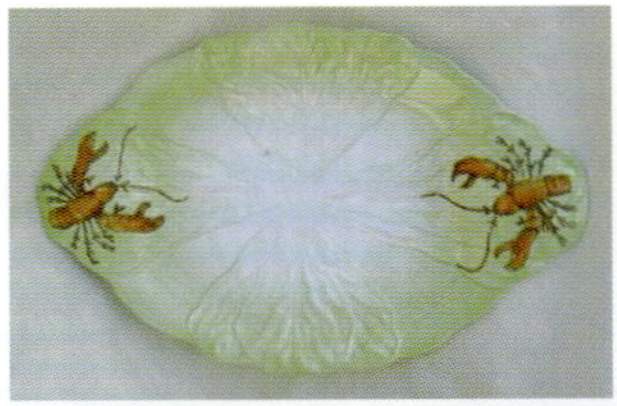

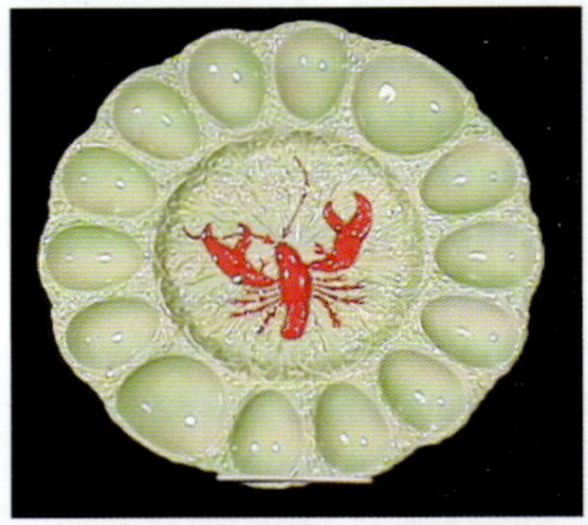

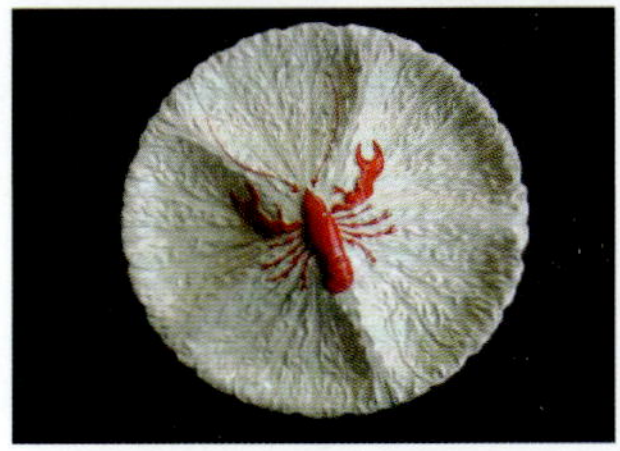

Lobster
2125 Plate £20 - £30
2185 Tray, 1 lobster, 3 sizes £20 - £50
2186 Salt & Pepper £20 - £40
2218 Serving Tray, 2 lobsters, 2 sizes £30 - £60
2231 Egg Tray £60 - £80
2230 3 Way Round Tray £40 - £70
2232 5 Way Round Tray £50 - £80
2242 5 Way Round Tray, Low Relief £40 - £70
2243 3 Way Round Tray, Low Relief £40 - £70
Salad Set with servers (lobster feet) £100 - £160

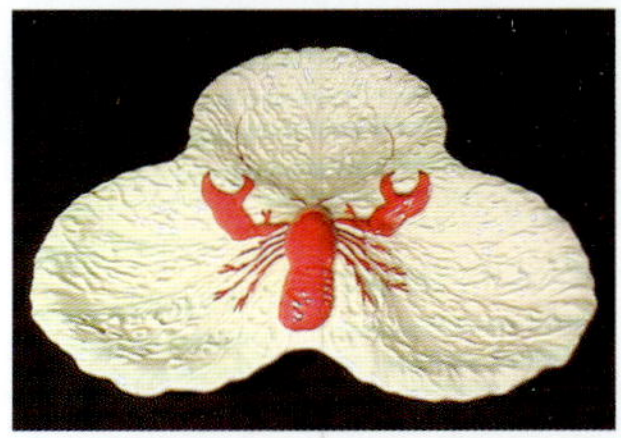

Langouste
2470 Serving Dish, 2 lobsters, 2 sizes £30 - £60
2471 5 Way Round Tray £50 - £80
2473 Butter, no lobster £10 - £20
2474 Tray, 1 lobster, 3 sizes £20 - £50
2475 3 Way Round Tray £40 - £70
2476 Mayonnaise Set with stand & ladle £30 - £60
(sometimes called Sauceboat mistakenly)
2481 Salad Set with servers £60 - £80
2492 Plate £20 - £30
2493 Salt & Pepper £20 - £40
2546 Butter, with lobster £15 - £25
Egg Tray, same as Lobster £60 - £80

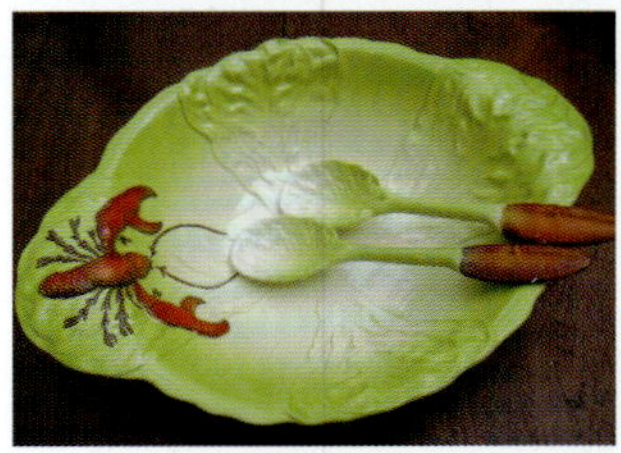

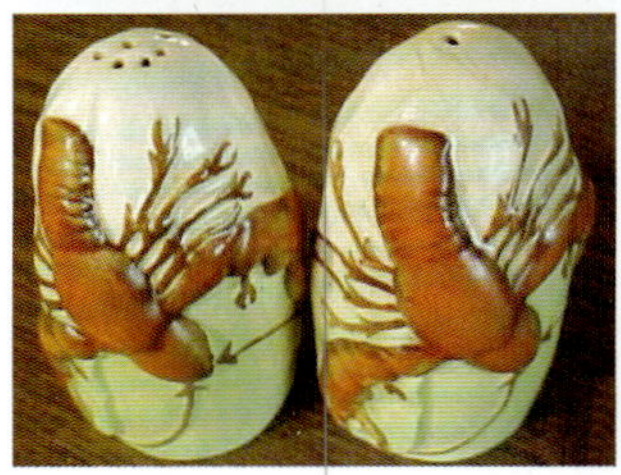

Grape

Carlton Ware introduced this rather unusual design in 1953/4. It was obviously very popular with Carlton Ware collectors of the day because it was produced in a large variety of shapes. Carlton Ware named this pattern *Vine, Grape Embellishment* and *Grape*; we have used the commonly used name *Grape*.

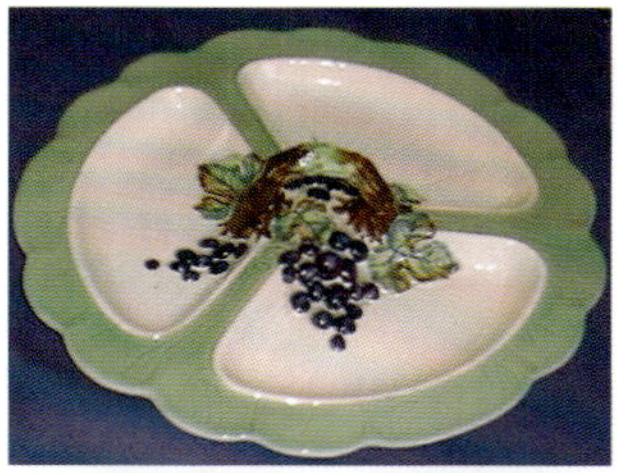

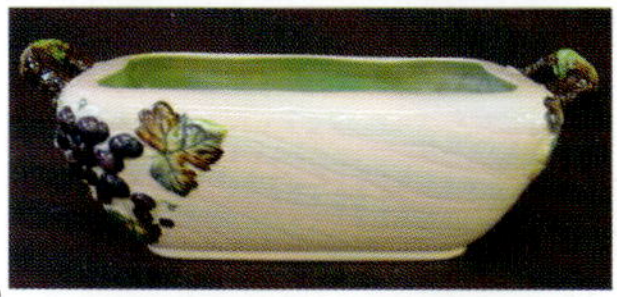

The design, not surprisingly, consists of bunches of grapes that are growing from a brown woody stem which is often modelled as the handle or handles of the piece. The grapes are in the mature stage of ripeness, which is illustrated by their vivid dark purple colour. Likewise the leaves convey maturity with dark colouring on the edges. The vine leaves are also reminiscent of a climbing plant with their clinging tendrils.

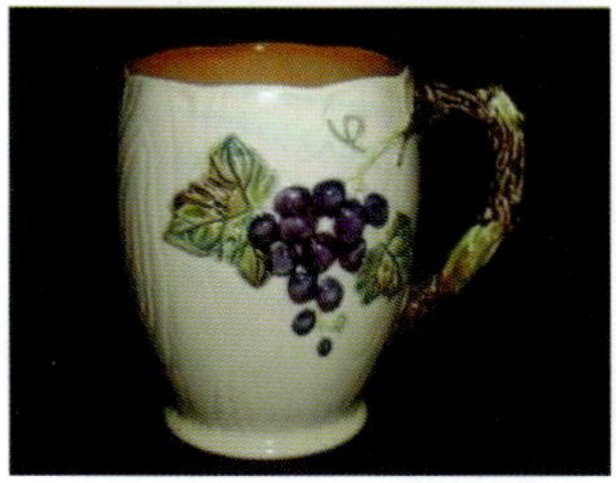

It was produced in two colourways. Both have a background beige colour. Pattern 4463 has the edges and interior in a green colour whilst pattern 4464 uses a sandy brown colour. The two-tone colours are used with great effect to compliment the unusual and attractive design to its full effect. The detail that the paintresses applied to this hand painted design can be appreciated to the full.

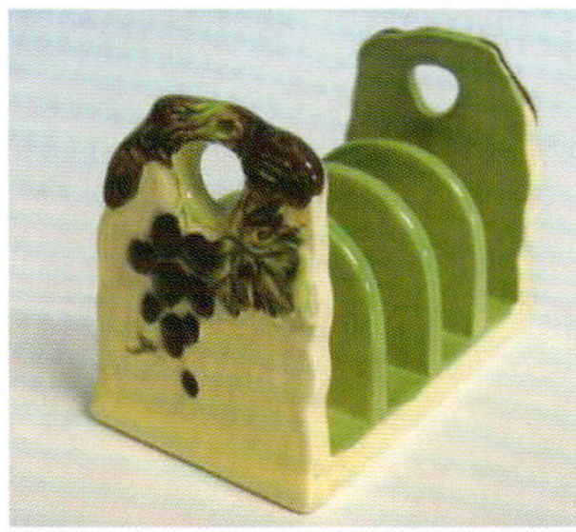

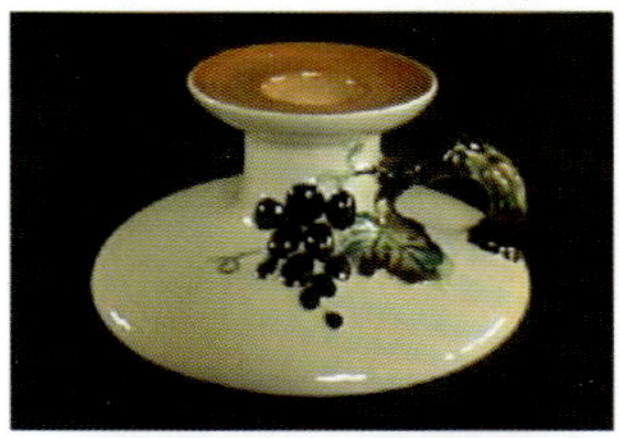

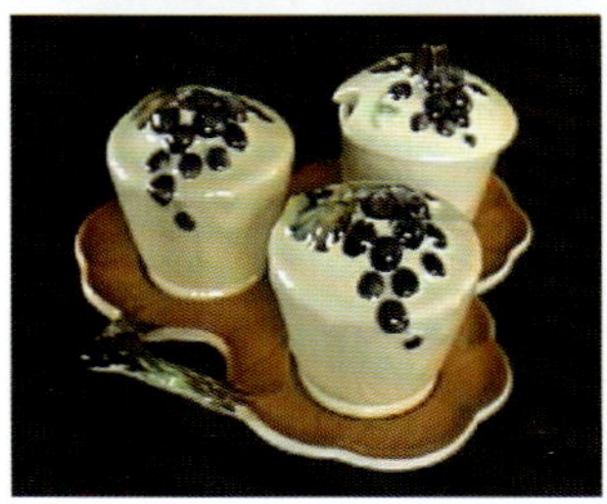

2195 & 2197 Round Dish £50 - £70
2203 Two Way Tray £50 - £80
2208 Preserve and Stand £60 - £90
2211 Jug, 2 sizes £50 - £90
2214 Three Way Tray, handled £70 - £100
2217 Cruet Set £120 - £160
2220 Five Way Tray, handled £90 - £130
2221 Planter, Oblong Dish, 2sizes £60 - £80
2224 Cigarette Box, Covered Box £60 - £90
2225 Mug or Beaker £40 - £60
2226 Sugar & Cream £40 - £60 each
2227 Toast Rack £70 - £100
2228 Candlestick £40 - £60
2253 Five Way Tray, unhandled £80 - £120
2254 Three Way Tray, unhandled £60 - £80
2268 Round Dish, 13" £50 - £70
2269 Oval Tray £50 - £70
2272 Dessert Plate, 5" £30 - £40
2295 Cigarette Box, different to 2224 £60 - £90
2296 Oval Bowl £50 - £70
2297 Ashtray £30 - £50
2299 Bon Bon £40 - £60
2301 Comport £50 - £70
2303 Turned over Bowl £50 - £70
2304 Candlestick £40 - £60

Guinness

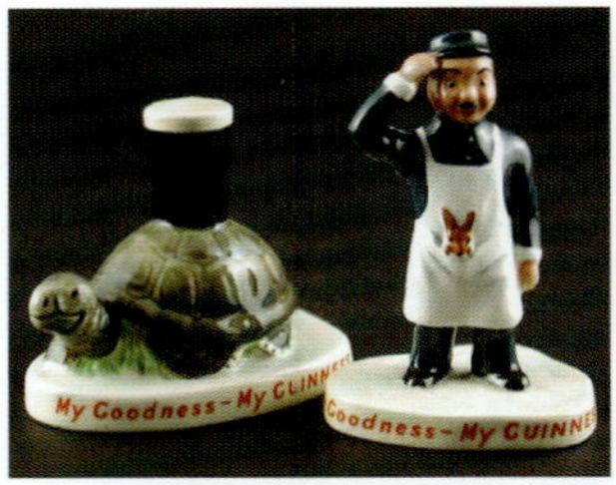

Carlton Ware were commissioned by several companies to produce advertising ware. The range produced for Arthur Guinness is probably the most well known.

The first piece to be produced was the Toucan in 1955. The beak of the Toucan is orange changing to deep yellow at the top.

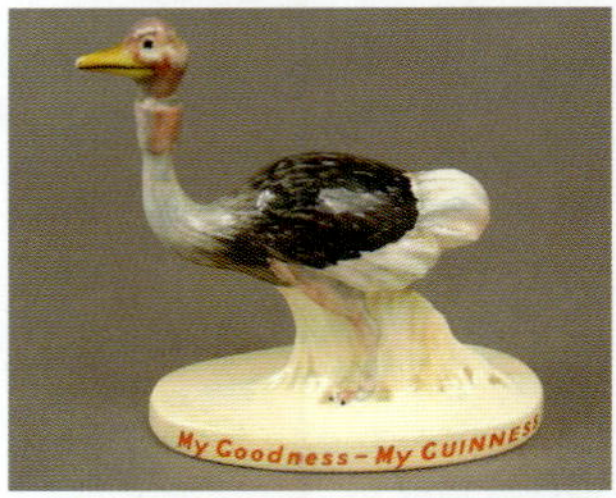

In 1956 the Zoo collection was introduced. This consisted of a Zoo Keeper, Ostrich, Tortoise, Kangaroo, small Toucan and Sea Lion.

The Toucan Lamp, the Flying Toucans and the Drayman were introduced in 1957. The Toucan lamp is like the Toucan but has a hole in the Toucan's head for the electrical fitting.

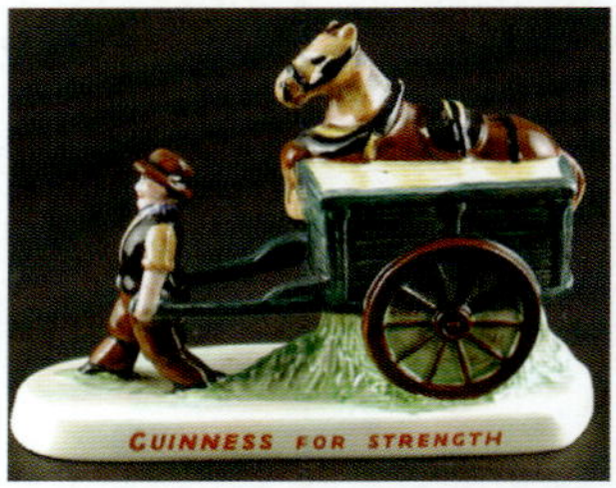

Other pieces such as the Toucan Jug and Penguin were introduced in later years.

When Carlton Ware was liquidated in 1989 some of the original moulds ended up in the hands of some disreputable people and many fakes were made. These fakes often appear for sale. See the chapter on *Fakes*, page 106, for more information on how to identify fakes.

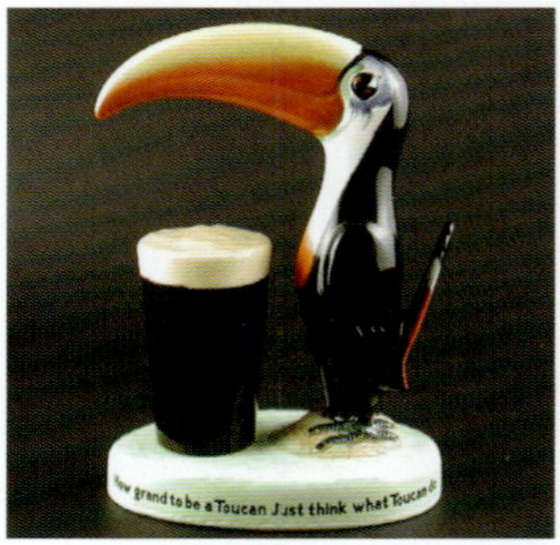

2298 Glass & Toucan £250 - £350
2308 Kangaroo £100 - £150
2317 Ostrich £100 - £150
2319 Tortoise £100 - £150
2320 Seal £100 - £150
2322 Small Glass & Toucan £100 - £150
2325 Toucan Lamp, with shade £300 - £400
2331 Zoo Keeper £100 - £150
2398 Drayman (man pulling horse in cart) £250 - £350
2399 3 Flying Toucans £300 - £400
2401 Drayman Plaque £100 - £150
2421 Toucan Jug £100 - £150
2556 Salt & Pepper £50 - £80
2566 Toucan Wall Plaque £100 - £150
2584 Mug, half pint £50 - £80
2637 Penguin Lamp, with shade £300 - £500
2663 Sea Lion Lamp Base & Revolving Shade £400 - £600
2689 Flower Pot £30 - £50
2690 Cheese Containers, 2 sizes £45 - £80
2703 & 2704 Pickle Jar & Store Jar £30 - £50 each
2705 Penguin £100 - £150

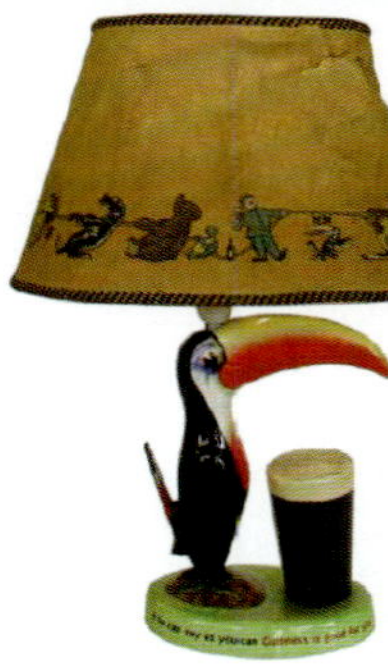

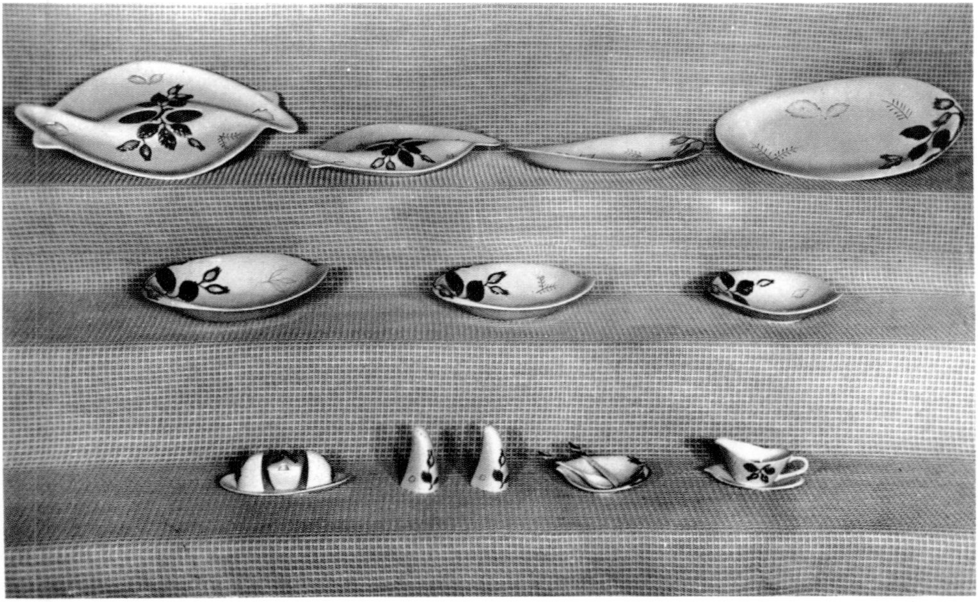

HAZEL NUT DESIGN

Carlton Ware

4504 MATT CREAM
4505 GREEN
4620 BLUE

HAZELNUT DESIGN

4504 Matt Cream
4505 Green
4620 Blue

Prices—each

2-way Tray l/s .. 16/11

2-way Tray s/s .. 12/6

Oval Serving Dish s/s .. 12/6

Oval Serving Dish l/s 16/11

Oval Bowl l/s .. 6/10

Oval Bowl m/s .. 5/5

Oval Bowl s/s 3/11

Cruet Set .. 5/5

Pepper & Salt l/s .. 4/–

Butter & Knife or Jam & Spoon .. 2/9

Sauce Boat & Stand 3/9

Pepper & Salt s/s boxed	2/10
Pepper & Salt s/s not boxed	2/4
Cruet Set boxed	7/2

Pepper	2/–
Salt	2/–
Pepper & Salt l/s boxed	5/6

Butter & Knife or Jam & Spoon boxed	3/3
Individual Butter or Jam in cellophane box	2/–
Butter or Jam	1/6
Knife or Spoon	1/2

Sauce Boat	2/6
Stand	1/3

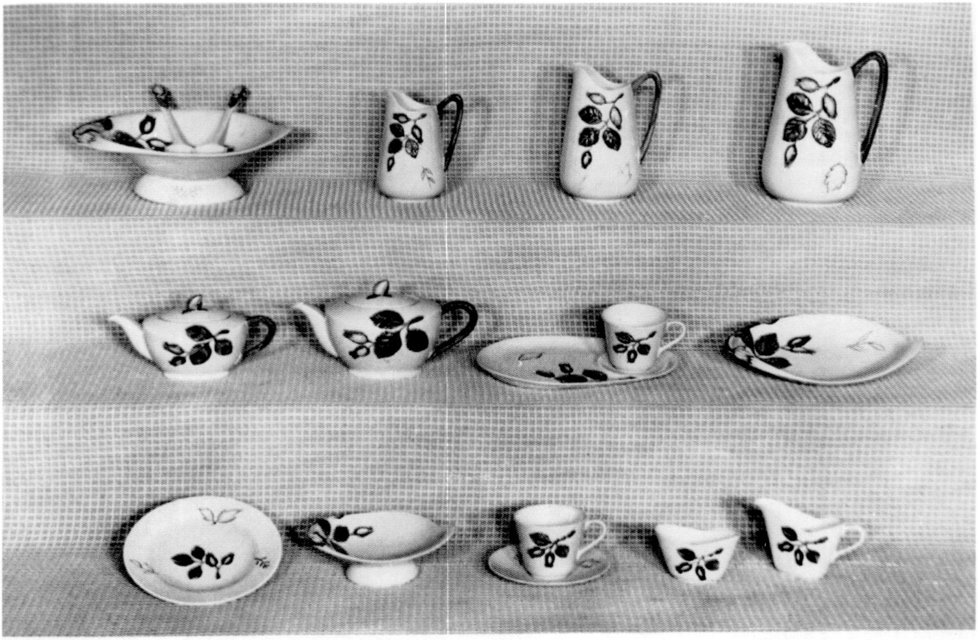

HAZEL NUT DESIGN Carlton Ware **4504** MATT CREAM **4505** GREEN 4620 BLUE

HAZELNUT DESIGN

4504 Matt Cream
4505 Green
4620 Blue

Prices—each

Salad Set 15/2 ({Bowl 10/10, Servers 4/4})	Jug s/s ½ pint 4/6	Jug m/s 1 pint 5/8	Jug l/s 6/10	
Teapot 2 cup 5/11	Teapot 4 cup 7/9	Television Set 6/10	Tray 4/5	
Plate 5″ 2/4	Bon Bon 3/11	Cup & Saucer 3/9	Sugar 2/9	Cream 2/11

Hazel Nut

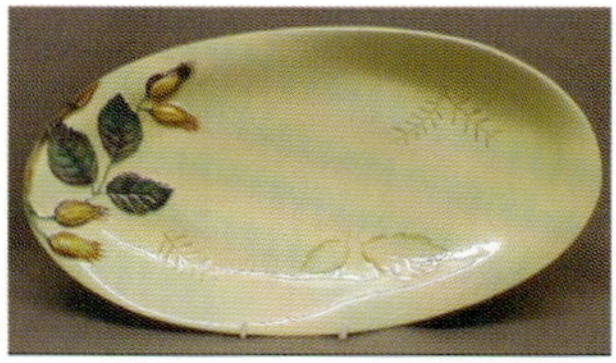

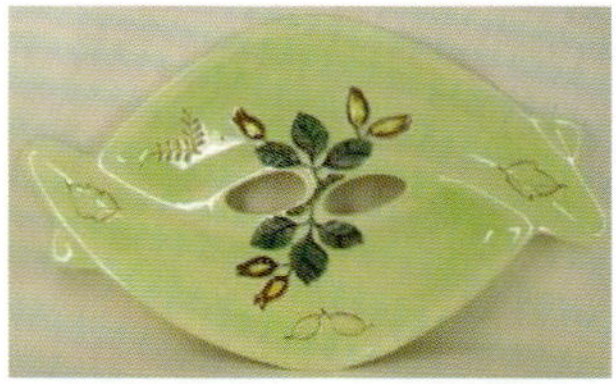

The *Hazel Nut* design was introduced in the mid 1950's. The Black & White sales literature shows that it was first introduced in two colours, 4504 Matt Cream and 4505 Green. Later on the colour 4620 Blue was introduced. Our experience is that the blue is not very common, perhaps because it wasn't such a popular colour or because the colour was introduced towards the end of the *Hazel Nut* production.

The design incorporates a Hazel Nut branch with twig, leaves and some hazel nuts. In addition you'll often find other isolated leaves and bits of fern.

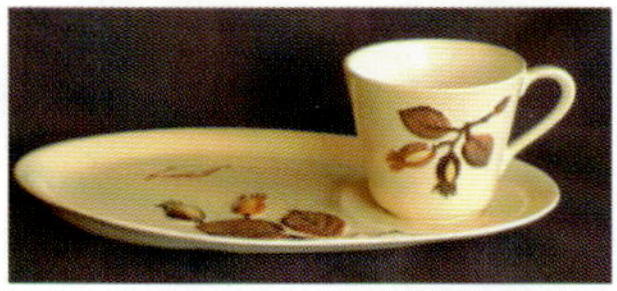

About fifteen different "shapes" were produced although, as we have mentioned for other designs, one shape number may contain several different pieces. For example the shape number used for the Tea Set was used for almost all the pieces within the tea set including the cup, saucer, sugar, cream and plate but not including the tea pot.

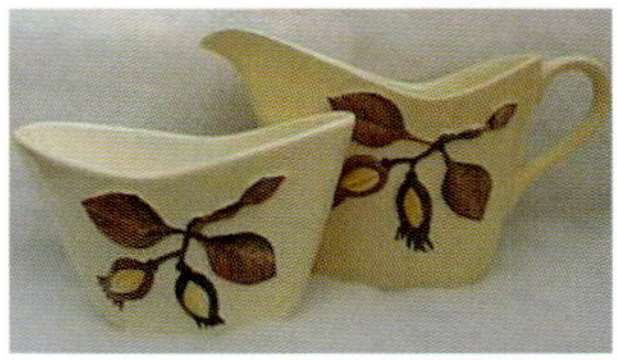

2277 Tray/Dish £20 - £40
2306 & 2327 Butter & Knife £20 - £40
2306 & 2327 Jam & Spoon £20 - £40
2307 Sauce Boat and Stand £20 - £40
2309 Salt & Pepper, large £15 - £35
2310 Oval Serving Dish, 2 sizes £30 - £50
2311 Jug, 3 sizes £40 - £80
2313 & 2321 Salad Bowl & Servers £50 - £80
2316 Oval Bowl, 3 sizes £25 - £50
2318 Boomerang Tray, 2 sizes £30 - £60
2324 Tea Pot £35 - £60
2326 Bon-bon Dish £20 - £40
2330 Cruet £25 - £50
2357 Television Set (Cup & Tray) £40 - £50
2358 Morning Tea Set (Tea for two) £120 - £200
Tea Pot £35 - £60, Cup & Saucer £20 - £30
Sugar £15 - £25, Cream £15 - £25, Plate £10 - £25

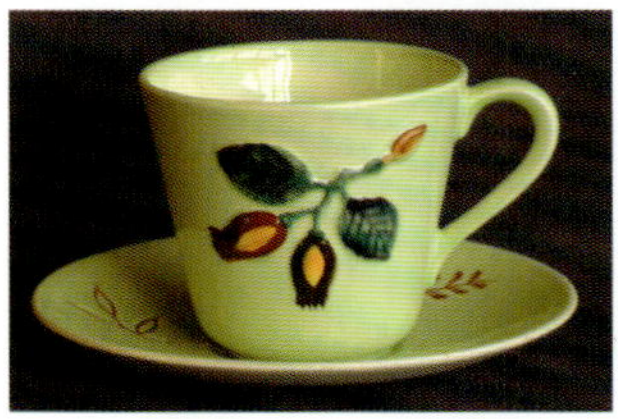

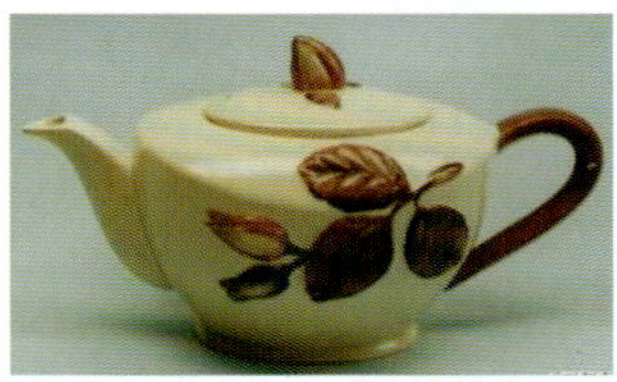

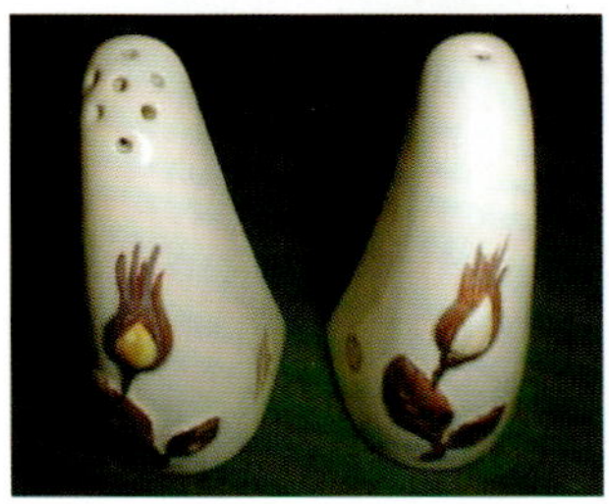

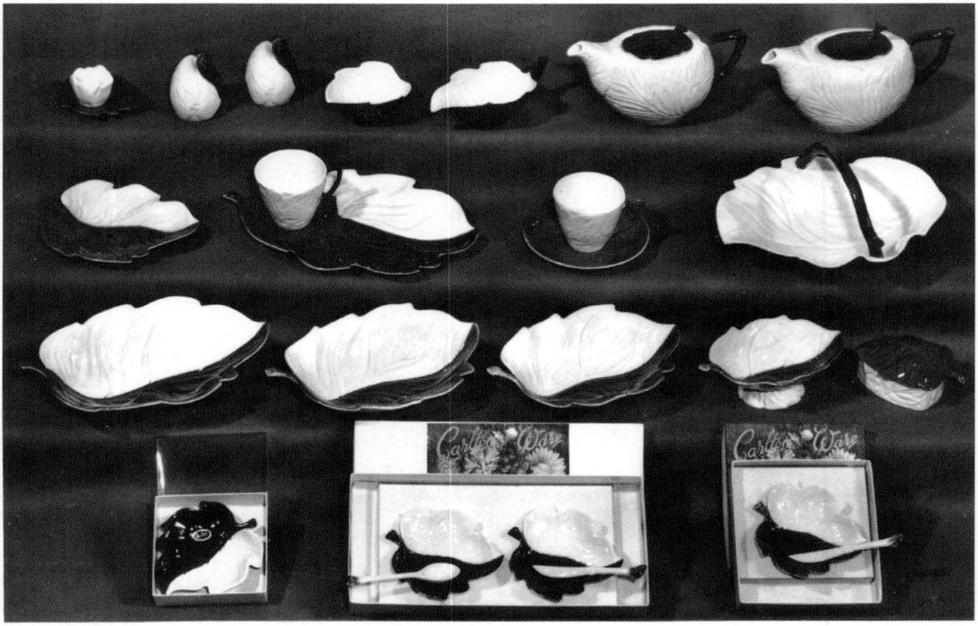

LEAF DESIGN Carlton Ware

LEAF DESIGN

4551 Twin-tone Green
4552 Twin-tone Grey
4553 Brown/Cream
4601 Twin-tone Chartreuse

Prices—each

Candlestick 2/5	Pepper & Salt l/s 3/10	Sugar 2/7	Cream 2/10	Teapot 2 cup 5/8	Teapot 4 cup 7/4

Pepper 1/11
Salt 1/11
Pepper & Salt Boxed 5/3

Plate 5″ 2/4	Television Set 6/6	Cup & Saucer 3/6	Handled Basket 10/11

Oval Bowl l/s 6/6	Oval Bowl m/s 5/1	Oval Bowl s/s 3/8	Bon Bon 3/1	Pin Box 2/10

Individual Butter boxed 2/–	Combined Butter & Knife and Jam & Spoon boxed 5/8	Butter & Knife or Jam & Spoon boxed 3/–

Butter or Jam 1/5
Knife or Spoon 1/2

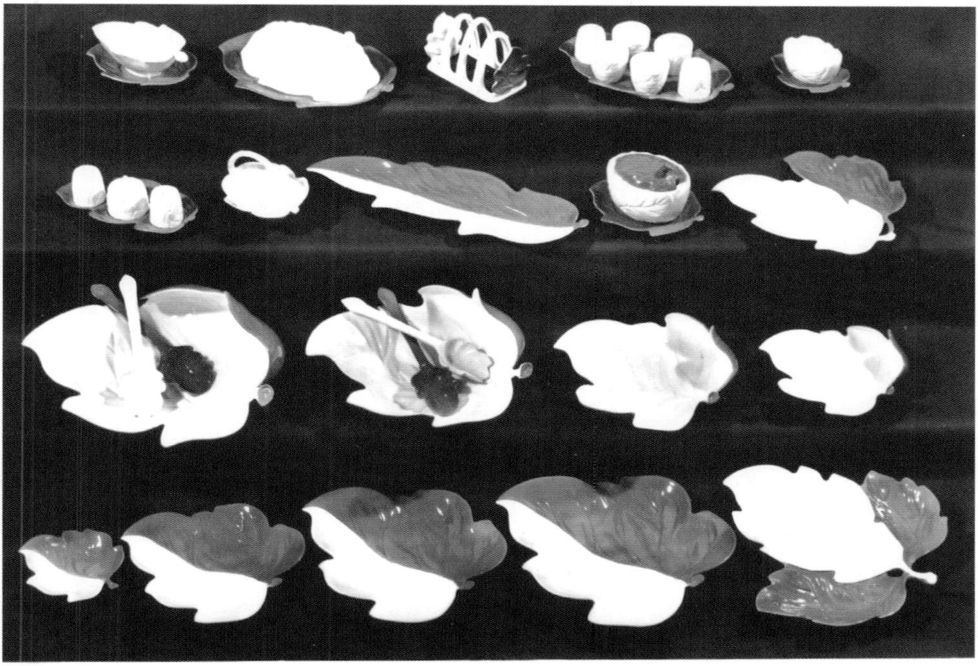

LEAF DESIGN Carlton Ware

LEAF DESIGN

4551 Twin-tone Green
4552 Twin-tone Grey
4553 Brown/Cream
4601 Twin-tone Chartreuse

Prices—each

Sauce Boat & Stand	Covered Cheese	Toastrack	Egg Set	Posy Holder
3/3	6/3	3/8	7/5	2/5

{Sauce Boat 2/2
{Stand 1/1

Cruet Set	Basket l/s	Basket s/s	Long Tray	Preserve & Stand	2-way Tray
5/-	4/8	3/7	3/7	4/2	4/-

{Pepper & Salt not boxed s/s 2/2 pr.
{Pepper & Salt s/s Boxed 2/9
Cruet Set Boxed 6/9

{Preserve 3/3
{Stand 11d.
{Preserve, Stand & Spoon 5/4
Preserve & Spoon 4/5

Salad Set l/s	Salad Set s/s	Turned-over Leaf l/s	Turned-over Leaf s/s
18/2	14/-	6/10	5/6

{Bowl 14/-
{Servers 4/2

{Bowl 9/10
{Servers 4/2

Butter	Tray 6″	Tray 8″	Tray 9″	3-way Tray
1/5	2/7	4/-	5/-	5/2

Leaf

Carlton Ware introduced this well known embossed range in 1957/58. It was obviously very popular as production at the Copeland St works continued well into the 1960's and 1970's.

The *Leaf* design doesn't really need a lot of explanation because as its name suggests the design very closely resembles the shape of a leaf. This includes the veins and serrated edges of the leaf, which are incorporated into the embossed design. This range was made in quite a large collection and variety of colours. This can be seen from evidence of the original advertisements literature. It was first produced in Twin -Tone Green, Twin -Tone Grey and Brown & Cream. Twin -Tone Chartreuse was added soon afterwards.

During the late 1960's and into the 1970's during re-runs of the design numerous colours were added to the collection. This included colours such as Rouge, Noir, Turquoise and a very opulent Gold as well as Twin -Tone variations.

2336 Salad Set with Servers, 2 sizes £40 - £70
2346 Sauce Boat & Stand £15 - £30
2359 Sauce Boat £10 - £20
2361 Butter & Knife or Jam & Spoon £25 - £40 each set
2363 Long Tray £20 - £40
2366 Turned-over Leaf Bowl, 2 sizes £20 - £40
2367 Tray, 4 sizes £10 - £30
2368 Two way Tray £20 - £40
2369 Cruet Set (Pepper, Salt, Mustard and Frame) £30 - £50
2370 Egg Set £40 - £60
2371 Covered Cheese £40 - £60
2372 Preserve Jar and Saucer £30 - £50
2373 Posy Holder £20 - £30
2374 Toast Rack £25 - £45
2376 Handled Basket, 2 sizes £15 - £35
2377 Three way Tray £25 - £45
2381 Morning Tea Set (Tea Pot, Sugar, etc) £80 - £150
Tea Pot £25 - £50, Cup & Saucer £15 - £30
Sugar £10 - £20, Cream £10 - £20, Plate £10 - £20
2382 Salt & Pepper, large £10 - £25
2383 Television Set (Tray with cup) £15 - £25
2385 Tea Pot, 2 sizes £25 - £50
2386 Candlestick £10 - £20
2387 Bon Bon £10 - £20
2388 Oval Bowl, 3 sizes £10 - £40
2389 Pin or Trinket Box £10 - £20
2390 Handled Basket £15 - £35
2417 Mayonnaise Bowl, Ladle & Stand £40 - £60

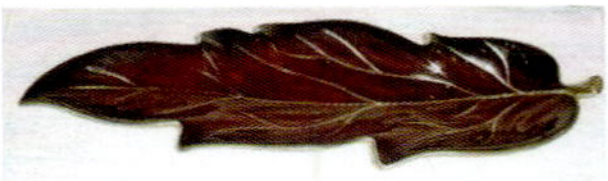
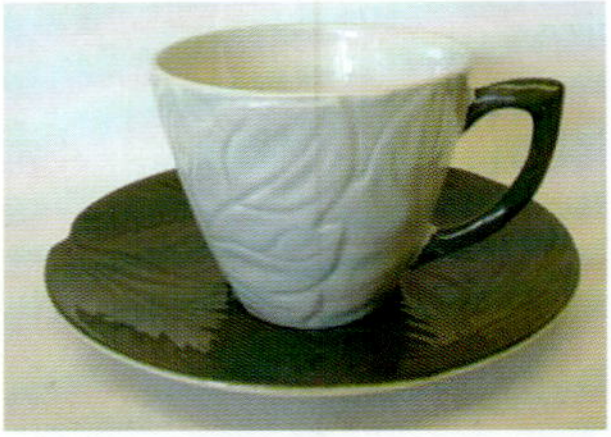
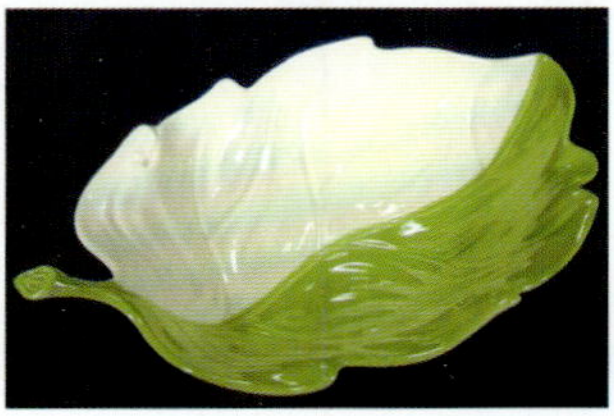
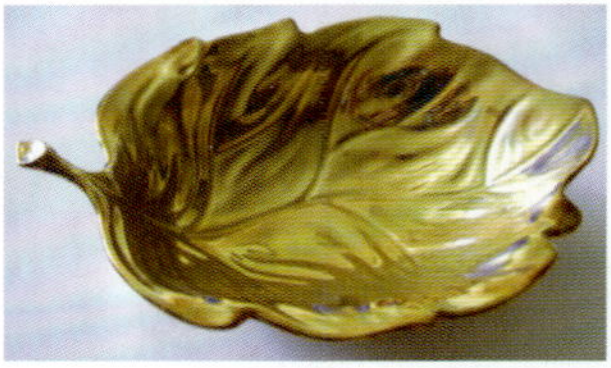
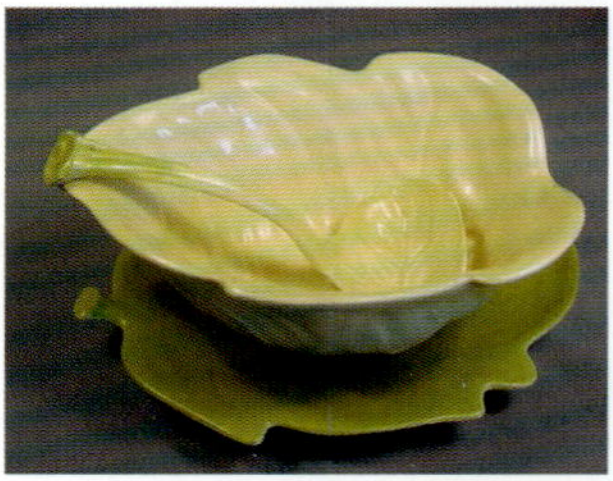
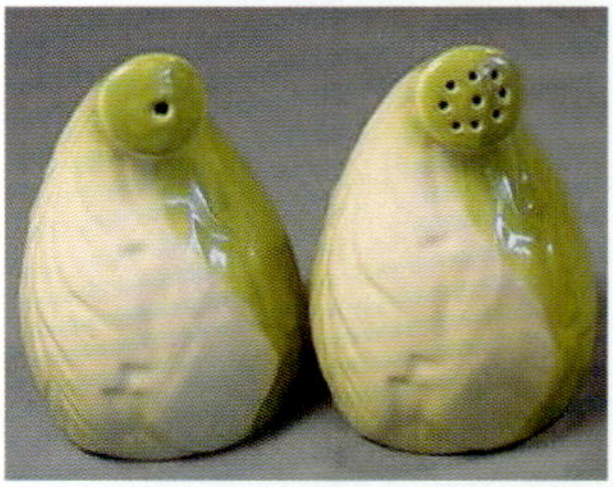
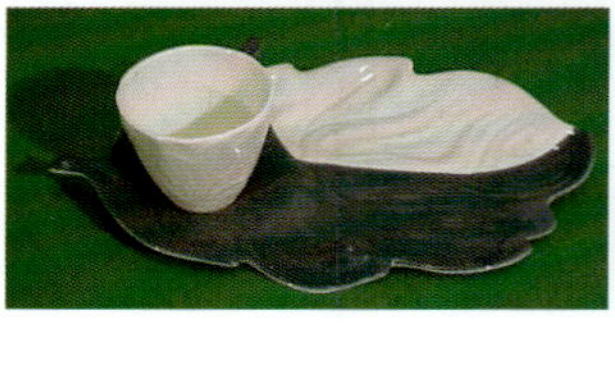

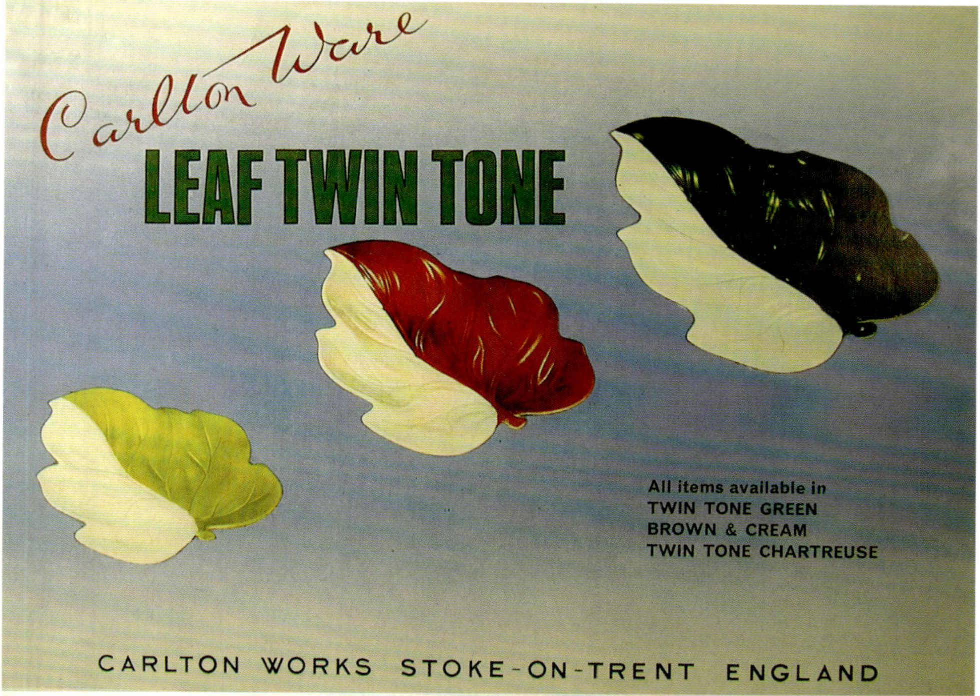
Carlton Ware
LEAF TWIN TONE
All items available in
TWIN TONE GREEN
BROWN & CREAM
TWIN TONE CHARTREUSE
CARLTON WORKS STOKE-ON-TRENT ENGLAND

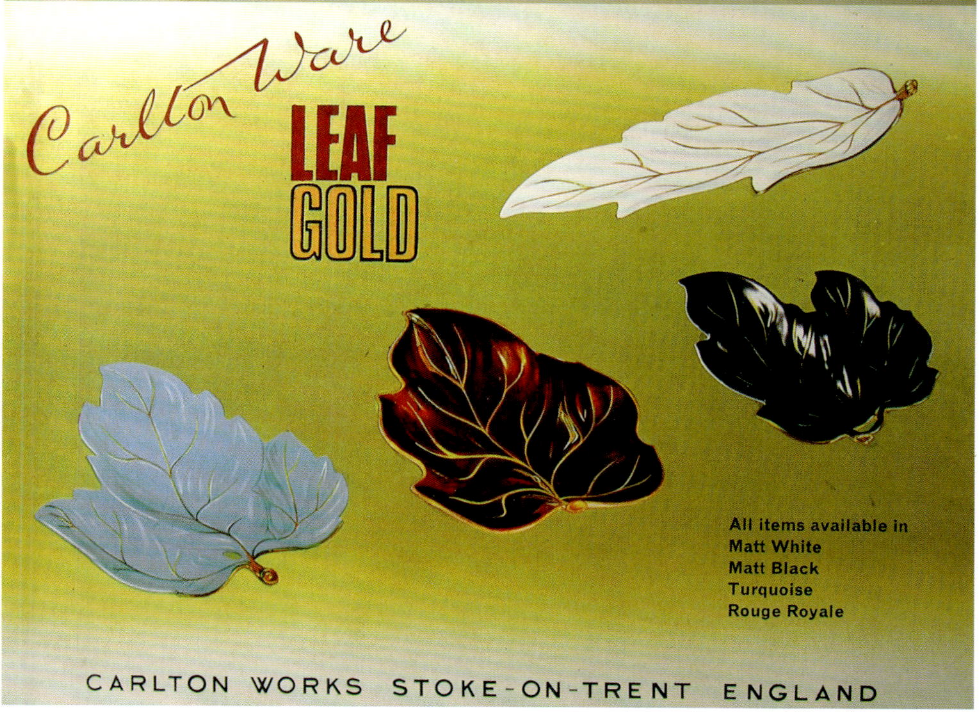
Carlton Ware
LEAF
GOLD
All items available in
Matt White
Matt Black
Turquoise
Rouge Royale
CARLTON WORKS STOKE-ON-TRENT ENGLAND

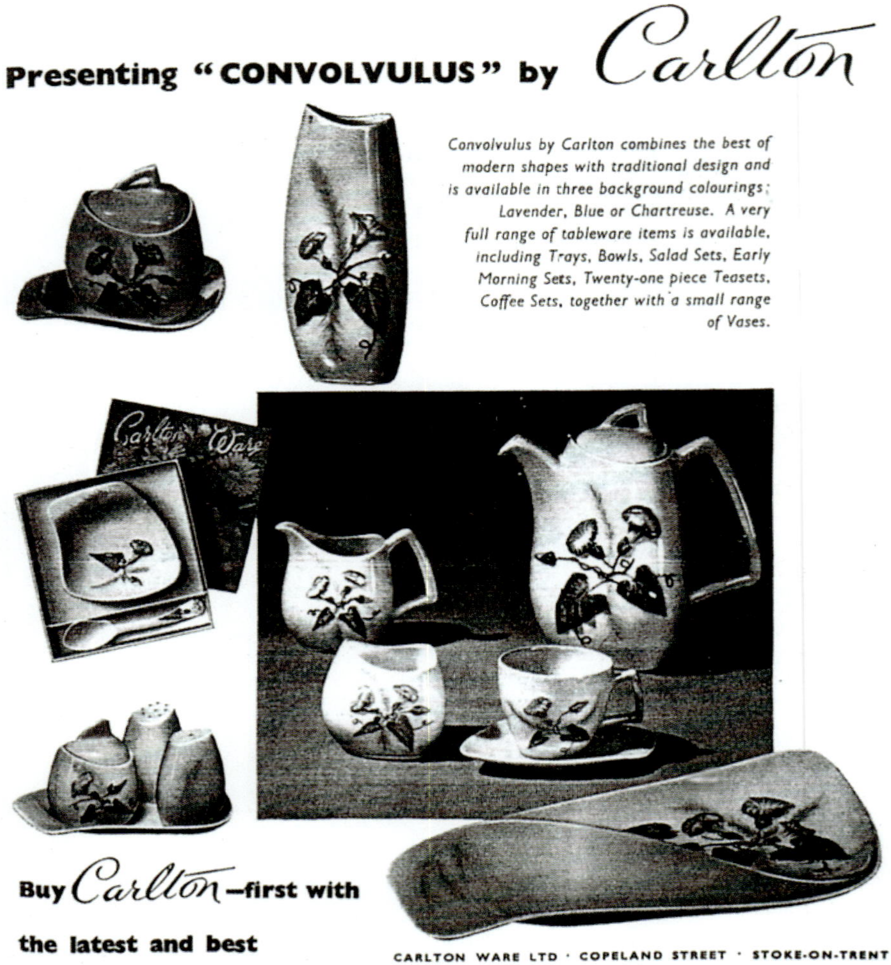
Presenting "CONVOLVULUS" by Carlton
Convolvulus by Carlton combines the best of modern shapes with traditional design and is available in three background colourings; Lavender, Blue or Chartreuse. A very full range of tableware items is available, including Trays, Bowls, Salad Sets, Early Morning Sets, Twenty-one piece Teasets, Coffee Sets, together with a small range of Vases.
Carlton Ware
Buy Carlton—first with the latest and best
CARLTON WARE LTD · COPELAND STREET · STOKE-ON-TRENT

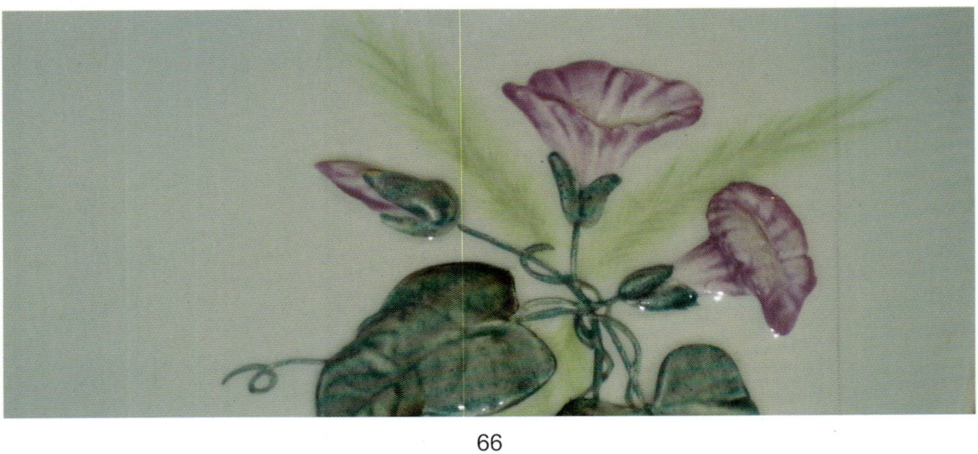

Convolvulus

One of the pretty weeds that you can find in a garden is Convolvulus or Bindweed. This is quite an invasive plant and as its common name Bindweed suggests - it binds itself around every other plant. If you've ever tried to rid a garden of this weed then you'll understand the fun you can have trying to get rid of the weed whilst trying to save the plants that have been entwined. The roots are also amazingly long.

Nevertheless the flower does look pretty and it's not surprising that Carlton Ware produced a range called *Convolvulus* in 1958/59. The design had a realistic depiction of the Convolvulus plant with green leaves and light purple flowers. *Convolvulus* was available in three background colourings: Lavender, Blue and Chartreuse.

2480 Tray, 3 sizes £25 - £35
2485 Jug £30 - £50
2488 Preserve Pot and Tray £30 - £50
2489 Morning Tea Set (Tea for two) £90 - £150
Tea Pot £30 - £60, Cup & Saucer £15 - £30
Sugar £10 - £20, Cream £10 - £20, Plate £10 - £20
2490 Salt & Pepper £25 - £40
2491 Butter & Knife or Jam & Spoon £25 - £40
2494 Two way Tray £25 - £35
2495 Cruet £30 - £50
2496 Tray, short width, 2 sizes £20 - £30
2497 Vinegar and Oil Pots (with stoppers) £25 - £40
2498 Three way Tray £25 - £35
2499 Salad Bowl and Servers £50 - £80
2500 Covered Cheese £40 - £60
2501 Bowl, 2 sizes £30 - £40
2504 Tea Pot, 2 sizes £30 - £60
2507 Tray, long width £30 - £40
2508 Sauceboat and Tray £25 - £40
2509 Lamp Base £35 - £50
2510 Soup Cup £10 - £20
2511 Coffee Pot £40 - £70
2512 Mayonnaise, Ladle and Tray £40 - £70
2513 Toast Rack £25 - £45
2518 Vase, medium £20 - £30
2519 Vase, tall £25 - £35
2520 Vase, squat £20 - £30
2521 Bowl £20 - £30
2523 Vase, tall £25 - £35
2524 Double Vase, crescent £25 - £40
2537 Hot Water Pot £35 - £60
2609 Bud Vase (from large Salt) £20 - £30

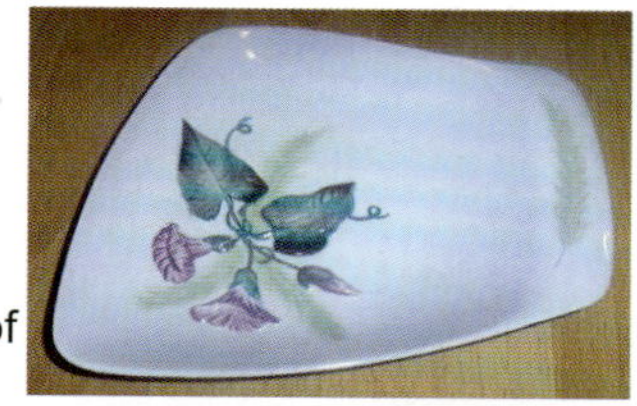
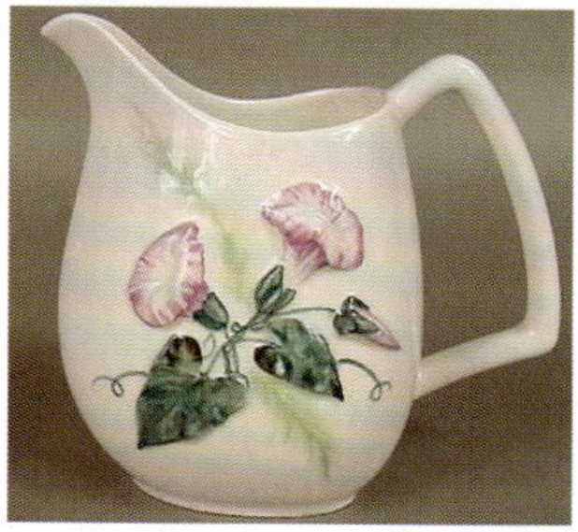
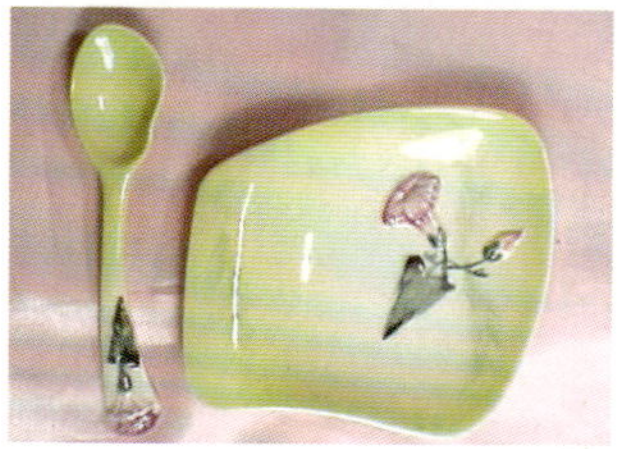
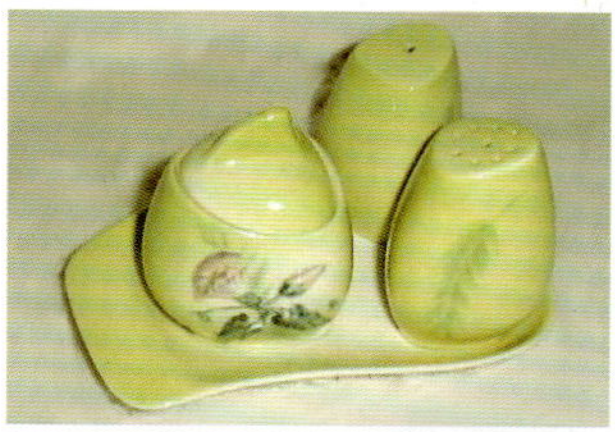
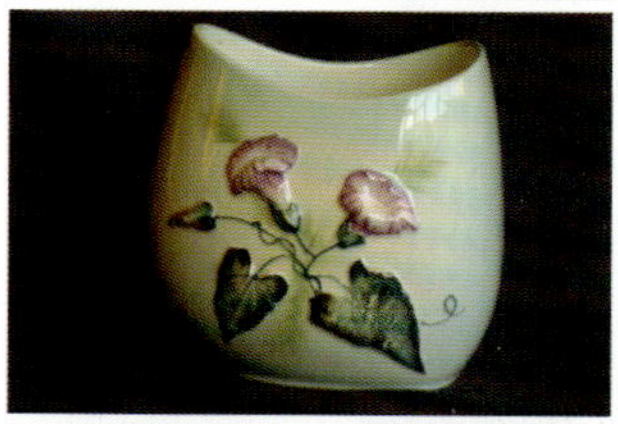
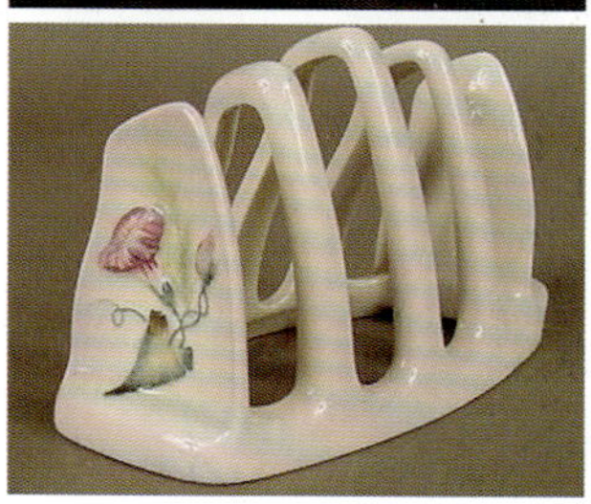

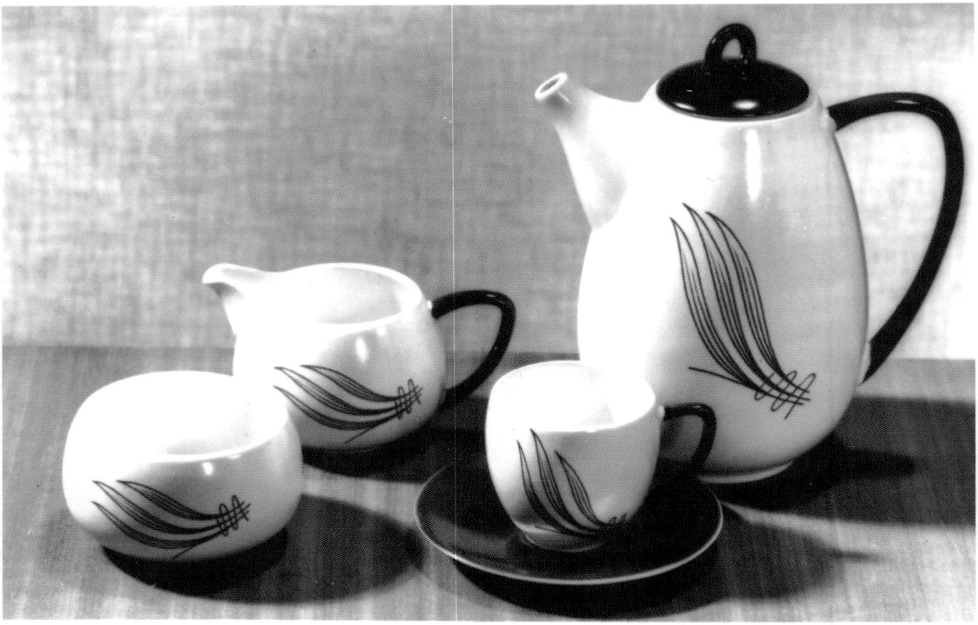

EDINBURGH COFFEE SET
"WINDSWEPT"

Carlton Ware

4581 MATT CREAM & BROWN
~~4582 MATT CREAM & SAGE GREEN~~
4583 GLOSSY PALE BLUE & BOTTLE GREEN
4622 DUSKY PINK & PALE BLUE

EDINBURGH COFFEEWARE "WINDSWEPT" DESIGN

4581 Matt Cream & Brown
4583 Glossy Pale Blue & Bottle Green
4622 Dusky Pink & Pale Blue

	Each	Each
Coffeeset	40/–	Boxed 42/6
Coffeepot	8/9	
Sugar	3/4	
Cream	3/11	
Cup & Saucer	4/–	

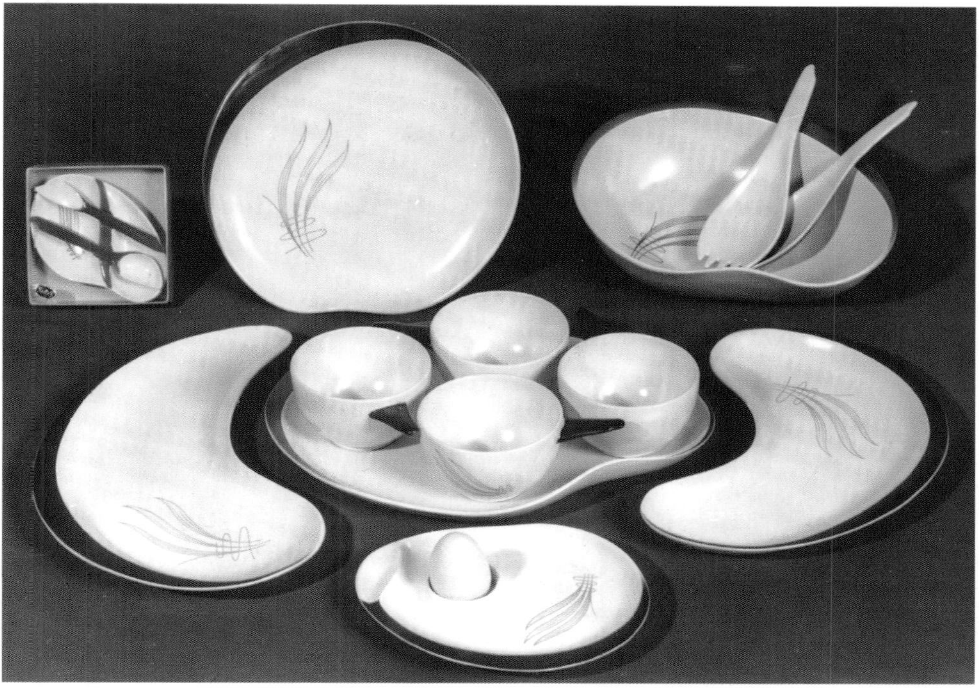

WINDSWEPT DESIGN

4581 Matt Cream/Brown
4583 Glossy Pale Blue/Glossy Bottle Green
4622 Dusky Pink/Pale Blue

Prices—each

Boxed Combined Individual
Jam/Butter and Knife & Spoon
4/4

Jam/Butter	1/6
Spoon	1/2
Knife	1/2

..

Plate l/s
5/6

..

Salad Set
15/2

Bowl	10/10
Servers	4/4

Barbecue Set
20/–

Side Tray l/s
6/3

..

Stand	8/8
Cup	2/10

..

Side Tray s/s
5/6

Egg Dish
3/2

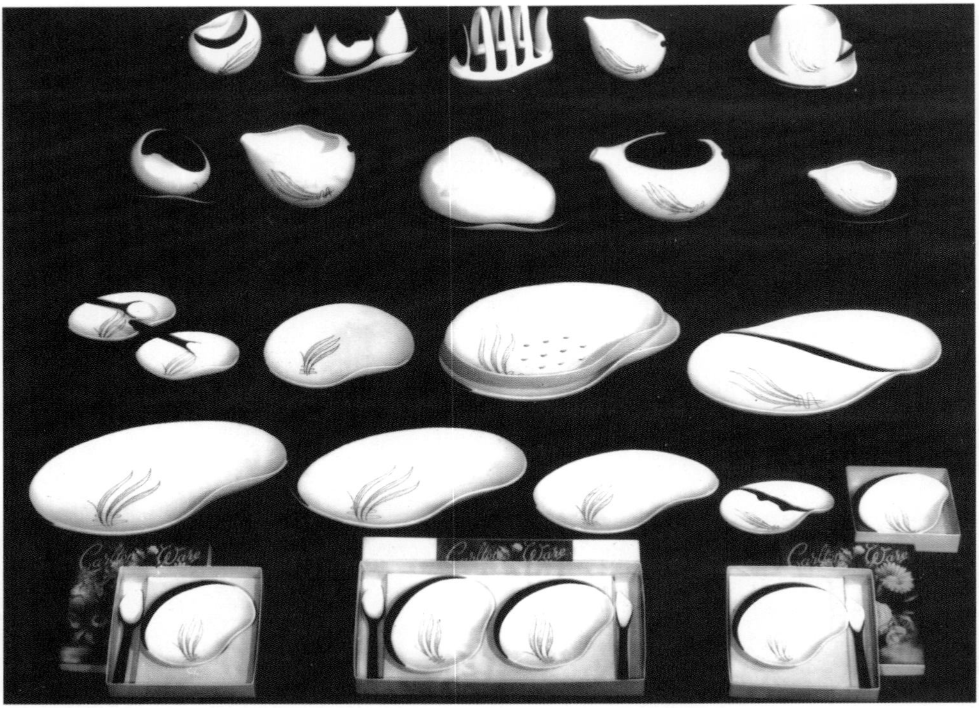

WINDSWEPT DESIGN

4581 Matt Cream/Brown
4583 Glossy Pale Blue/Glossy Bottle Green
4622 Dusky Pink/Pale Blue

Prices—each

Sugar	Cruet Set	Toastrack	Cream	Cup & Saucer
2/9	5/5	3/10	2/11	3/9

Pepper & Salt s/s 2/4 pr.
Cruet Boxed 7/2

Preserve & Stand	Jug ½ pint	Covered Cheese	Teapot 2 cup	Sauce Boat & Stand
4/7	4/6	6/10	5/11	3/9

Preserve 3/4
Preserve & Spoon 4/6
Preserve, Stand & Spoon 5/9

Teapot 4 cup 7/9

Sauce Boat 2/6
Stand 1/3

Jam & Spoon	Butter & Knife	Plate	Cress Dish & Stand	2-Way Tray
2/8	2/8	2/7	12/6	5/3

Jam 1/6
Spoon 1/2

Butter 1/6
Knife 1/2

Tray l/s	Tray m/s	Tray s/s	Ashtray	Individual Butter Boxed
5/6	4/5	2/11	1/6	2/–

Jam & Spoon Boxed	Combined Butter & Knife and Jam & Spoon boxed	Butter & Knife Boxed
3/3	6/2	3/3

Windswept

In 1958 Carlton Ware introduced a new range called *Windswept*. The decoration is very simple but effective. It consists of three long grass-like leaves blowing in the wind. The shapes of the various pieces reflect this decoration to great effect.

Windswept was produced in twin-tone colours. The colours were matt cream with brown, glossy pale blue with glossy bottle green and dusky pink with pale blue. Another colour, matt cream with sage green was abandoned. The dusky pink with pale blue is quite rare compared with the other colours; perhaps it was less popular back in those days.

The range proved to be very popular and continues to adorn many collectors shelves.

2394 Tray £10 - £20
2395 Jug £10 - £20
2396 Preserve and Stand £20 - £30
2403 Cream £10 - £20 Sugar £10 - £20
Cup and Saucer £10 - £20
2404 5" Plate £10 - £20
2405 Tea Pot (2 sizes) £20 - £45
2406 Sauceboat and Stand £20 - £35
2407 Toast Rack £20 - £30
2408 Butter & Knife or Jam & Spoon £15 - £25 each
2409 Ashtray £10 - £20
2411 Two way Tray £15 - £25
2414 Cruet Set (Pepper, Salt, Mustard and Frame) £20 - £40
2415 Cheese Dish and Stand £15 - £30
2416 Cress Dish and Stand £25 - £40
2422 Coffee Set (inc 6 C&S) £100 - £150
Coffee Pot £20 - £35, Cup & Saucer £10 - £20
Sugar £10 - £20, Cream £10 - £20
2423 Egg Tray £15 - £30
2424 Salad Bowl and Servers £25 - £50
2425 Barbecue Set (4 cups on stand) £25 - £40
Crescent Plate (Side Tray) £15 - £25
2426 Plate (large size) £10 - £20
2438 Soup Jug (Hot Water Jug) £20 - £40

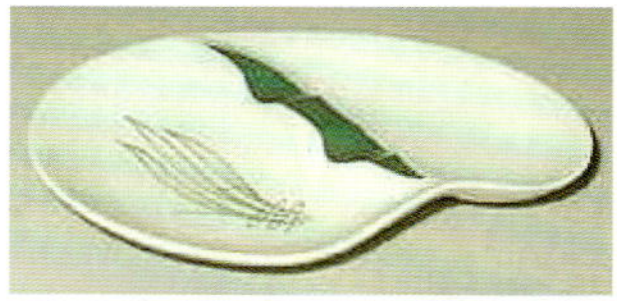

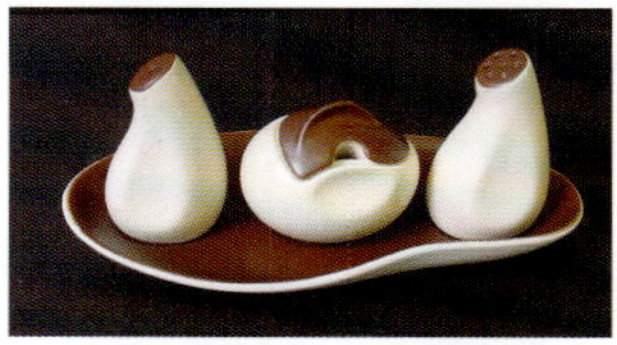

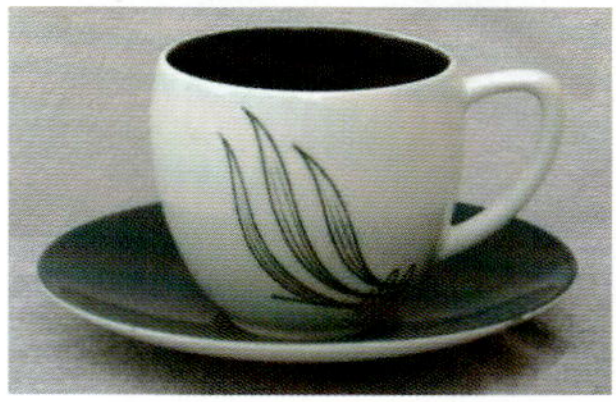

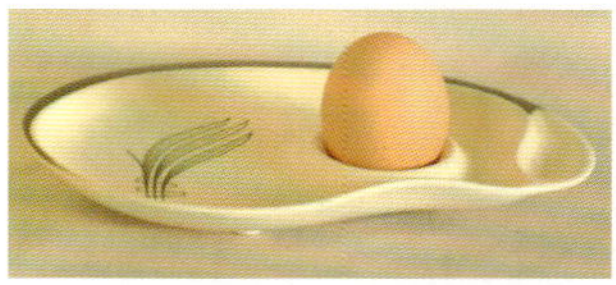

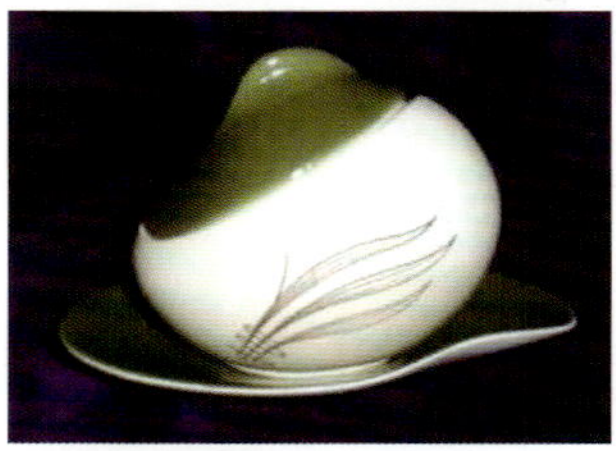

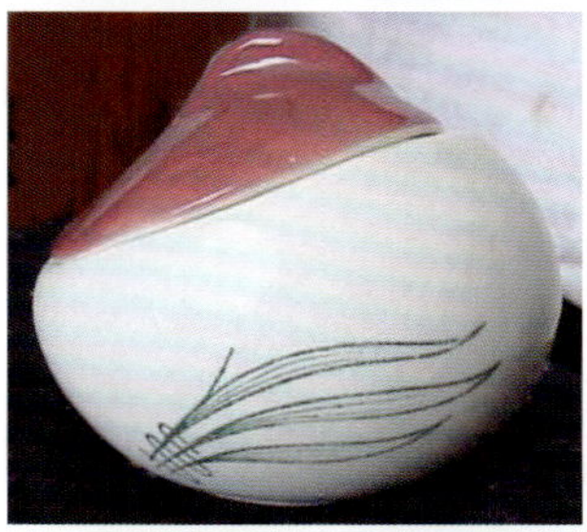

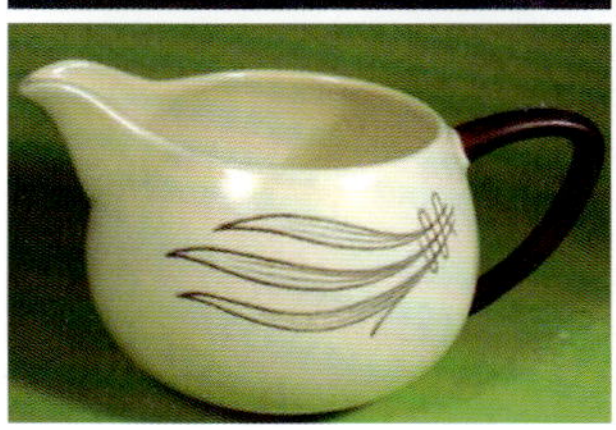

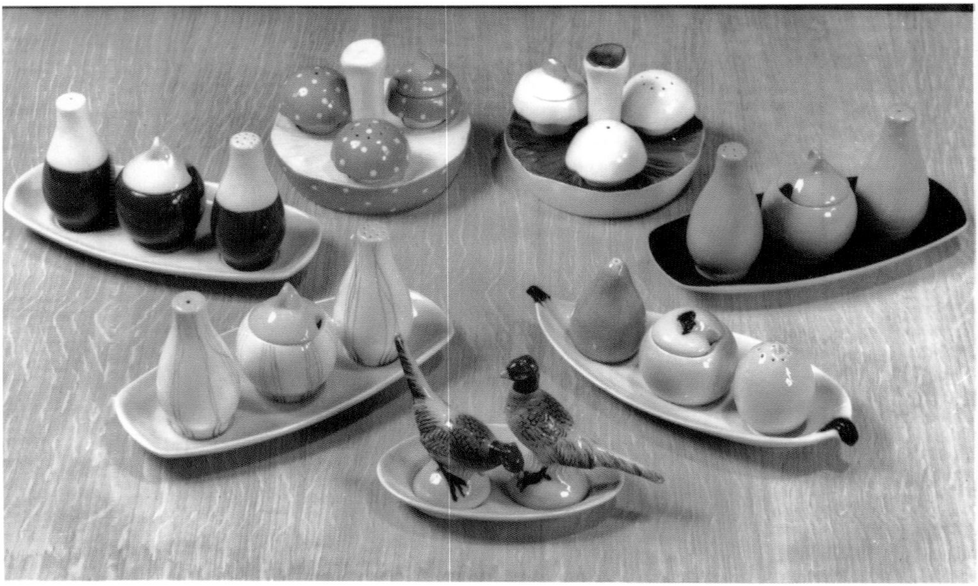

NOVELTY Carlton Ware CRUET SETS

NOVELTY CRUETS

Prices—each

MUSHROOM No. 4617 (Orange & Yellow with spots) 9/4

Pepper	1/5
Salt	1/5
Mustard	1/9
Stand	4/9

MUSHROOM No. 4618 (Brown & Cream) 9/4

Pepper	1/5
Salt	1/5
Mustard	1/9
Stand	4/9

MODERN No. 4615 (Grey & Pink) 6/3

Pepper	1/3
Salt	1/3
Mustard	1/8
Stand	2/1

MODERN No. 4614 (Black & Orange) 6/3

Pepper	1/3
Salt	1/3
Mustard	1/8
Stand	2/1

MODERN No. 4616 (Green & Stripe) 6/3

Pepper	1/3
Salt	1/3
Mustard	1/8
Stand	2/1

FRUIT 5/7

Pepper	1/2
Salt	1/2
Mustard	1/6
Stand	1/9

PHEASANT (only sold complete) 7/6

Novelty Cruet Sets

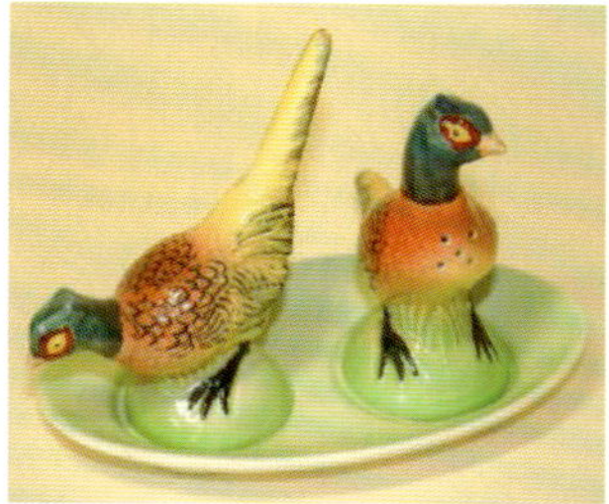

A cruet set is a stand or container that holds salt & pepper or salt, pepper & mustard containers.

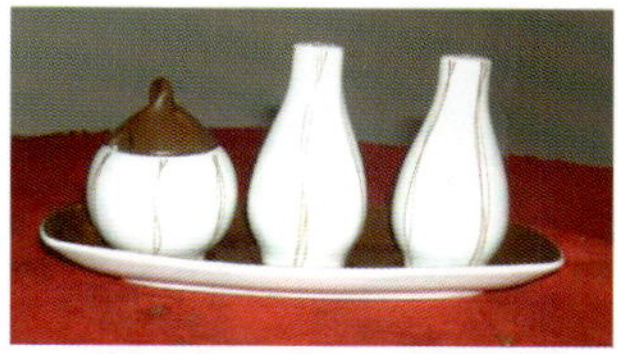

Carlton Ware made cruet sets in just about every pattern that they produced. In addition they produced some *Novelty Cruet Sets*. The Black & White catalogue shows four varieties. This includes Mushroom in two colours, 4617 Orange & Yellow with spots, and 4618 Brown & Cream. The Modern pattern was available in three colours, 4614 Black & Orange, 4615 Grey & Pink, and 4616 Green & Stripe. The other two cruet sets, *Fruit* and *Pheasant,* were available in a single colour version.

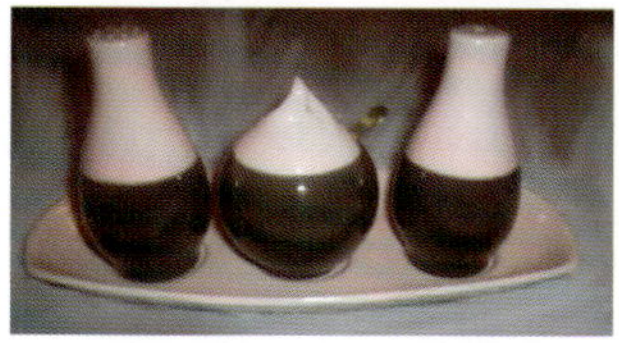

A *Squirrel Cruet Set* (Rd 727287) consisting of a tray, squirrel, salt, pepper and mustard was made around 1927. The salt, pepper and mustard took the shape of acorns. Another version was made in the 1960's which consisted of a tray with two squirrels, one of which was salt and the other pepper. A *Squirrel Preserve* was also produced.

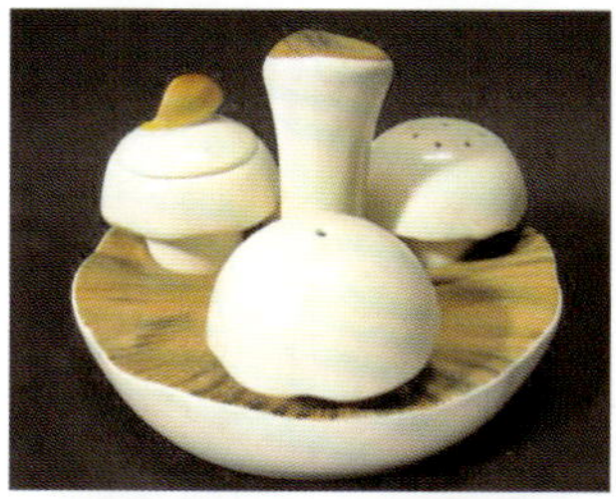

Squirrel with 3 acorn condiments £40 - £70

2400 Pheasant £40 - £70
2440 Modern £25 - £45
2441 Mushroom, brown & cream £50 - £75
2441 Mushroom, orange & yellow with spots £75 - £100
2503 Squirrel £40 - £70
2544 Shelf £30 - £50
2572 Shell £30 - £50

2792 Squirrel Preserve £40 - £70

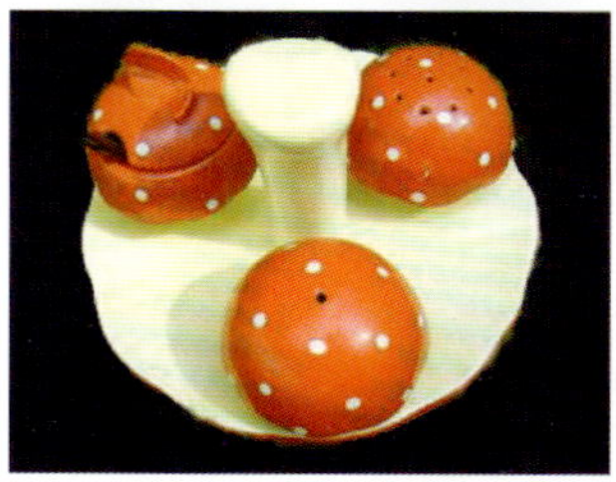

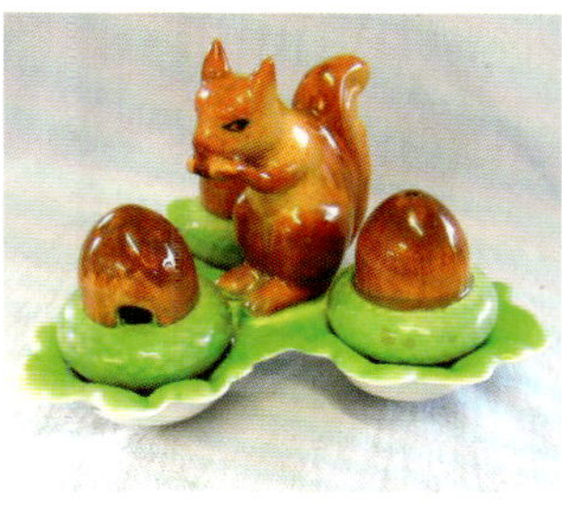

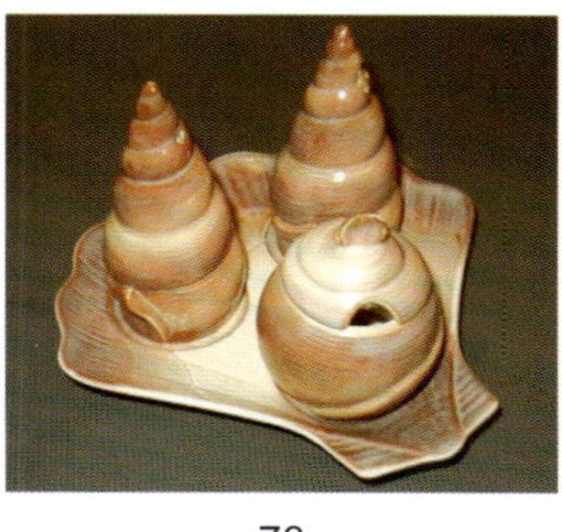

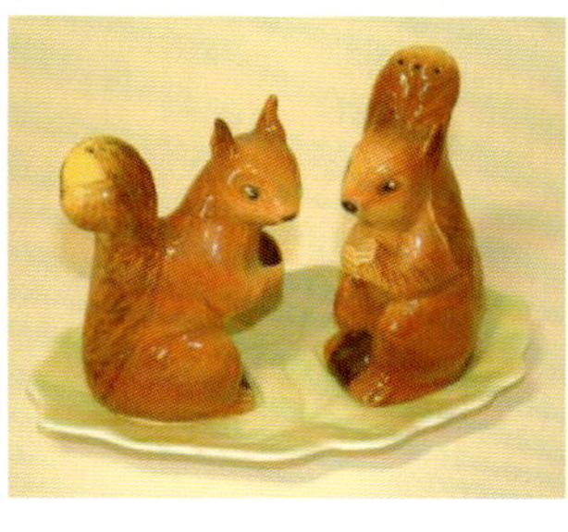

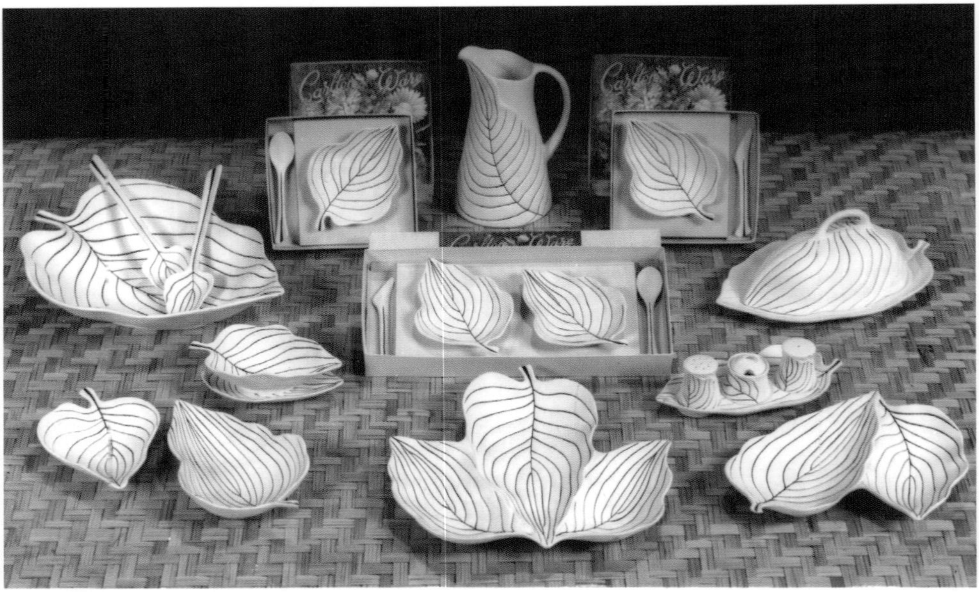

PIN STRIPE DESIGN

Carlton Ware

4609 LIME GREEN
4610 BROWN
4611 SAND

4609 Lime Green
4610 Brown
4611 Sand

PIN STRIPE DESIGN

Prices—each

Jam & Spoon Boxed
3/3

Jam 1/6
Spoon 1/2

Tall Jug
5/8

Butter & Knife Boxed
3/3

Butter 1/6
Knife 1/2

Salad Set
15/2

Bowl 10/9
Servers 4/5

Combined Butter & Knife and
Jam & Spoon
6/2

Cheese Dish
6/10

Sauce Boat & Stand
3/9

Boat 2/6
Stand 1/3

Cruet Set
5/5

Pepper & Salt s/s
2/4 pr.

Pin Tray
2/2

Bowl s/s
3/11

3-way Tray
5/2

2-way Tray
3/7

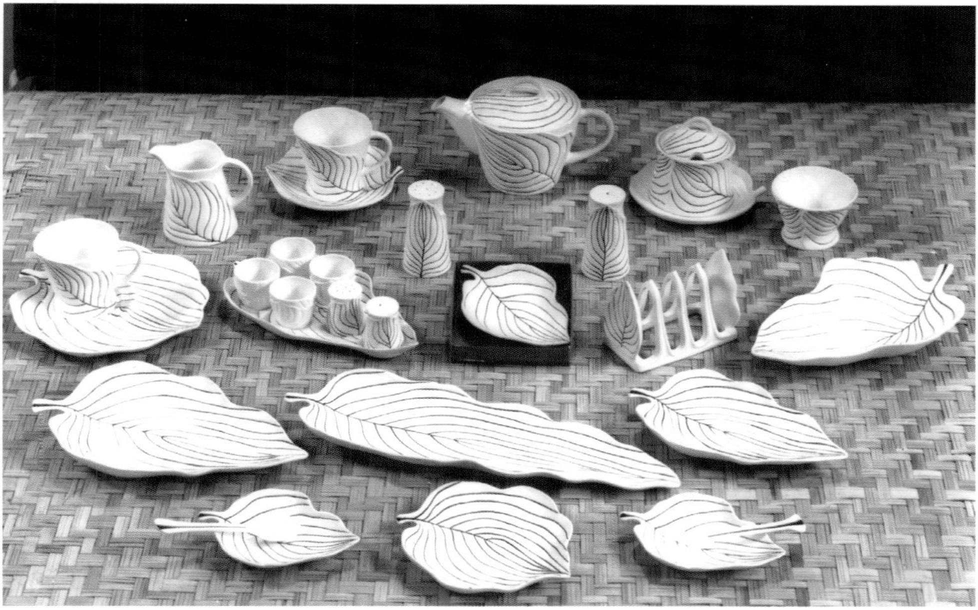

4609 Lime Green
4610 Brown
4611 Sand

PIN STRIPE DESIGN

Prices—each

Cup & Saucer
3/9

Teapot
5/11

Preserve & Stand
4/7

Preserve	3/4
Stand	1/3
Preserve, Stand and Spoon	5/9
Preserve and Spoon	4/6

Cream
2/11

Pepper l/s
2/–

Salt l/s
2/–

Sugar
2/10

Television Set
6/6

Egg Set
7/9

Individual Boxed Butter
2/–

Toastrack
3/11

Bowl l/s
5/5

Tray 8″
4/5

Long Tray
3/8

Tray 6″
2/11

Jam & Spoon
2/8

Jam	1/6
Spoon	1/2

Plate 5″
2/7

Butter & Knife
2/8

Butter	1/6
Knife	1/2

Pinstripe

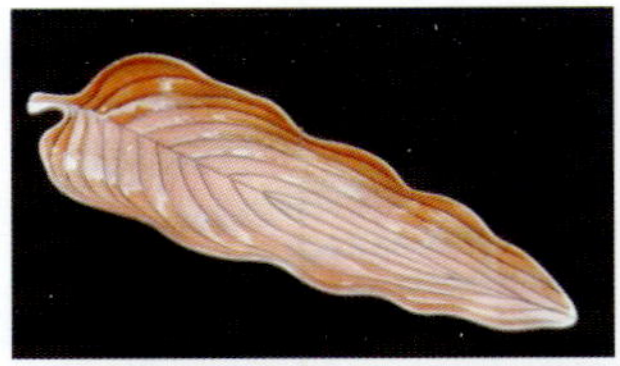
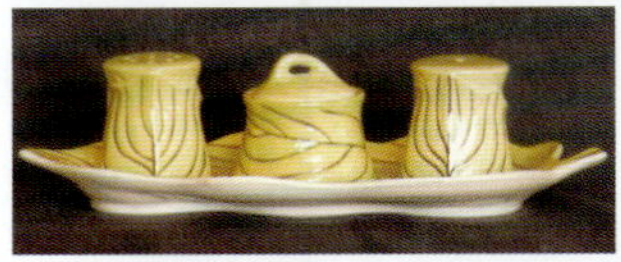
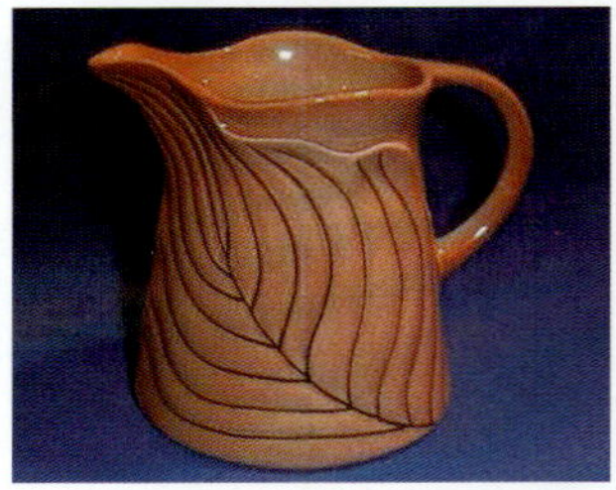
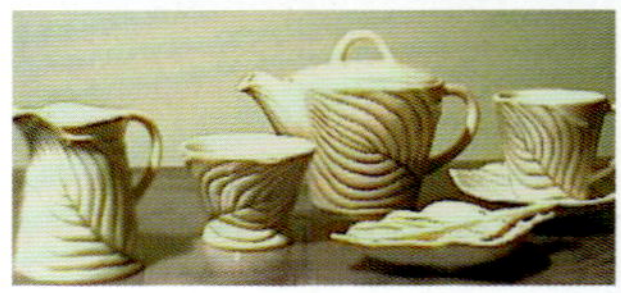
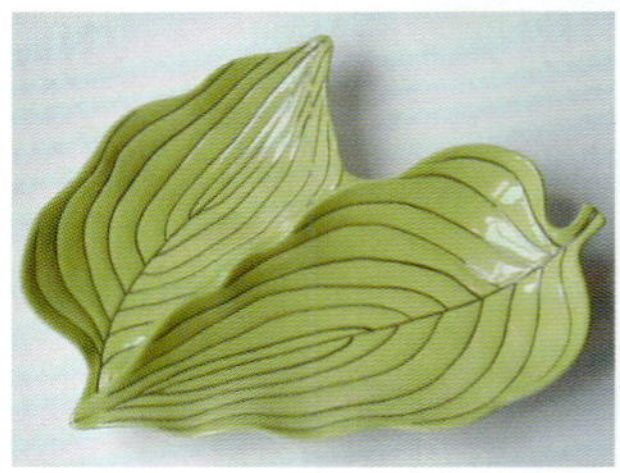
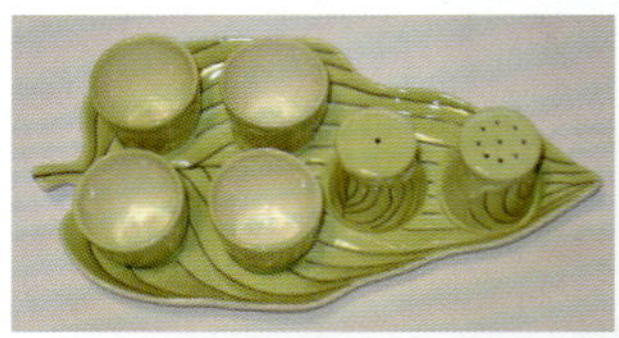
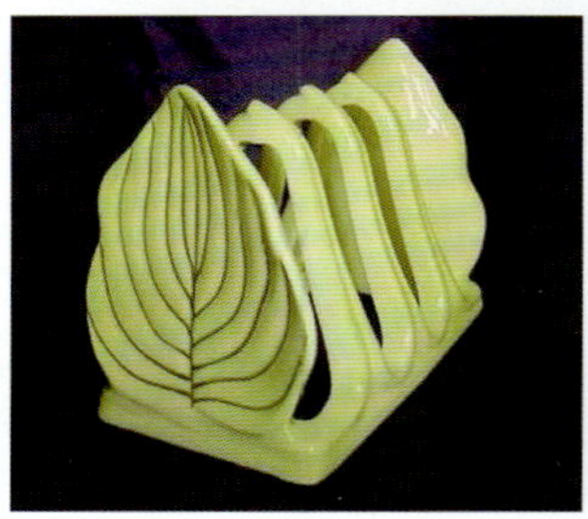

Carlton Ware introduced their *Pinstripe* range in the late 1950's. The pattern is aptly described by its name, pinstripe, of which some definitions include:

a fine vertical stripe, usually in white or grey
a thin stripe on a fabric
a kind of fabric with thin stripes, often used for men's suits.
a thin line over the body colour that accentuates the body lines and contours.

Carlton Ware originally produced the *Pinstripe* range in three colours, 4609 Lime Green, 4610 Brown, and 4611 Sand. The Black & White catalogue pages on the two previous pages shows the vast array of different shapes.

2419 Tall Jug £15 - £25
2428 Butter & Knife £20 - £40
2428 Butter & Knife, Boxed £30 - £50
2428 Butter, Individual Boxed £20 - £40
2428 Butter, Jam, Knife, Spoon, Combined Set £50 - £70
2428 Jam & Spoon £20 - £40
2428 Jam & Spoon, Boxed £30 - £50
2429 Plate 5" £10 - £20
2430 Long Tray £20 - £40
2435 Cruet Set (Pepper, Salt, Mustard and Frame) £30 - £50
2439 Tray 2 sizes £15 - £30
2451 Morning Tea Set (Tea for two) £80 - £150
Tea Pot £25 - £50 Cup & Saucer £10 - £20
Cream £10 - £20 Sugar £10 - £20 Plate £10 - £20
2452 Preserve and Stand £30 - £50
2453 Two way Tray £20 - £35
2454 Three way Tray £25 - £45
2455 Sauceboat and Stand £20 - £30
2456 Tall Cup with Saucer £15 - £25
2457 Pin Tray £10 - £20
2458 Television Set (Tray with cup) £20 - £30
2461 Cheese Dish and Stand £40 - £60
2462 Toast Rack £30 - £50
2464 Tea Pot £25 - £50
2465 Egg Set £40 - £60
2466 Salad Set - Bowl with Servers £40 - £60
2467 Salt & Pepper, large £10 - £25
Bowl small size £10 - £20
Bowl large size £15 - £25

Linen

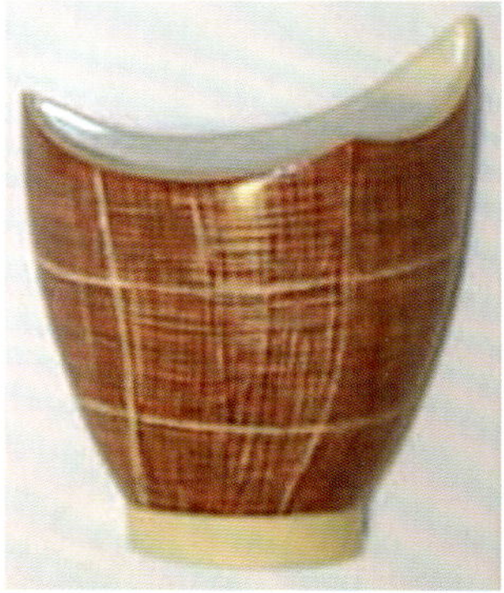

Introduced in 1958. The name for this pattern is very apt as it does look like a piece of Linen, a material made from the fibers of the flax plant. A number of colourways were produced, red or terracotta, green, lemon-yellow, black and brown.

2442 Vase £20 - £30
2443 Coffee Pot £30 - £50 Cup & Saucer £20 - £40
Sugar £15 - £30 Cream £15 - £30
2444 Butter £10 - £20
2445 Triangular Plate, 3 sizes £20 - £60
2446 Bowl, 2 sizes £20 - £40
2447 Tall Narrow Vase £20 - £40
2448 Wall Vase £20 - £40
2449 Jug £30 - £50
2450 Candle Holders £25 - £35

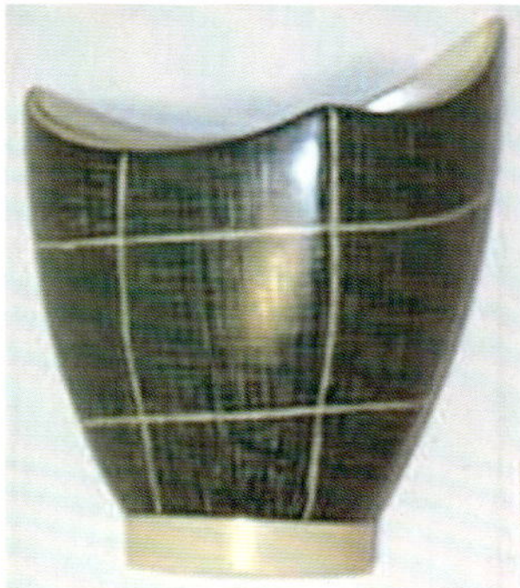

Carlton Ware also used these shape numbers for other patterns such as Lily of the Valley flowers.

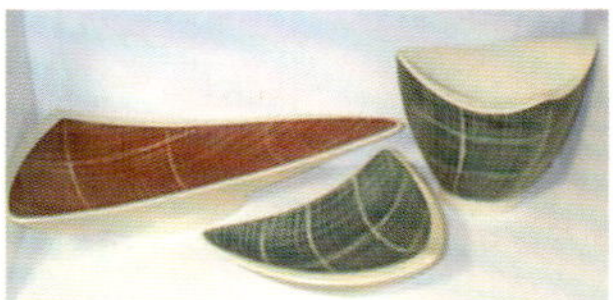

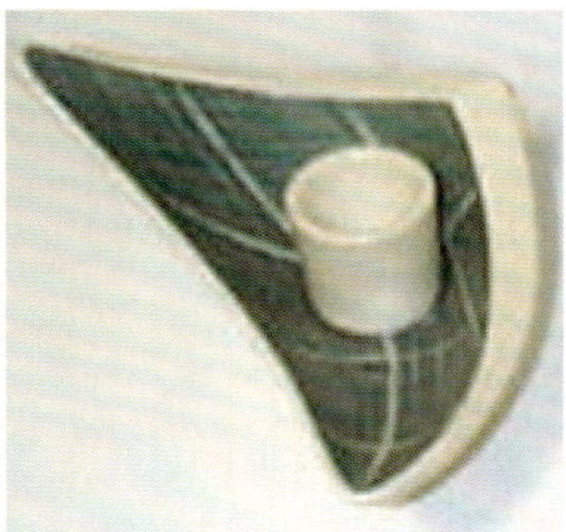

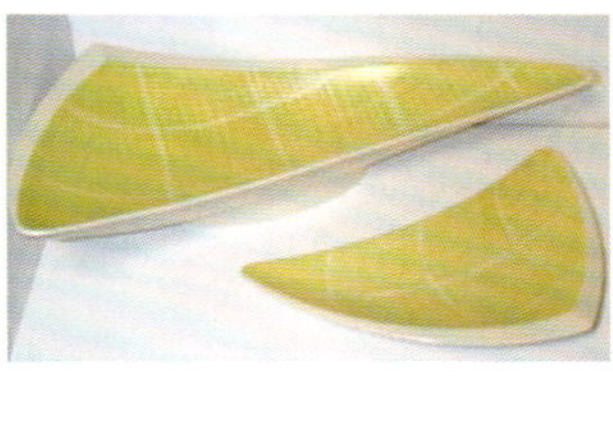

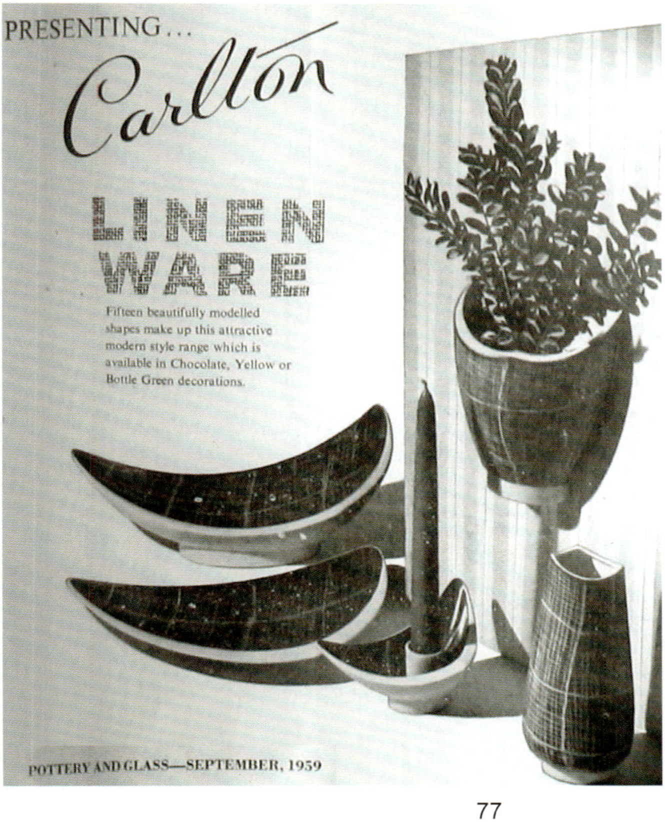

Fruit

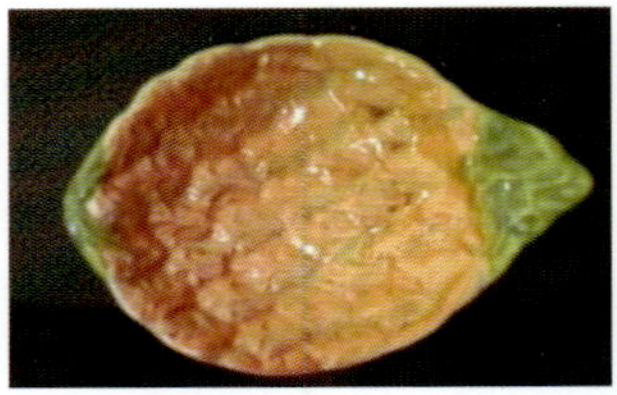

Carlton Ware produced a variety of colourful *Fruit Ware*. Most were produced from the late 1950's until the late 1970's. Carlton Ware was always very keen to keep up with their competitors.

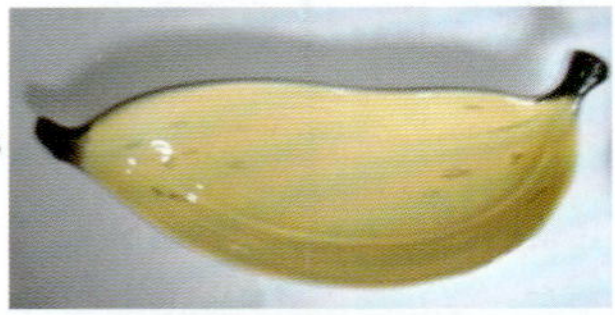

It seems that many of the potteries were influenced by each other's ideas and of course by what was selling well. Therefore many designs produced were adapted from designs of the time and fruit probably falls into this category. It was obviously a very popular range as is shown by the large number of shapes produced. Its popularity was probably due in some part to the novelty and fun factor of the naturalistic shapes and designs.

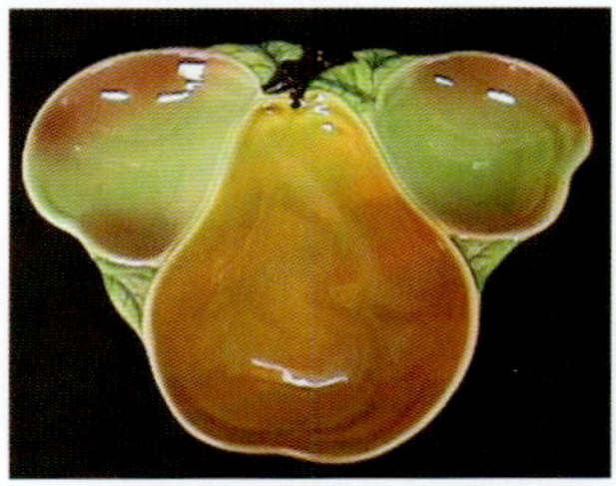

Fruit (and vegetables) seem an obvious choice for table and dinnerware patterns. The Carlton Ware range goes one step further as the pieces are actual representations of the fruit they are named after. Vegetables including mushrooms designs were also included into the fruit range as it was so named.

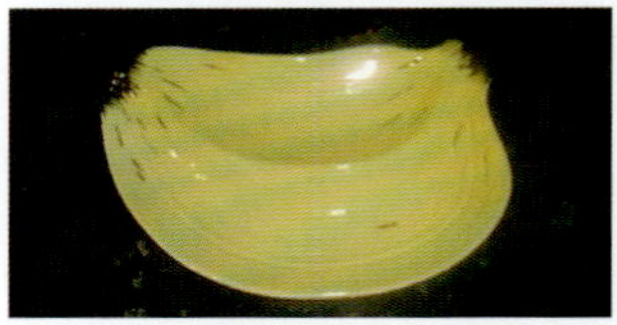

The designer at that time, Phillip Forster, must have had fun creating novelty cruet and preserve sets as well as dinner and tableware. The range was first sold in the *Apple* design, which was followed by *Pear* etc.

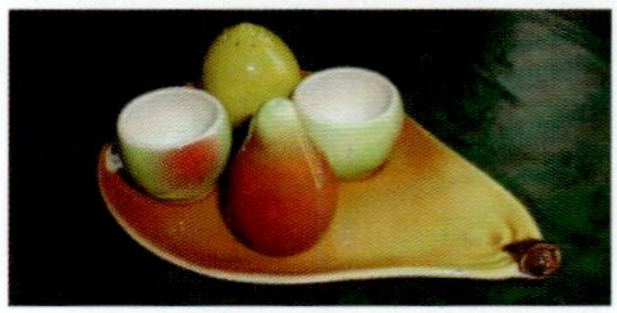

The Trade and Fair brochures of the time show that there was considerable interest and attention in the new lines of *Apple, Pear, Lemon* and *Banana Novelty Cruet Sets.*

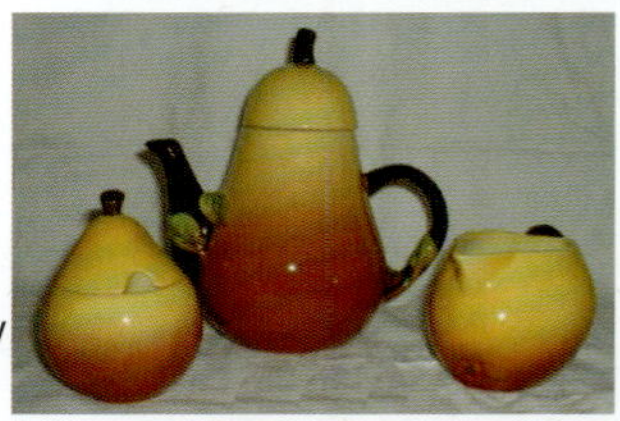

The *Orange* Preserve, also known as the *Jaffa* Preserve pot was originally introduced in the 1920's, possibly about 1926. The early ones can be found with a shape number of 331 but often do not have any shape number at all on the base. The *Orange* Preserve was then reintroduced as shape 3312 much later and continued into the 1980's.

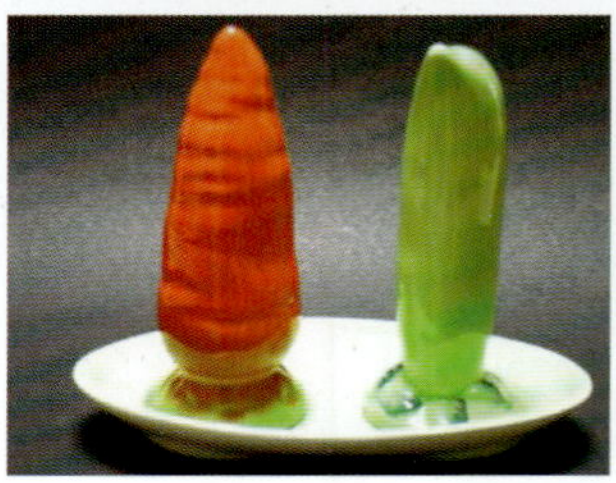

The copies of the advertising catalogue dated from 1959 show that the *Jaffa* pot was produced in two sizes, small and large. Both of the sizes were advertised with an optional circular stand that was embossed with leaves. The small one sold for 5s 5d (about 27p) and the large one for 6s 9d (about 34p). You could buy the pot and stand separately with prices being 4s 4d, 1s 1d respectively for the small size and 5s 5d, 1s 4d respectively for the large size. The leaflet does not show any spoons for the pots.

Although some pieces were produced in the early 1920's they continued to be produced into the 50's and 60's under Cuthbert Wiltshaw until he died in 1966. The company was sold to Arthur Wood who reintroduced the *Apple* range in the early 1970's.

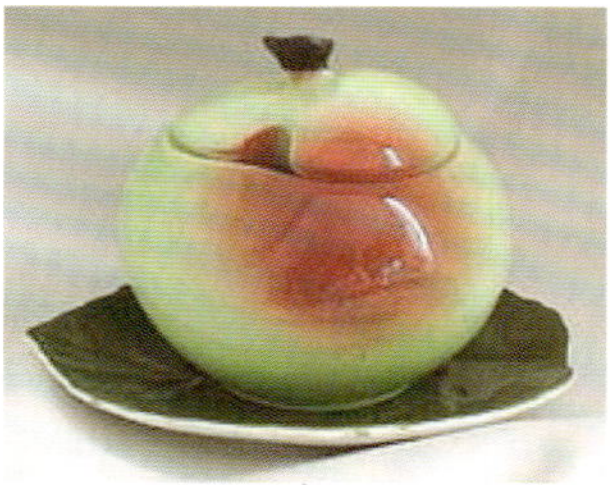

331 Jaffa Preserve and Stand £30 - £50
2431 Cruet Set (Fruit) £30 - £50
2514 Apple Preserve and Stand £20 - £35
2526 Pear Butter £10 - £20
2527 Apple Butter £10 - £20
2528 Lemon Butter £10 - £20
2529 Pineapple Butter £10 - £20
2530 Knife or Spoon for Butter Set £15 - £25 each
2591 Pear Preserve with Apple Preserve Stand £20 - £35
2630 Vegetable Cruet Set £30 - £50
2635 Tomato Cruet Set £30 - £50
2661 Apple Salt and Pepper £20 - £30
2662 Pear Salt and Pepper £20 - £30
2769 Banana Split Tray £10 - £20
2771 Apple Individual Preserve £15 - £25
2772 Lemon Individual Fruit Dish £10 - £20
2773 Apple Salad Bowl and Servers £30 - £50
2774 Banana Long Tray £15 - £25
2775 Pear Egg Frame and Apple Egg Frame £40 - £60
2776 Fruit Range Centre Piece £35 - £55
2777 Fruit Knob for covered Butter £20 - £35
2778 Apple and Pear Three Way Tray £25 - £40
2779 Banana Salt and Pepper Stand £20 - £20
2780 Banana Two Way Tray £15 - £25
2781 Lemon Cream or Sauceboat £15 - £25
2782 Combination Toast Rack, Pear £60 - £80
2783 Lemon Individual Preserve £15 - £25
2784 Individual Apple and Lemon Preserve Stand £10 - £20
3063 Strawberry Preserve £20 - £40
3064 Pineapple Preserve £20 - £40
3065 Blackberry Preserve £20 - £40
3066 Raspberry Preserve £20 - £40
3067 Peach or Plum Preserve £20 - £40
3277 Banana Tray £10 - £20
3296 Apple Tea Pot £40 - £60
3297 Pear Tea Pot £50 - £65
3312 Orange Preserve £20 - £40
3340 Apple Sugar £20 - £30 Cream £20 - £30
Cup and Saucer £25 - £40

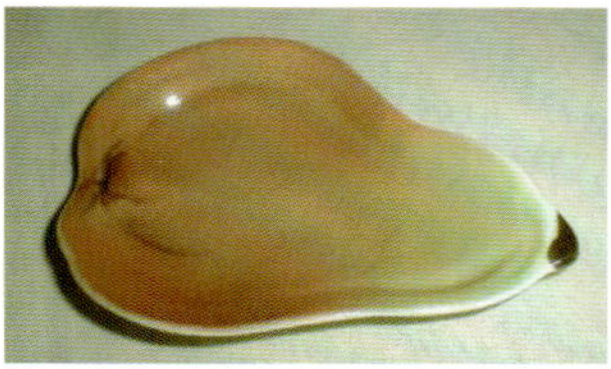

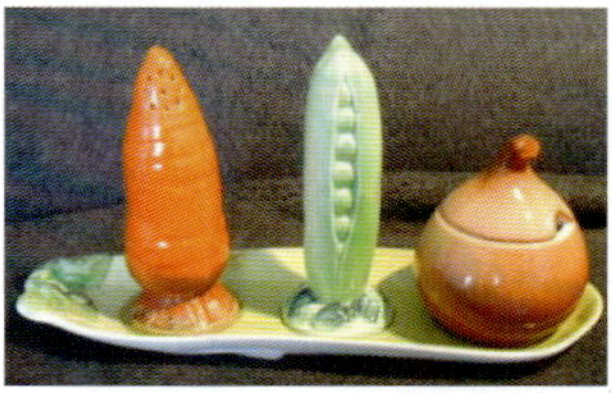

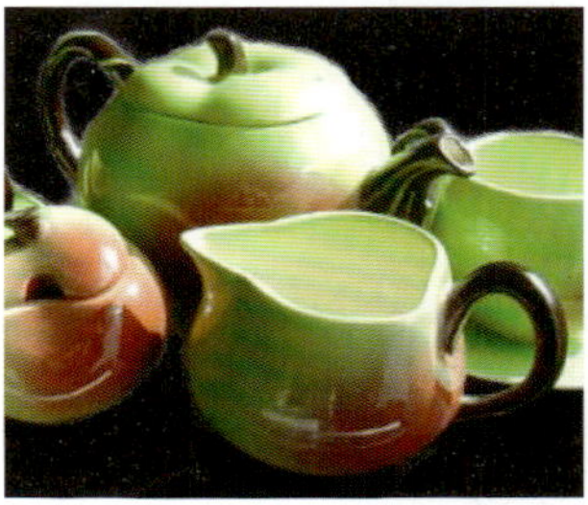

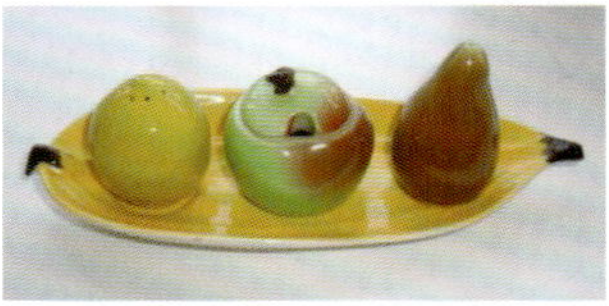

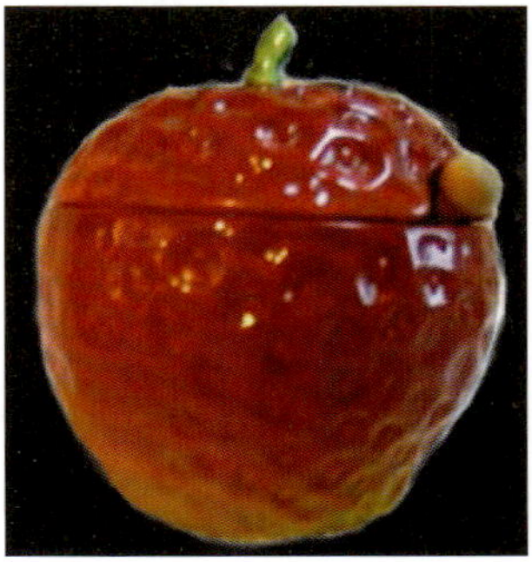

Aladdins Lamp

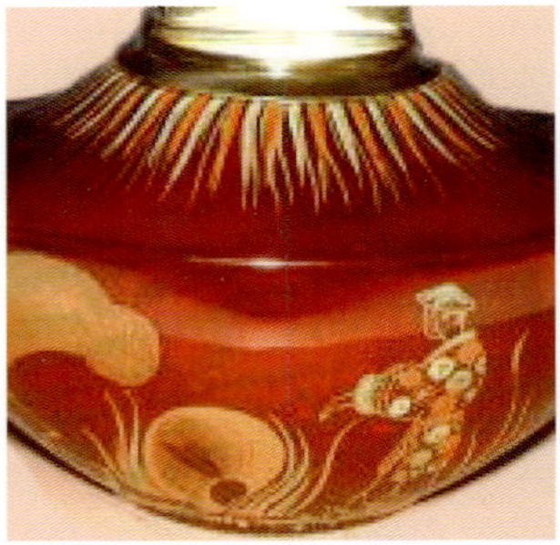

As the name suggests, this is a lighter in the shape of Aladdins Lamp. The lighter part is removable and has a receptacle for the lighter fluid. It was first made in 1959. Several different patterns were painted on it's surface, including Mikado as well as one with Aladdin.

A Carlton Ware retail price list from the 1980's shows that you could buy the lamp with one of the following patterns for the price indicated.

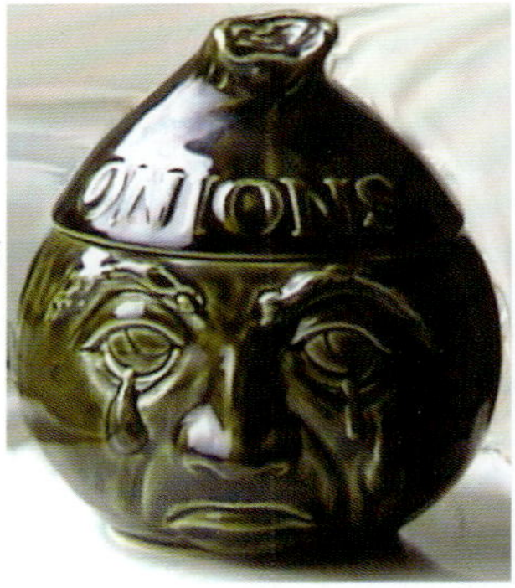

Rouge Royale with best gold finish £10.95
Powder Blue with best gold finish £10.95
Pagoda on Rouge Royale with best gold finish £16.55
Pagoda on Powder Blue with best gold finish £16.55
Bird of Paradise on Rouge Royale with best gold finish £16.55
Bird of Paradise on Powder Blue with best gold finish £16.55
Burnt Orange/Gold (Plain) £7.15
Almond/Gold (Plain) £7.15
Cherry Blossom Burnt Orange (Decorated) £8.20
Cherry Blossom Almond (Decorated) £8.20

2525 Lighter Holder £20 - £50

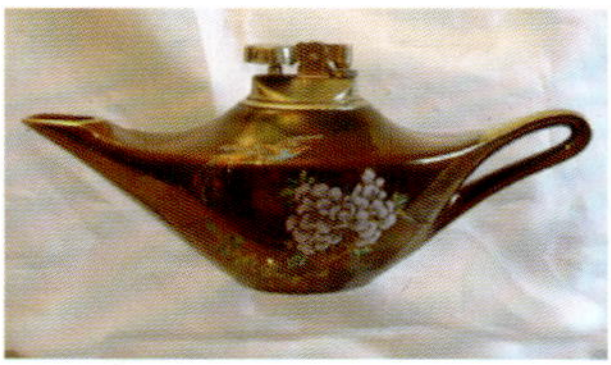

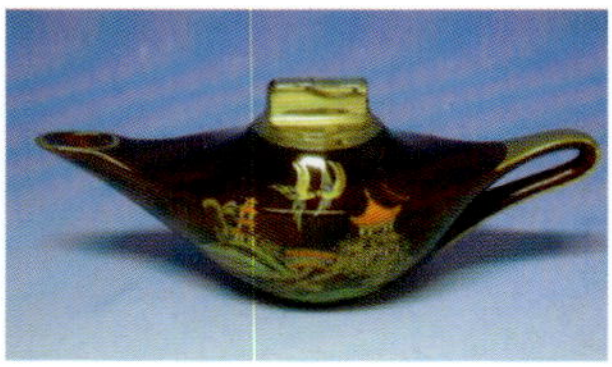

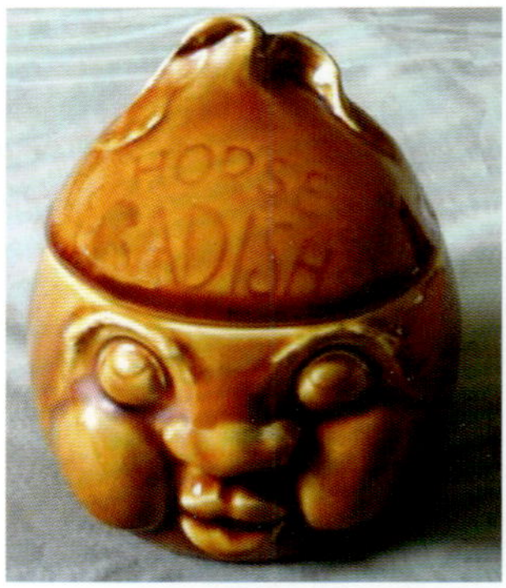

Vegetable Preserve

Four of these were produced by Carlton Ware and are often seen at Fairs and Internet auctions.

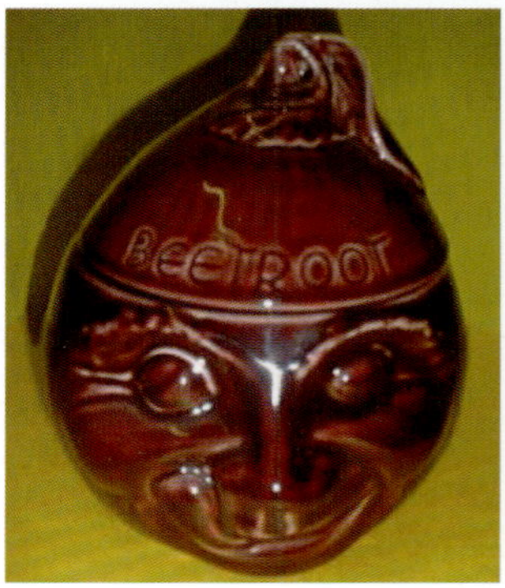

2763 Onion Preserve Pot £10 - £20
3090 Horse Radish Preserve Pot £10 - £20
3092 Red Cabbage Preserve Pot £10 - £20
3093 Beetroot Preserve Pot £10 - £20

Magnolia

Carlton Ware introduced the *Magnolia* pattern in the late 1950's, early 1960's. The *Magnolia* design was produced in three colourways; pale green, yellow and pinky-peach. The pale green has a realistic flower painted in the shade of purple. The yellow colourway has a green flower and the pink colourway is complemented with a flower in a darker shade of pink.

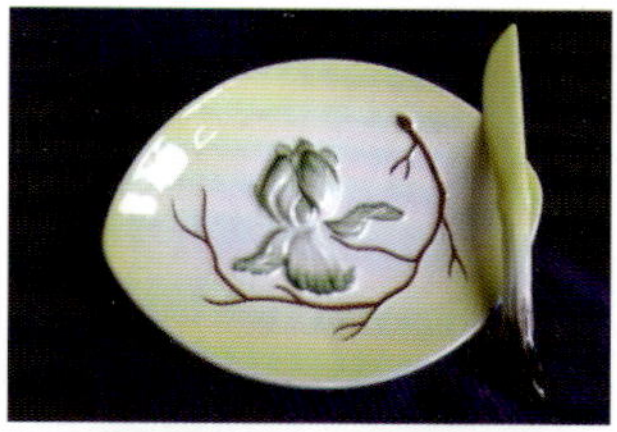
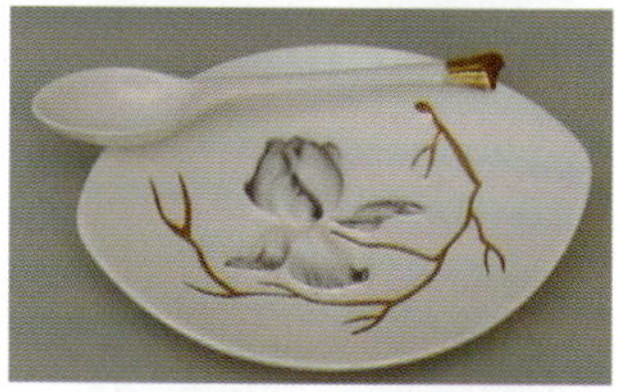
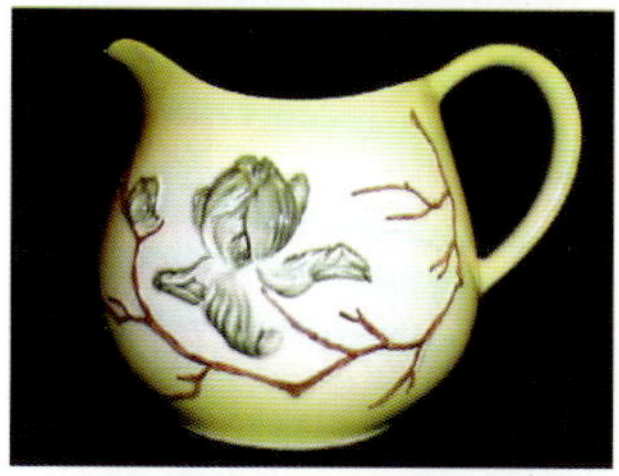
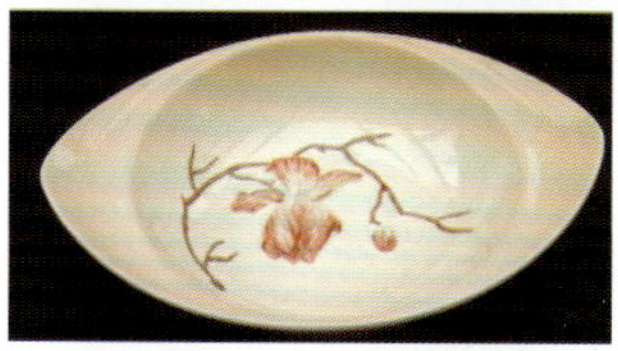
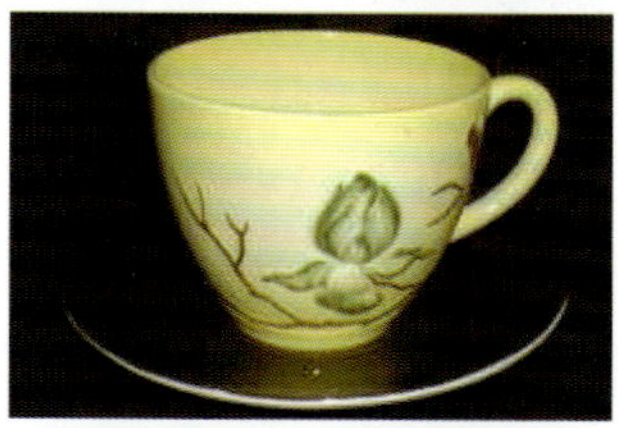
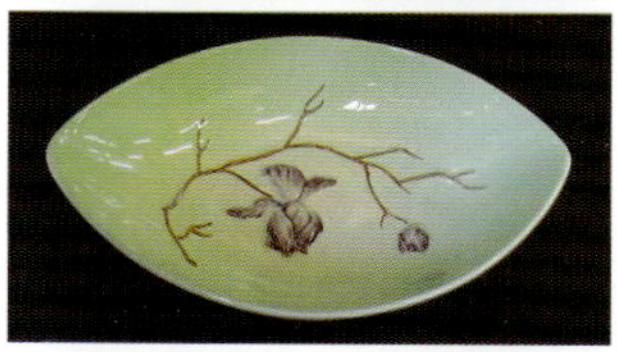
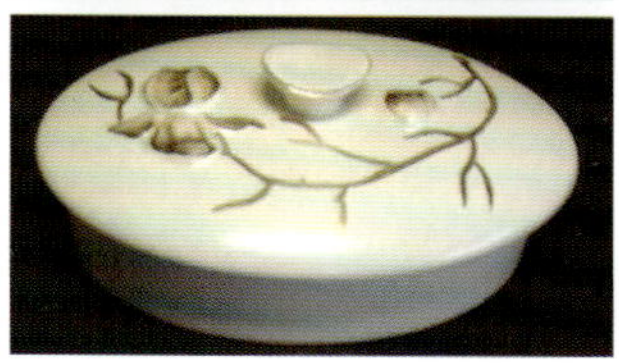

2515 Preserve Pot and Tray £30 - £50
2531 Oval Plate, 2 sizes £20 - £30
2558 Butter & Knife or Jam & Spoon £25 - £40
2559 Double Candlestick £15 - £30
2560 Jug, 1 pint £15 - £30
2561 Pin Box, Covered £20 - £30
2562 Covered Bon Bon, Trinket Box £20 - £30
2563 Single Candlestick £10 - £25
2564 Long Tray £25 - £35
2571 Covered Cheese £50 - £80
2592 Cup & Saucer £20 - £30
Sugar £20 - £30 Cream £20 - £30
2593 Two way Tray £25 - £35
2594 Double Butter £20 - £30
2595 Salad Bowl and Servers £60 - £80
2596 Salt & Pepper £25 - £40
2597 Sugar Shaker £25 - £40
2598 Dessert Bowl £20 - £30
2599 Tea Pot, 2 sizes £90 - £120
2601 Three way Tray £25 - £40
2604 Coffee Pot £80 - £100 Cup & Saucer £20 - £30
2605 Tray, 3 sizes £20 - £30
2607 Bowl, 2 sizes £15 - £30
2610 Hot Milk Jug £80 - £100
2611 Sauceboat and Tray £30 - £60
2612 Soup Jug £80 - £100
2613 Egg Set £40 - £60
2615 Handled Soup Cup £15 - £30
2616 Cruet £40 - £55
2617 Oil and Vinegar £30 - £50
2618 Mayonnaise, Ladle and Tray £30 - £60
2620 Toast Rack £45 - £65
2621 Vase, Tall £40 - £60
2622 Vase, Squat £30 - £50
2623 Vase, Bud £30 - £50
2624 Vase, Open Top £30 - £50
2625 Covered Butter, rectangular £40 - £60
2626 Large Stand for Oil etc £20 - £30
2627 Bowl £15 - £30

Orchid

Apparently around 120 million years ago, flowering plants were evolving and one of the first of these was the Orchid. The Orchid is a sub-tropical plant that survives in a hot and humid climate. Today there are around 35,000 different species of orchid in existence around the world. Orchids are not parasitic plants, they do grow on trees, but they do not feed from them, they use the host merely as somewhere to reside. So, it's not really that surprising that Carlton Ware used this beautiful exotic flower in one their floral range of designs. They obviously were not content just to feature the more common English garden flowers to entice collectors.

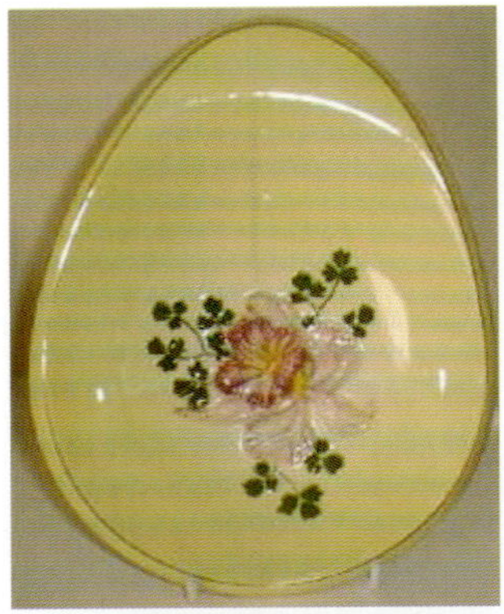

Carlton Ware introduced the embossed *Orchid* range in the early 1960's. This embossed design of an Orchid flower is a favourite of many Carlton Ware collectors.

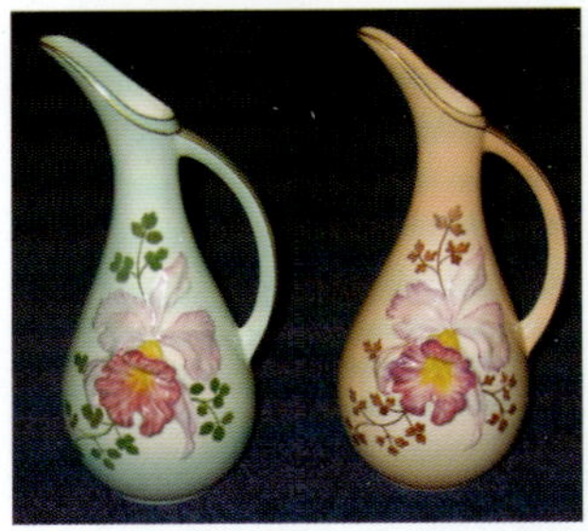

The pattern contains a very realistic representation of an Orchid and although there are many varieties to choose from the design looks very much like it is a copy of the *Labiate's Cattleya* Species named *Lueddamanniana Pterodactyl* (sounds like a well known dinosaur).

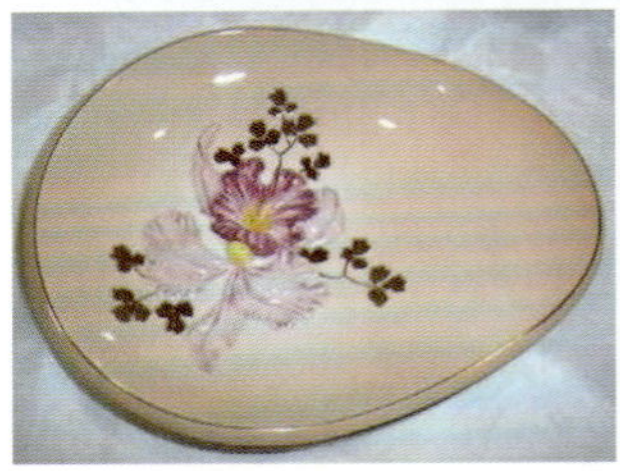

The *Orchid* and *Magnolia* designs are very similar in many ways and it's not unusual for people to confuse the two. Indeed, you often see *Magnolia* pieces being advertised or auctioned as *Orchid* and visa versa.

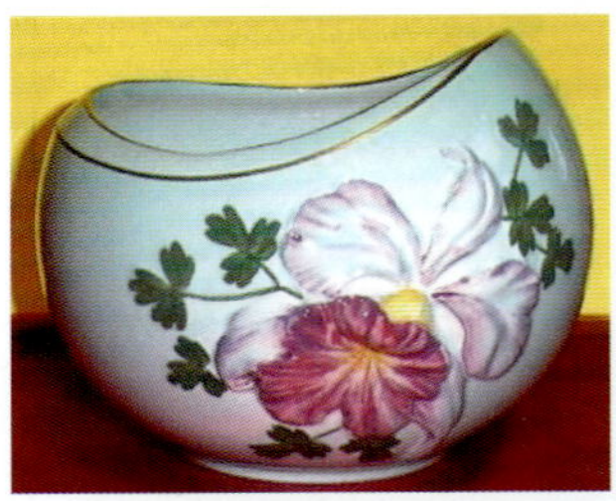

As with the *Magnolia* pattern, there are three colourways: creamy yellow, pale green and a pinky-peach colour. The flower head which is in full bloom includes some greenery, which for some reason looks more like shamrock leaves than Orchid foliage. On the pink colourway the shamrock like leaves are not green but a brownish/red colour, which complements the colour tones much better.

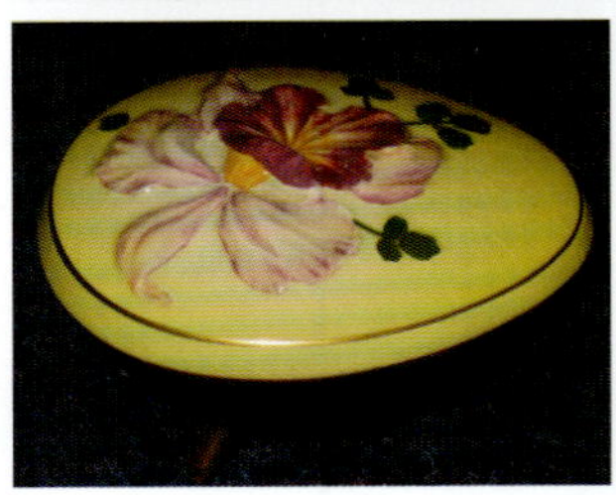

2533 Tray, large size £30 - £50
2574 Flower Jug £65 - £90
2575 Cigarette Box £45 - £70
2576 Trinket Box with legs, including lid £45 - £70
2577 Ashtray £25 - £40
2578 Bud Vase (no handle) £50 - £80
2579 Oval Bowl £25 - £40
2580 Vase, Squat £50 - £80
2582 Tray, 2 sizes £25 - £40
2585 Bon Bon Dish £40 - £60
2586 Low Vase £40 - £60

Floral Spray

Carlton Ware introduced this pattern in the mid 1960's. It consists of a simple yellow flower design. We have seen people use a variety of different names for the pattern but the correct factory name is *Floral Spray*.

The pattern was produced in either a yellow or brown trim.

The same shapes were used for *Orbit* (but with a different pattern and colour).

2639 Preserve & Stand £20 - £30
2641 Butter & Knife or Jam & Spoon £20 - £30
2642 Plate, 3 sizes £10 - £30
2644 Coffee Pot £40 - £70, Cup & Saucer £10 - £20
2654 Cruet Set (Frame is Magnolia) £30 - £50
2655 Sauce Boat (Stand is 2629) £20 - £30
2656 Mayonnaise Bowl & Ladle (Stand is 2629) £30 - £40
2657 Egg Frame (Cups are Magnolia) £30 - £40
2658 Salad Bowl & Servers £30 - £40
2659 Tray, Triangular, 3 sizes £15 - £30
2664 Cheese Dish & Stand £25 - £45
2665 Long Tray, Elongated £20 - £30
2666 Sugar £10 - £20, Cream £10 - £20
2666 Tea Cup & Saucer £10 - £20
2667 Oil & Vinegar £20 - £30
2668 Two way Tray £20 - £35
2669 Three way Tray £20 - £35
2670 Soup Jug £30 - £50
2671 Double Butter £10 - £20
2672 Salt & Pepper, large £20 - £30
2674 Individual Fruit £10 - £20
2675 Sugar Shaker £20 - £30
2676 Jug, 2 sizes £20 - £40
2677 Bowl, 2 sizes £10 - £25
2678 Soup Cup & Barbecue Tray £20 - £30
2679 Tea Pot, 2 sizes £40 - £70
2680 Hot Water Jug or Small Coffee Pot £30 - £50
2681 Covered Butter £20 - £30
2682 Five way Tray £20 - £35
2683 Vegetable Dish £20 - £35
2684 Powder Bowl £20 - £35
2685 Salt, Pepper & Stand, small £20 - £30
2686 Candlestick £15 - £30
2687 Divided Bowl £15 - £30
2688 Toast Rack £20 - £35

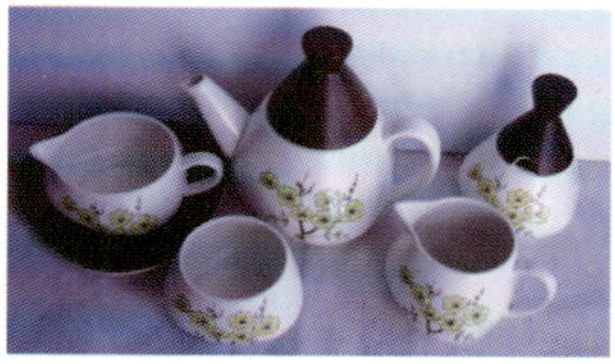
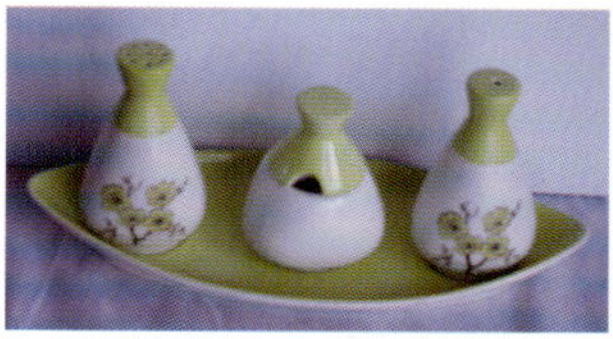
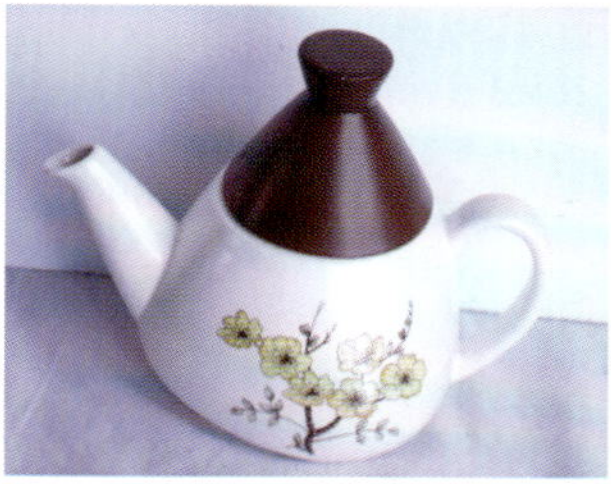
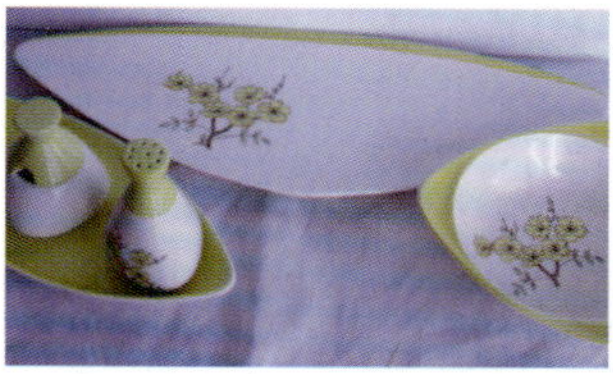
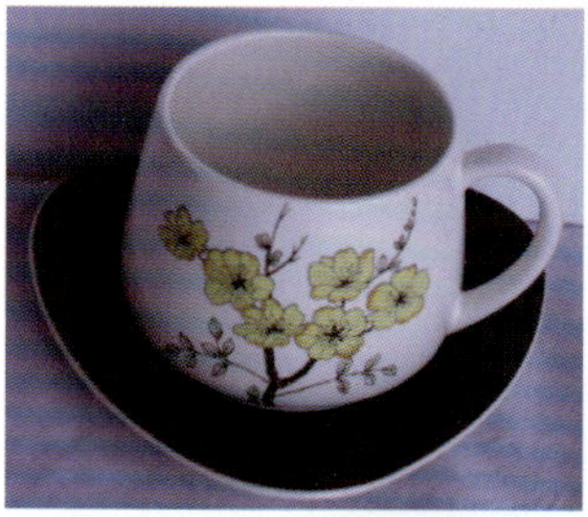
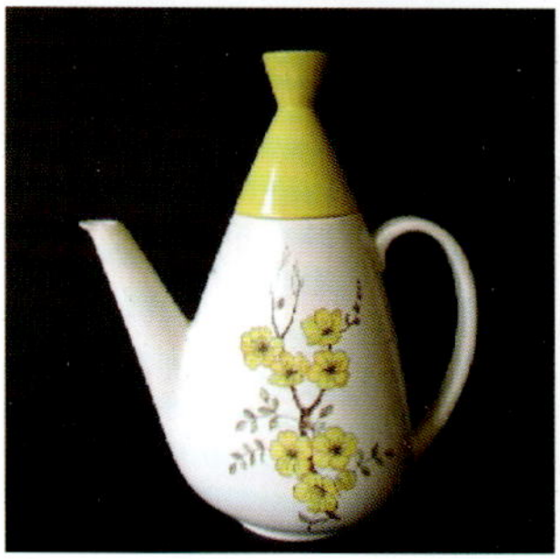

Orbit

Orbit was introduced in about 1965. What was the inspiration for this pattern? Was it the orbit of the various space satellites that were being launched? Was it the orbit of electrons in an atom? Perhaps we'll never know but pieces with this pattern are quite popular and can be seen for sale in various places. Its popularity may be because of its "retro" look.

The same shapes were used for *Floral Spray* (but with a different pattern and colour)..

2639 Preserve & Stand £30 - £50
2641 Butter & Knife or Jam & Spoon £30 - £40
2642 Plate, 3 sizes £20 - £50
2644 Coffee Pot £70 - £130, Cup & Saucer £25 - £40
2654 Cruet Set (Frame is Magnolia) £50 - £80
2655 Sauce Boat (Stand is 2629) £30 - £50
2656 Mayonnaise Bowl & Ladle (Stand is 2629) £40 - £60
2657 Egg Frame (Cups are Magnolia) £40 - £60
2658 Salad Bowl & Servers £40 - £60
2659 Tray, Triangular, 3 sizes £25 - £55
2664 Cheese Dish & Stand £45 - £65
2665 Long Tray, Elongated £30 - £40
2666 Sugar £25 - £35, Cream £25 - £35
2666 Tea Cup & Saucer £25 - £40
2667 Oil & Vinegar £30 - £50
2668 Two way Tray £30 - £50
2669 Three way Tray £30 - £50
2670 Soup Jug £50 - £70
2671 Double Butter £20 - £30
2672 Salt & Pepper, large £35 - £60
2674 Individual Fruit £20 - £30
2675 Sugar Shaker £40 - £60
2676 Jug, 2 sizes £40 - £60
2677 Bowl, 2 sizes £20 - £35
2678 Soup Cup & Barbecue Tray £30 - £45
2679 Tea Pot, 2 sizes £50 - £80
2680 Hot Water Jug or Small Coffee Pot £50 - £70
2681 Covered Butter £40 - £65
2682 Five way Tray £30 - £50
2683 Vegetable Dish £30 - £45
2684 Powder Bowl £30 - £50
2685 Salt, Pepper & Stand, small £35 - £60
2686 Candlestick £25 - £45
2687 Divided Bowl £25 - £35
2688 Toast Rack £30 - £50

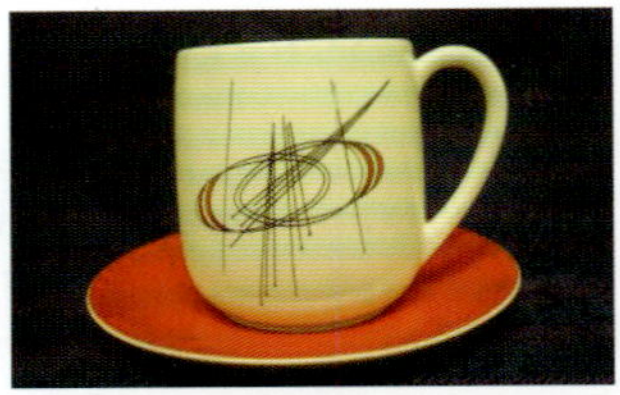
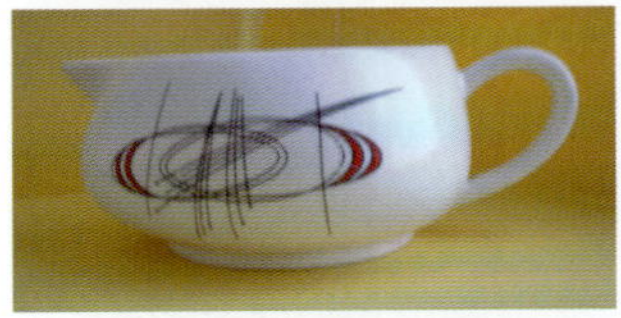
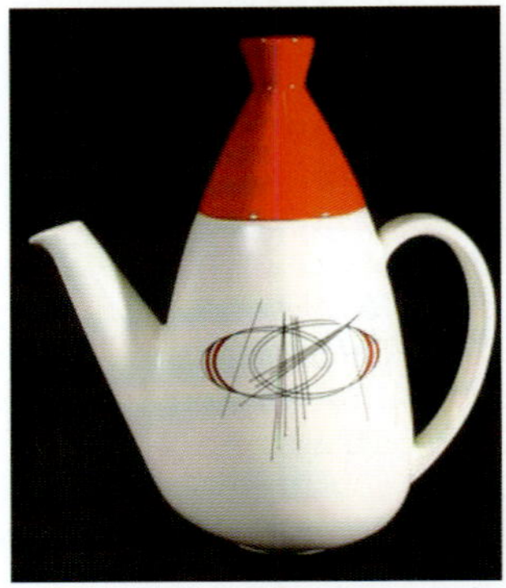
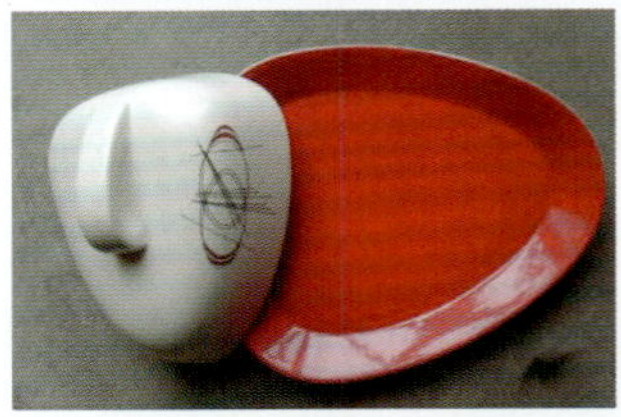
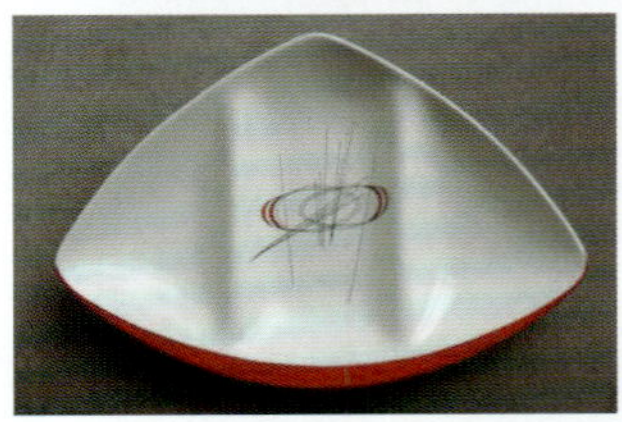
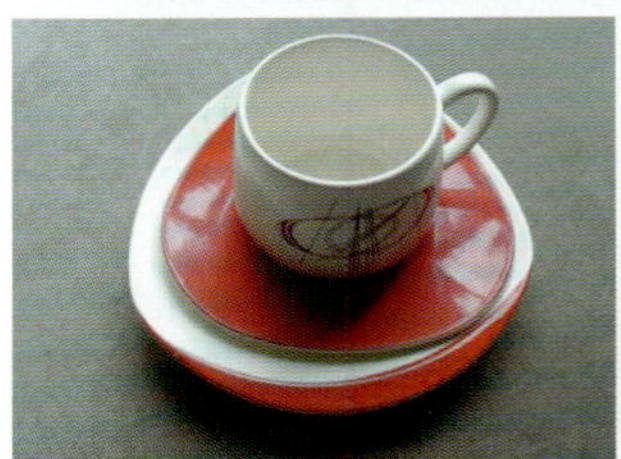

Carlton Village

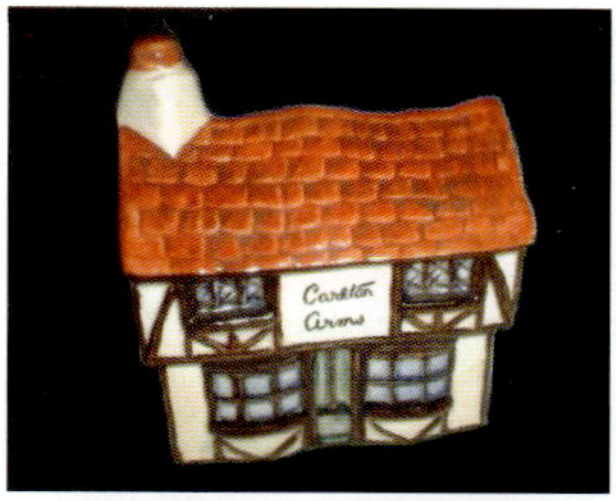

The *Carlton Village* set was introduced in the mid 1960's. There are nine buildings forming the village. The buildings were modelled in a realistic style, some resemble buildings that are several centuries old.

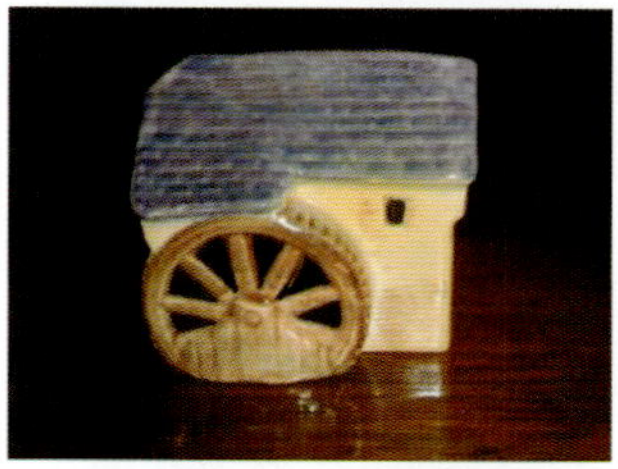

The Church, Smithy and Water Mill have a beige stone like exterior. The Wind Mill, Shop, Hall, Inn and Cottage appear to be timber framed. The Butter Market is a pillared building with decorations imitating stone.

The challenge for many collectors is to get a full set.

2645 Inn £40 - £60
2646 Smithy £40 - £60
2647 Water Mill £40 - £60
2648 Wind Mill £150 - £300
2649 Church £40 - £60
2650 Cottage £40 - £60
2651 Butter Market £100 - £170
2652 Shop £40 - £60
2653 Hall £40 - £60

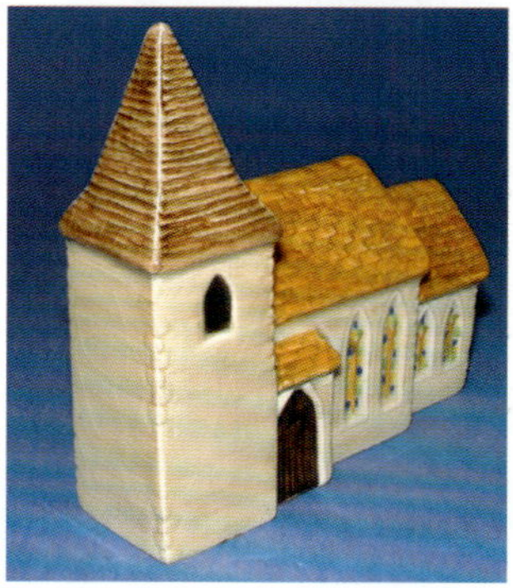

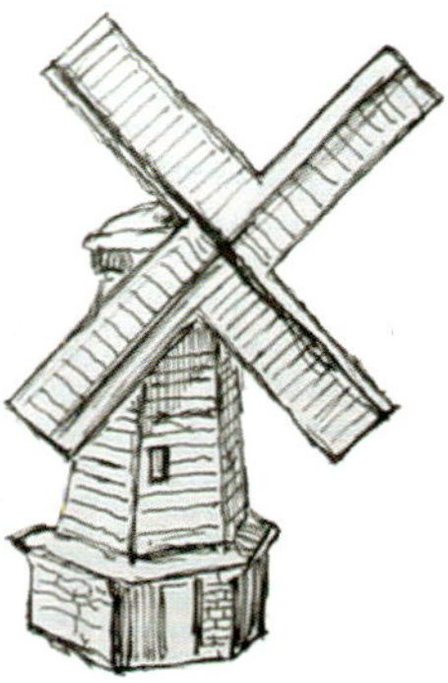

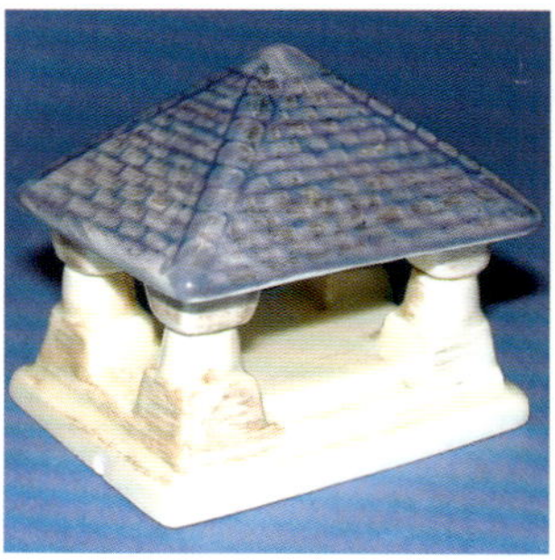

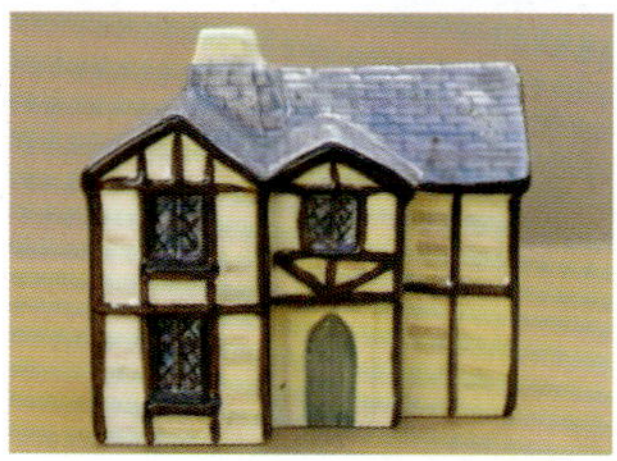

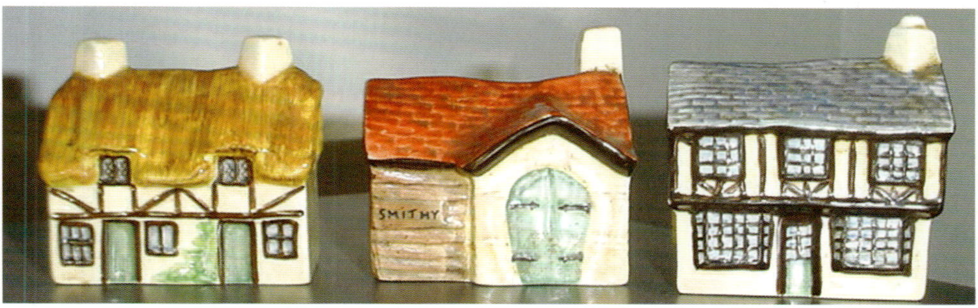

Tapestry and Daisy Chain

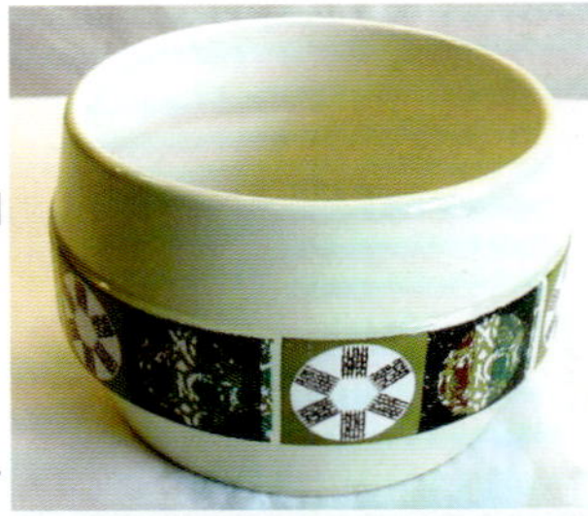

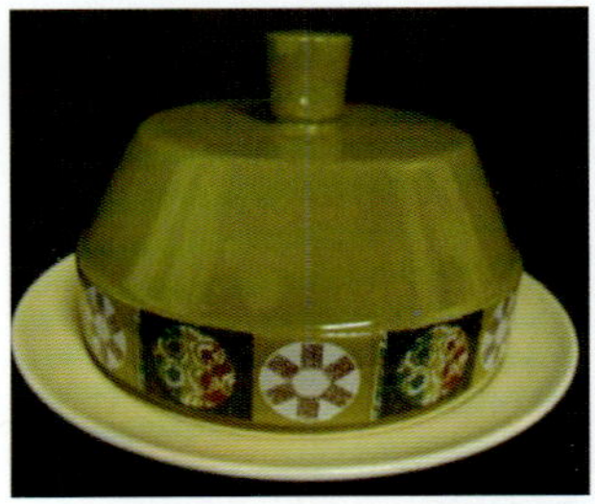

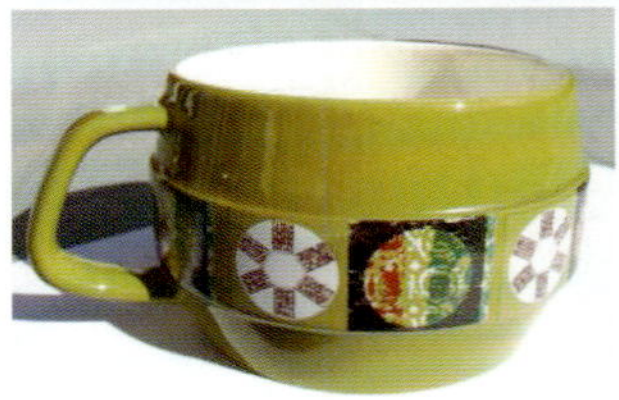

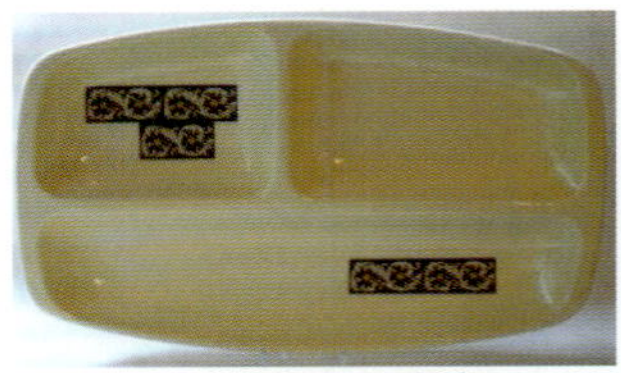

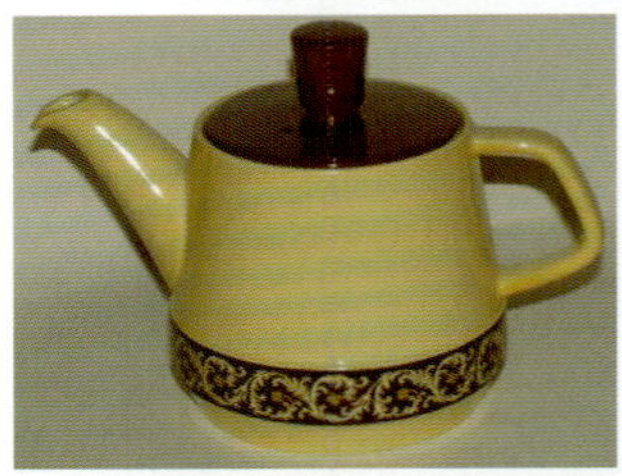

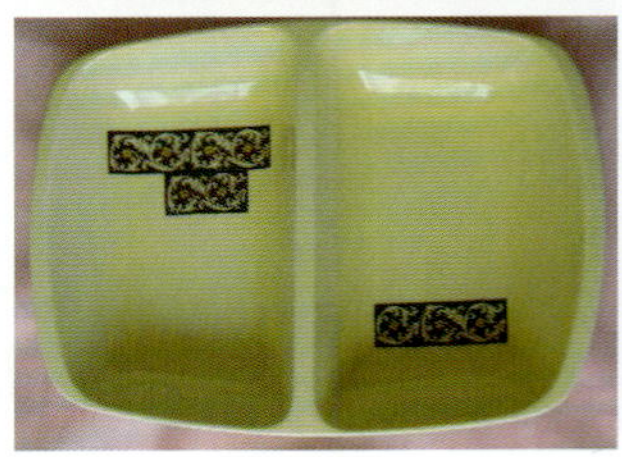

The *Tapestry* range was introduced in 1968. The principal pattern is a frieze containing a decorated band with a colourful pictorial design. It was produced on a number of different colourways.

Daisy Chain was introduced a little later on and used the same shapes as *Tapestry*. A Daisy Chain traditionally is flower chain consisting of a string of daisies linked by their stems. The pattern made by Carlton Ware is basically a frieze or part of a frieze that contains a pair of circular designs which are repeated.

2707 Preserve, Cover & Stand £20 - £30
2710 Coffee Pot £20 - £30, Cup & Saucer £10 - £20
2711 Sugar Shaker £20 - £30
2712 Cruet £25 - £40
2713 Long Tray £10 - £20
2714 Round Plate, 3 sizes £10 - £30
2715 Two way Tray £10 - £20
2716 Three way Tray £15 - £25
2717 Double Butter £10 - £20
2718 Cheese & Stand £20 - £30
2719 Vegetable Dish £10 - £20
2721 Five way Tray £15 - £25
2724 Butter & Knife or Jam & Spoon £20 - £30
2725 Mayonnaise Bowl, Stand & Ladle £20 - £30
2726 Oil & Vinegar £20 - £30
2729 Platters, 3 sizes £10 - £20
2730 Salad Bowl & Servers £20 - £30
2731 Tea Pot, 2 sizes £20 - £40, Cup & Saucer £10 - £20
2731 Sugar £10 - £20, Cream £10 - £20
2732 Salt & Pepper, large £20 - £30
2733 Oval Bowl, 2 sizes £10 - £25
2734 Individual Fruit £10 - £20
2737 Soup Cup £10 - £20
2738 Covered Bon Bon £15 - £25
2742 Sauce Boat & Stand £15 - £25
2743 Hot Milk Jug £20 - £30
2744 Jug £20 - £30
2745 Salt, Pepper & Stand £15 - £25
2746 Egg Frame £20 - £30
2747 Divided Bowl £10 - £20
2748 Covered Butter £15 - £25
2749 Toast Rack £20 - £30
2754 Sugar, small size £10 - £20

Athena

This set was introduced in 1969 in three colours as illustrated. The shape consists of grooves which are either vertical or radiate out. The look is very Grecian!

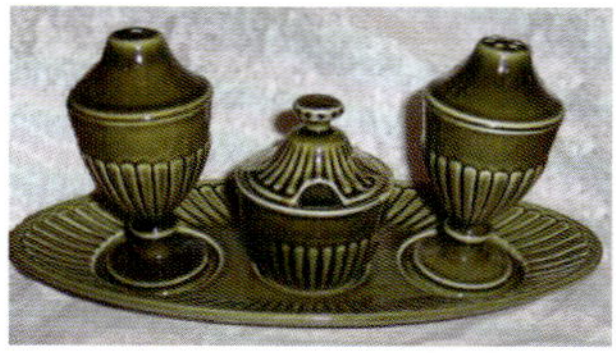

2794 & 2796 Salt, Pepper & Stand £15 - £25
Cruet £15 - £25
2795 Egg Set £20 - £30
2800 Covered Butter £15 - £25
2801 Long Tray £10 - £20
2802 Butter £10 - £20
2803 Vinegar Jug £15 - £25
2805 Preserve & Stand £15 - £25
2806 Coffee Mug £10 - £20
2807 Cheese £15 - £25
2808 Coffee Pot £15 - £25, Cup & Saucer £10 - £20
2808 Cream £10 - £20, Sugar £10 - £20
2809 Hot Milk Jug £15 - £25
2810 Bowl, 2 sizes £10 - £20
2811 Tray, 2 sizes £10 - £20
2812 Toast Rack £15 - £25
2836 Tea Pot £15 - £25
2837 Plate, 5" £10 - £20

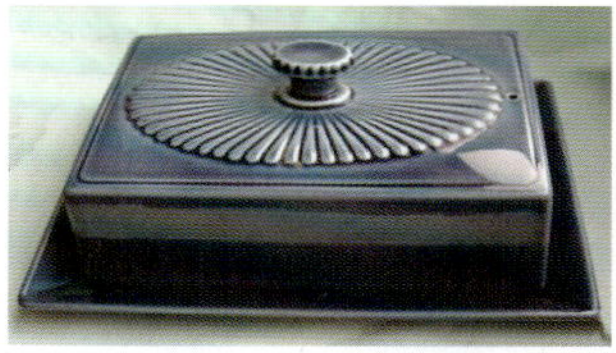

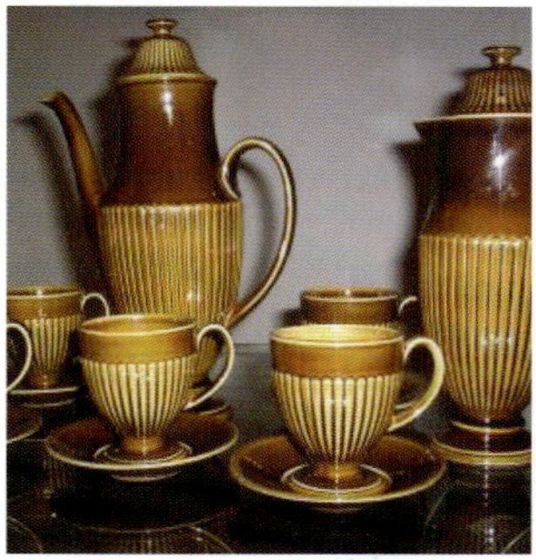

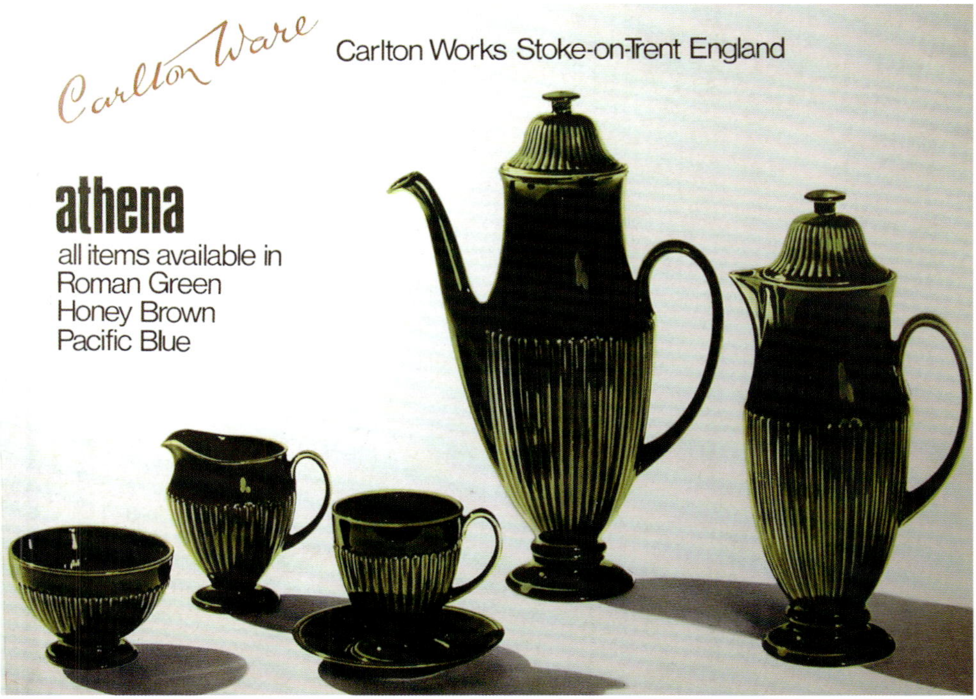

Skye

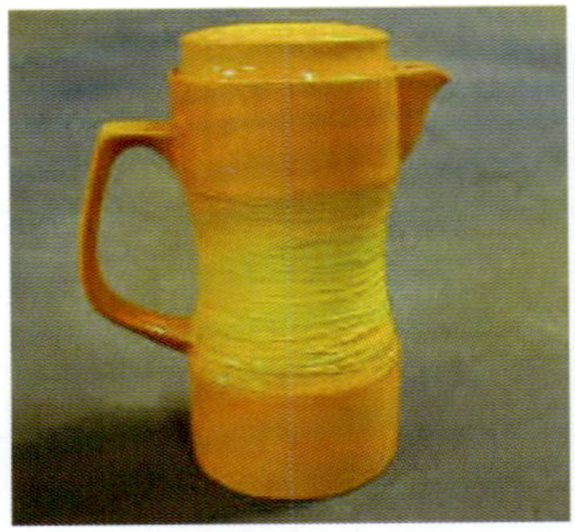

Another set introduced in 1969. The pattern is a textured embossing with criss-cross lines or just lines in a circle or lines in a radial design.

The usual and most common colour sunglow, a vivid yellow changing to orange towards the edges. Other colours are roman green and thistle (purple), in each case darker towards the edges. These latter colours were less popular and are rarely seen.

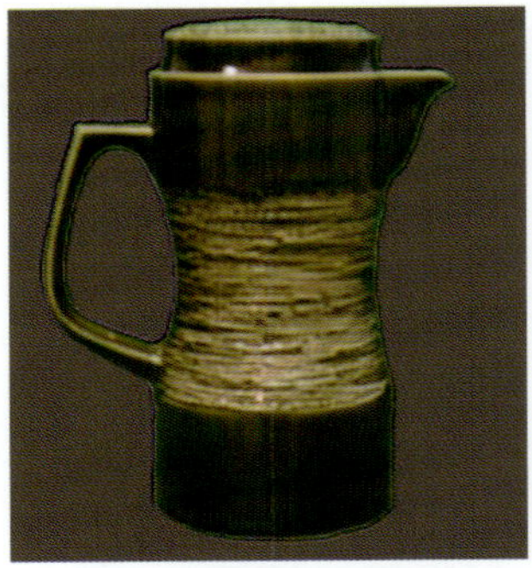

The pattern is also known as *Sunburst* for obvious reasons when you see the yellow version.

2804 Coffee Pot £20 - £30, Coffee Mug £10 - £15
2813 Long Rectangular Tray £10 - £15
2814 Circular Dish £10 - £15
2846 Square Tray, small £10 - £15
2847 Three way Tray, oblong £10 - £15
2849 Five way Tray, round £10 - £15
2850 Television Set (with cup) £15 - £20
2852 Two way Tray, oblong £10 - £15
2853 Triangular Tray £10 - £15
2854 Coffee Jug £20 - £30
2856 Butter £5 - £10
2857 Salt & Pepper £10 - £15
2888 Cream £10 - £15
2889 Covered Sugar £10 - £15

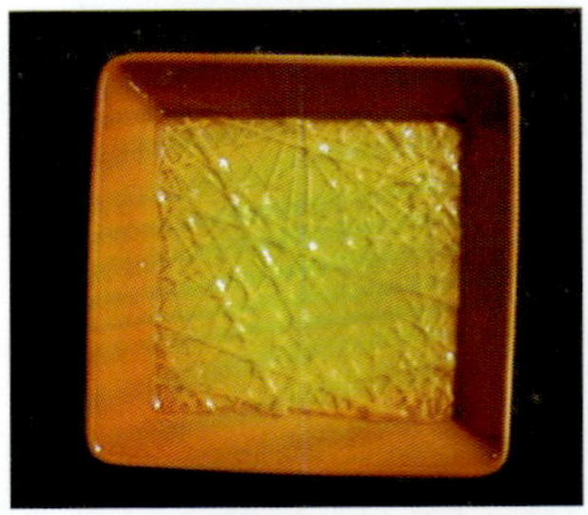

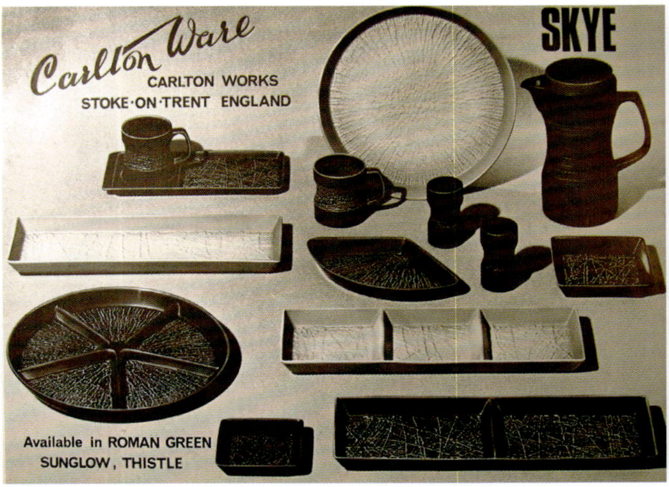

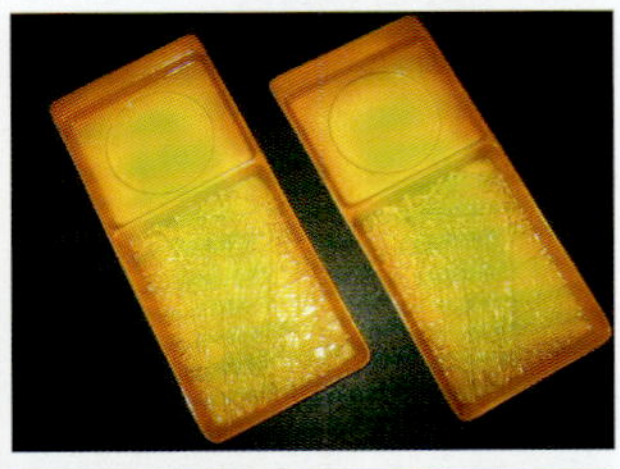

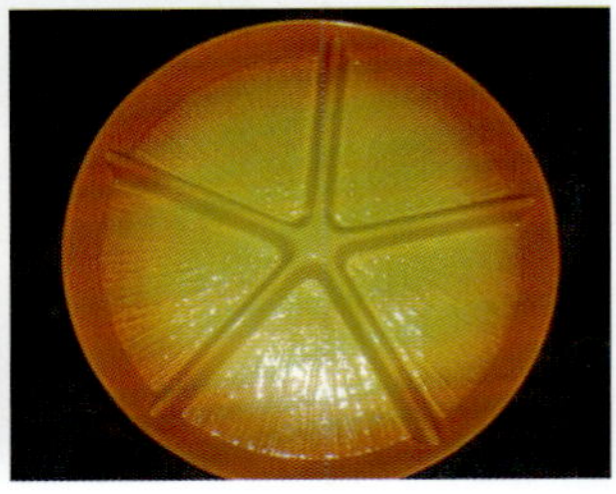

Military Figures

Several *Military Figures* were made by Carlton Ware in 1968/69.

2822 Royal Hussar ?
2824 Royal Horse Guard ?
2830 12th Royal Lancers ?
2835 Coldstream Guard ?
2861 Beefeater Yeoman £50 - £80

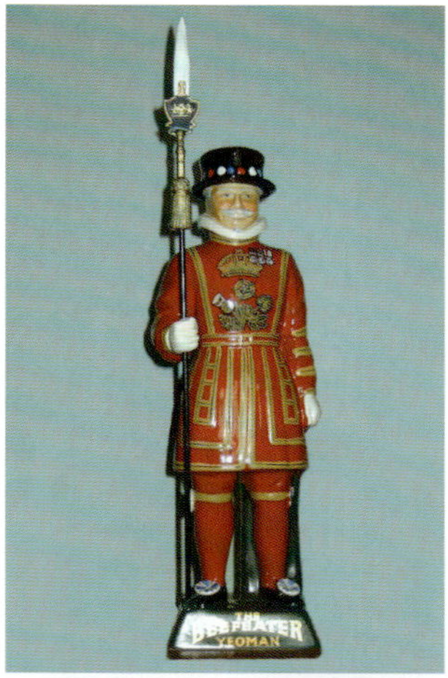

Vine or Canterbury

This range was introduced in the late 1960's. Although the Carlton Ware name for this is *Canterbury*, it is often called *Vine* which is more descriptive of the pattern.

2872 Coffee Pot £25 - £40, Cup & Saucer £15 - £20
2872 Cream £10 - £15, Sugar £10 - £15
2878 & 2872 Tea Cup & Saucer £15 - £20
2381 Cruet £20 - £30
2382 Egg Set £10 - £15
2384 Plate, 5" £10 - £15
2385 Three way Tray £10 - £15
2387 Long Tray £10 - £15
2391 Butter £10 - £15
2399 TV Tray £10 - £15
2901 Vinegar Jug £10 - £15
2902 Preserve, with cover £15 - £20
2907 Covered Butter £20 - £25
2908 & 2894 Salt, Pepper & Stand, large £15 - £20
2909 Beaker £10 - £15
2910 Covered Cheese £20 - £30
2917 Tea Pot £25 - £40
2920 & 2904 Sauce Boat & Stand £15 - £20

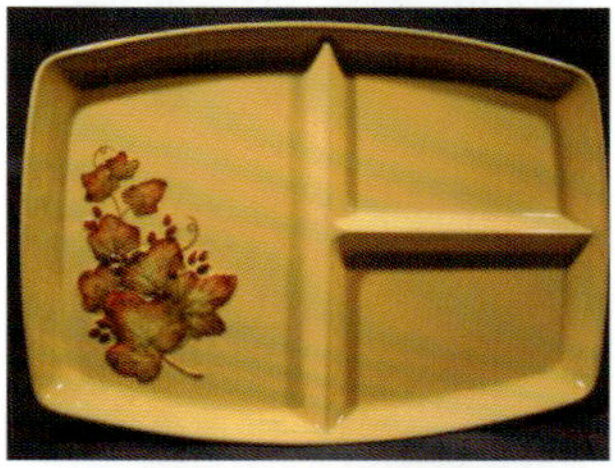

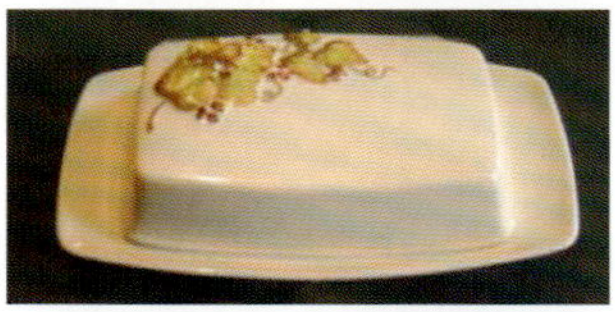

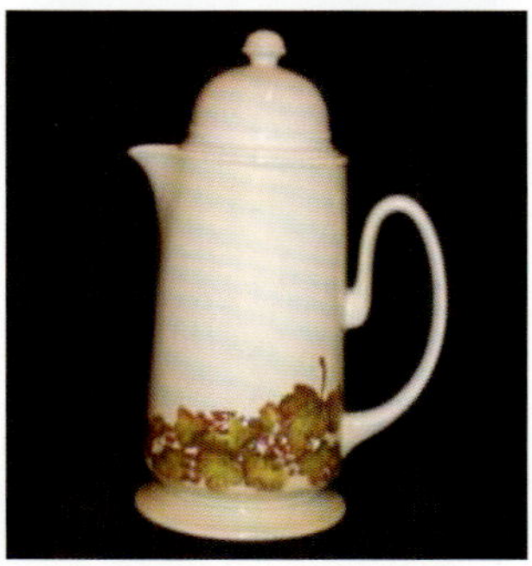

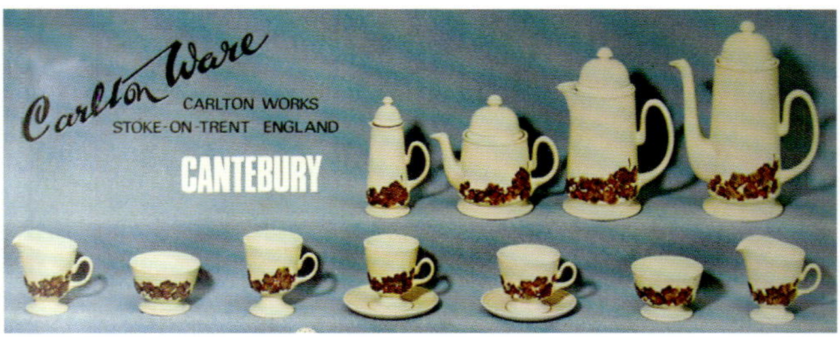

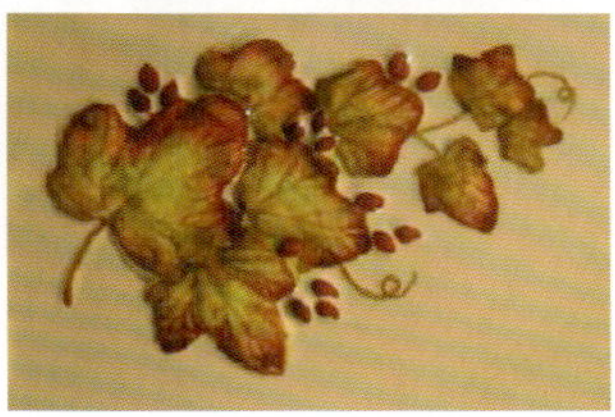

Wellington or Sunflower

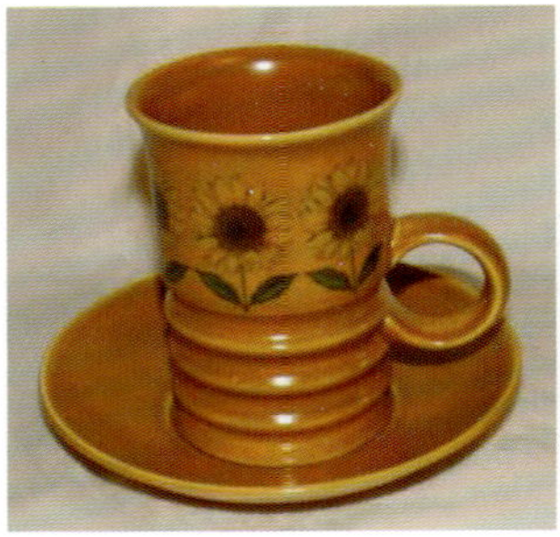

Wellington was introduced in the early 1970's. The shape is ribbed or flanged, consisting of grooves and flanges going around horizontally. The back stamp is usually the "curved" back stamp used from 1967 to 1989. Some pieces have the "yellow" back stamp used from 1967 to 1987.

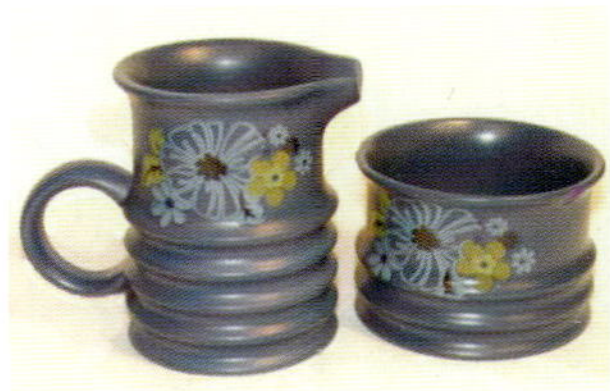

The range was produced in several bright colours such as yellow, lime green and orange. It was also produced in many darker colours, such as brown and blue, often with a realistic Sunflower design.

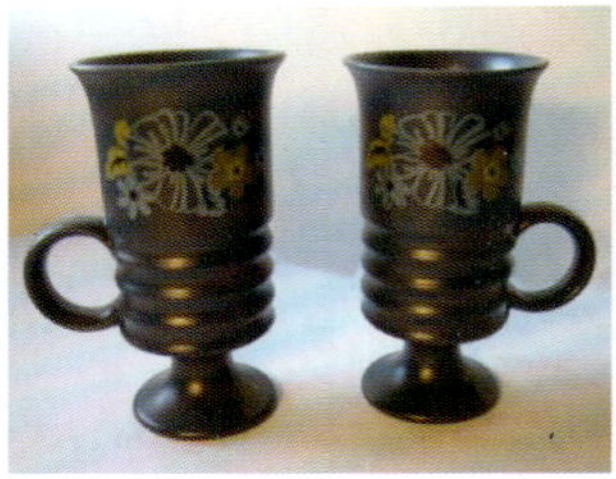

The more vividly coloured pieces are often damaged. This is because the pieces were originally bought for use, not for display. For instance, when you look at some of the candlesticks you can see that someone has been scraping away melted wax!

The brightly coloured un-patterned pieces usually fetch a higher price as they are considered to be more “retro”. Retro usually refers to the "modern" popular designs that appeared after the Second World War from the 1950's to 1970's. The designs were a reaction against the "traditional" designs that were considered dated.

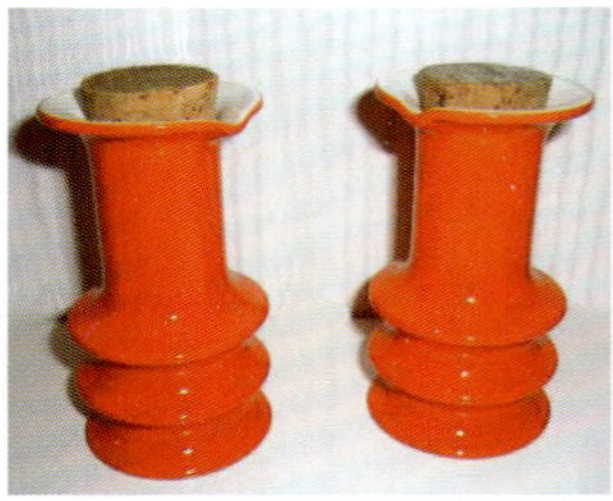

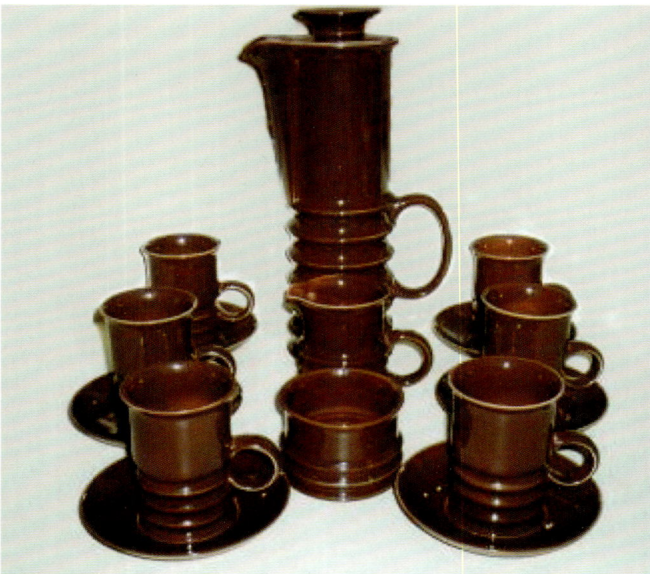

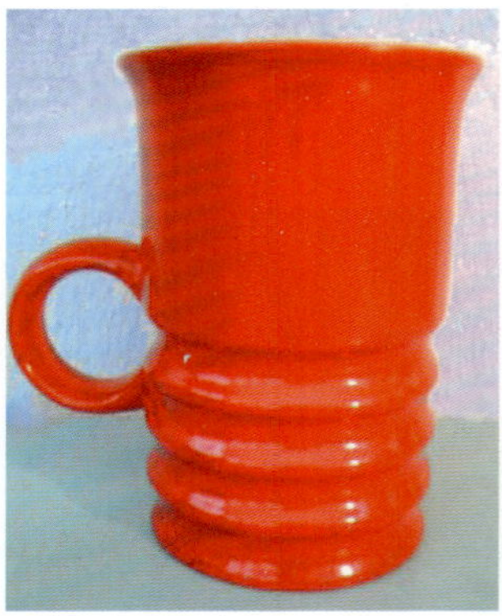

Sunflower and other flower designs.

2973 Vase, 3 sizes £10 - £20
2974 Lighter Holder £5 - £10
2975 Tray £5 - £10
2976 Footed Mug £5 - £10
2977 Cup & Saucer £5 - £10
2978 Ashtray £5 - £10
2979 Lighter Holder, tall £5 - £10
2980 Cigarette Box £10 - £15
2981 Candle Stick (5 flanges) £5 - £10
2982 Candle Stick (3 flanges) £5 - £10
2983 Coffee Pot £10 - £20, Cream £5 - £10, Sugar £5 - £10
2984 Ashtray, large £5 - £10
2990 Oil & Vinegar £10 - £15
2991 Soup Cup £5 - £10
2992 Tea Cup £5 - £10
2994 Cruet £10 - £15
2995 Butter Tray £5 - £10
2997 Covered Cheese £10 - £15
2998 Covered Butter £10 - £15
3000 Two way Tray £5 - £10
Salt & Pepper £5 - £10

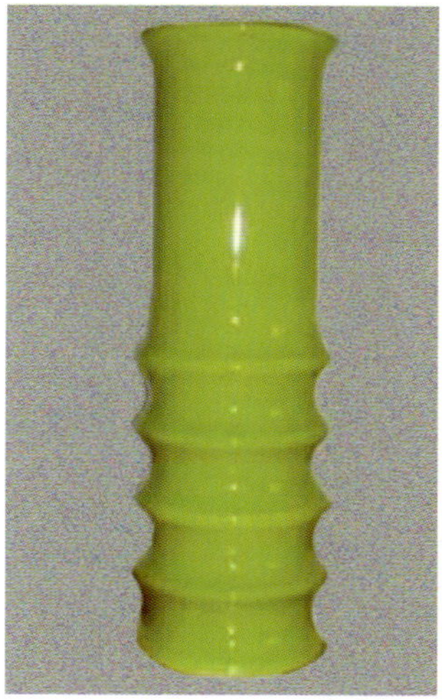

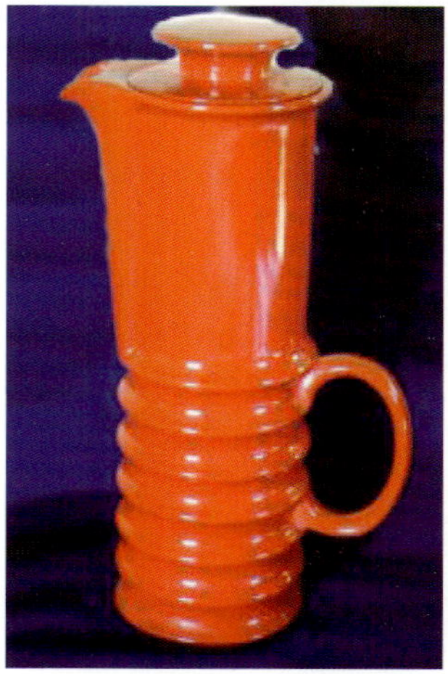

Plain Bright Colours.

2973 Vase, 3 sizes £20 - £30
2974 Lighter Holder £10 - £20
2975 Tray £10 - £20
2976 Footed Mug £15 - £20
2977 Cup & Saucer £10 - £20
2978 Ashtray £10 - £20
2979 Lighter Holder, tall £10 - £20
2980 Cigarette Box £20 - £30
2981 Candle Stick (5 flanges) £10 - £15
2982 Candle Stick (3 flanges) £10 - £15
2983 Coffee Pot £20 - £30
2983 Cream £10 - £15, Sugar £10 - £15
2984 Ashtray, large £10 - £20
2990 Oil & Vinegar £15 - £25
2991 Soup Cup £10 - £20
2992 Tea Cup £10 - £20
2994 Cruet £20 - £30
2995 Butter Tray £10 - £20
2997 Covered Cheese £20 - £30
2998 Covered Butter £20 - £30
3000 Two way Tray £10 - £20
Salt & Pepper £15 - £25

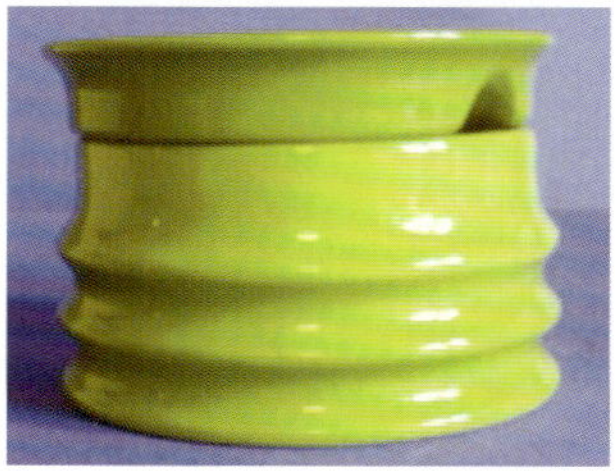

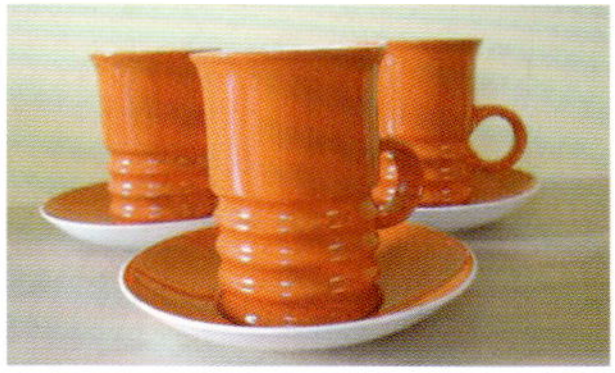

Money Box - Flat Back

The "flat" money boxes were mainly designed by Vivienne Brennan in the early 1970's. They were produced over a period of eight years. The flat surfaces were ideal for decorating and each shape was produced in a number of different decorations.

2922 Owl £35 - £50
2923 Horse £35 - £50
2944 Cat £35 - £50
2946 Ark £35 - £50
2950 Engine £35 - £50
3080 Face £35 - £50
3086 Pig £35 - £50
3104 Soldier £35 - £50
3141 Boot £35 - £50
3142 Peacock £35 - £50

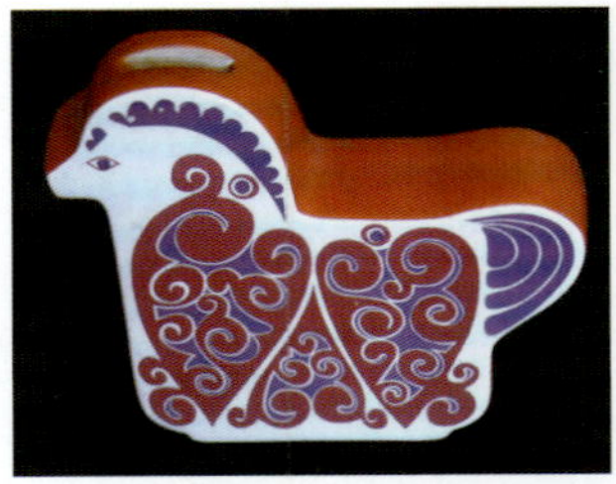

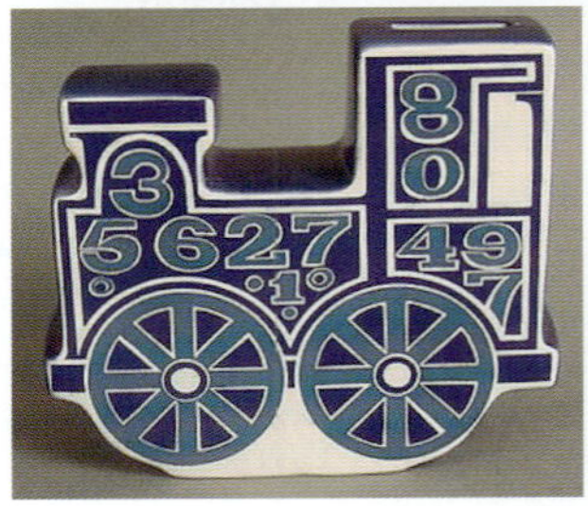

Money Box

A mixed bag of money boxes, some made as advertising items.

3056 Cube £20 - £30
3149 Tram Car £40 - £70
3150 Carousel £30 - £40
3159 Rocking Horse £35 - £50
3174 Pig £30 - £50
3288 Fred £35 - £55
3377 Rumbelows £35 - £55
3382 Rumbelows £35 - £55
3385 Access ?

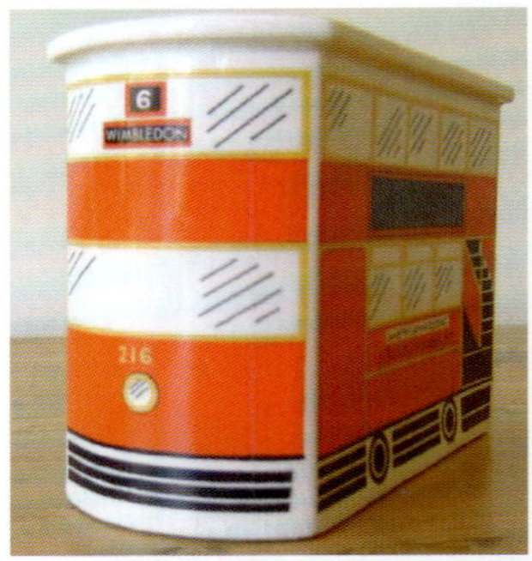

Money Box - Bug Eyes

In the mid 1970's four rounded money boxes with protruding eyes, called "bug eyes", were produced.

3128 Owl £35 - £55
3129 Snail £35 - £55
3130 Bird £35 - £55
3131 Frog £35 - £55

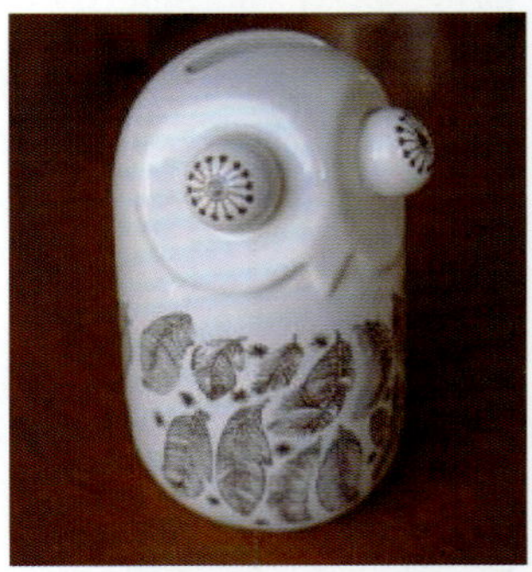

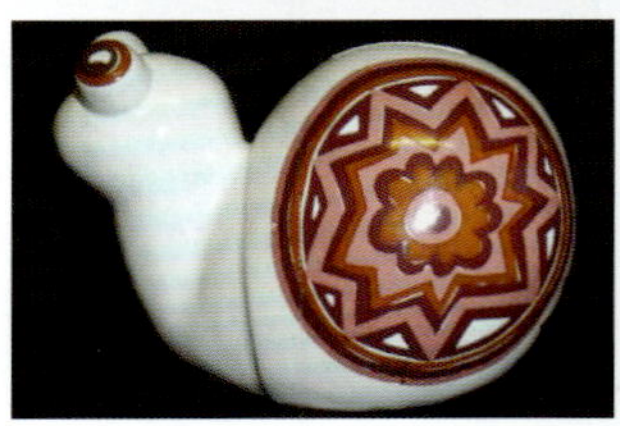

Walking Ware

In 1967 Carlton Ware was sold to Arthur Wood & Sons who operated it independently of the group. Under their direction sales rose dramatically in the 1970's due to designs of the *Walking Ware* range introduced and designed by Roger Michell and Danka Napiorkowska. The *Walking Ware* gained immediate popularity, and it was probably this range that kept the company afloat during the 1970's.

Roger Michell and Danka Napiorkowska owned a small pottery in Yorkshire called Lustre Pottery. They were studio potters and exhibited a Walking Ware Dinner and Tea service at an exhibition in London. This received rave reviews and orders poured in from all over the world. But, Lustre Pottery could not cope with the demand and had to consider sub-contracting to a larger manufacturer. After a few rejections from some Staffordshire potteries, Arthur Wood & Sons expressed an interest. This resulted in a working relationship for about eight years.

First Walking Ware Range

The initial range of *Walking Ware* included various sizes of tea pots, sitting sugar bowls, mugs, cups, egg cups etc.

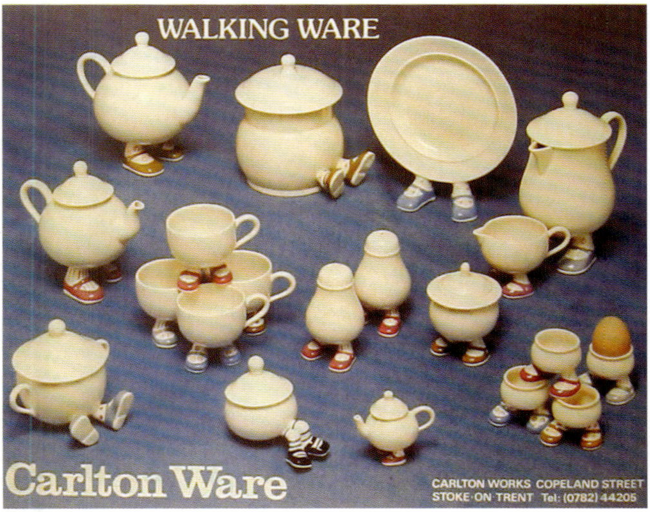

3143 Cup £30 - £50
3143 Egg Cup £25 - £40
3143 Milk £30 - £50
3143 Sugar with lid, standing £45 - £65
3143 Tea Pot, small £80 - £120 Miniature £150 - £200

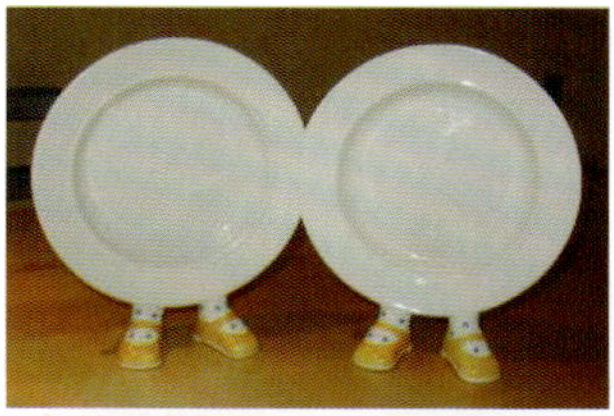

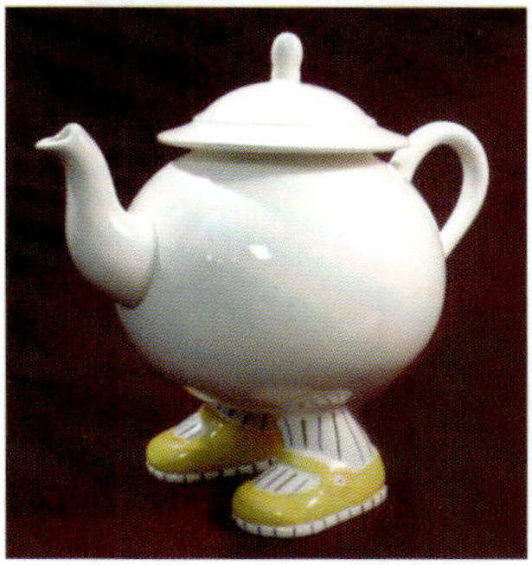

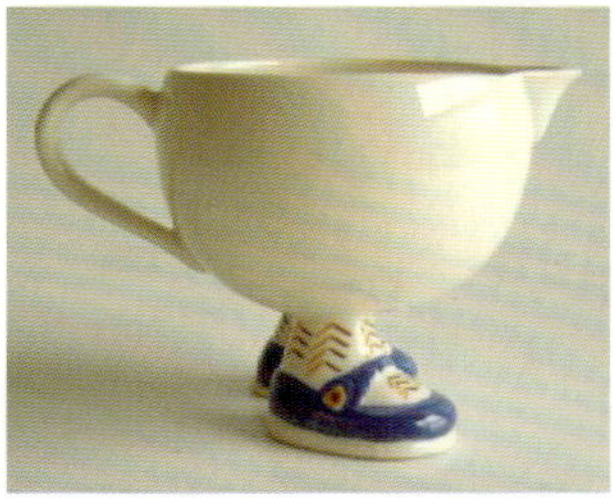

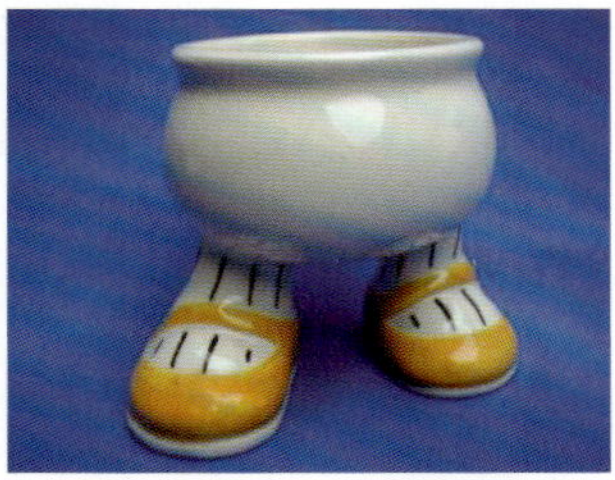

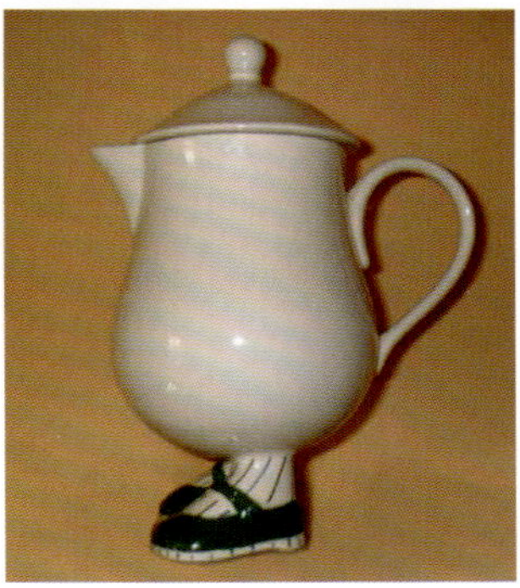

3194 Salt & Pepper £50 - £80
3195 Tea Pot, large £100 - £150
3196 Coffee or Water Jug £70 - £130
3197 Sugar with lid, sitting cross legged £55 - £85
3198 Plate £60 - £90
3199 Soup Bowl with lid £55 - £85
3228 Tea Pot, miniature £150 - £200
3229 Biscuit Barrel £70 - £130

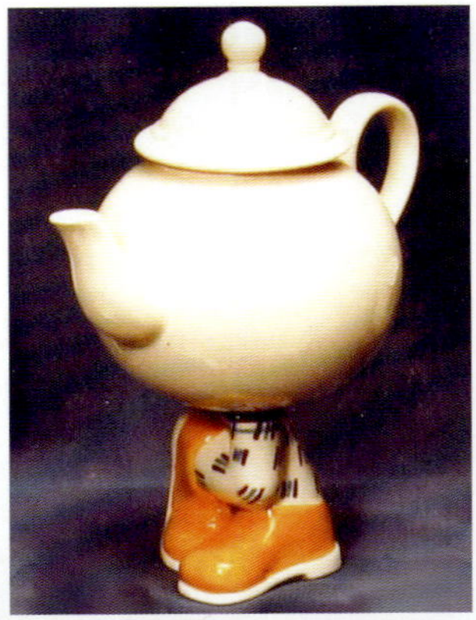

RJS Series

The next range was the RJS tea service (Running, Jumping and Standing Still), which had plaid, socks and sandals.

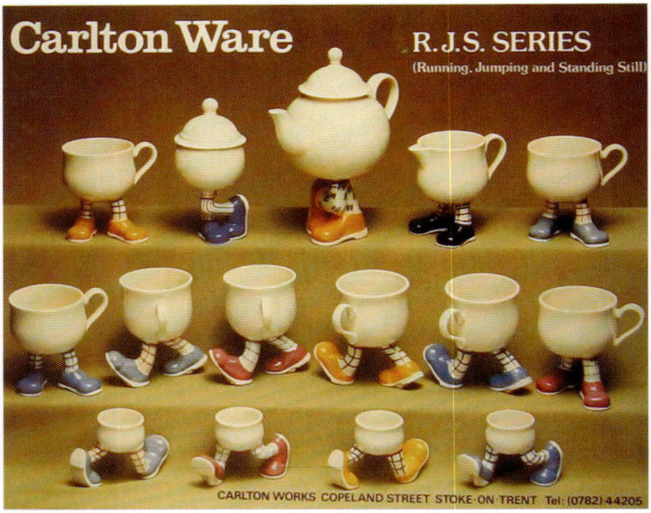

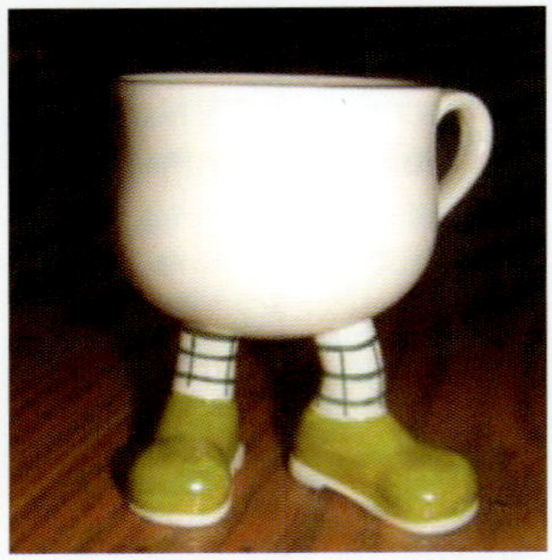

3290 Cup £45 - £70
3290 Egg Cup £30 - £50
3290 Milk £45 - £70
3290 Sugar with lid £55 - £85
3290 Tea Pot £90 - £160

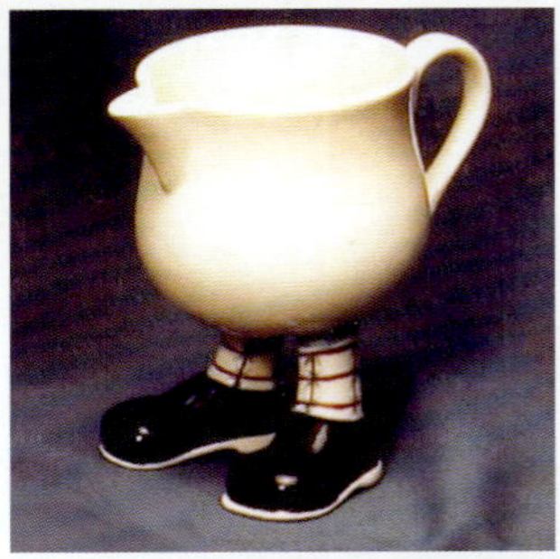

Caribbean Series

The moulds from the first series were used to produce the Caribbean series. These had a palm tree and sunset scene with yellow shoes and blue line for socks.

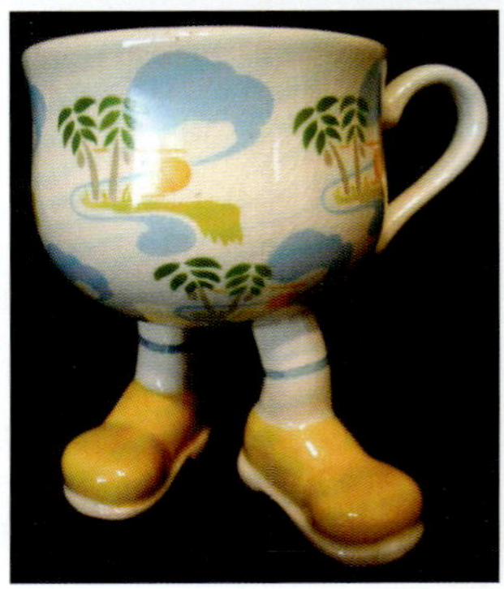

3290 Cup £50 - £75
3290 Egg Cup £35 - £55
3290 Milk £50 - £75
3290 Sugar with lid £50 - £80
3290 Tea Pot £100 - £160

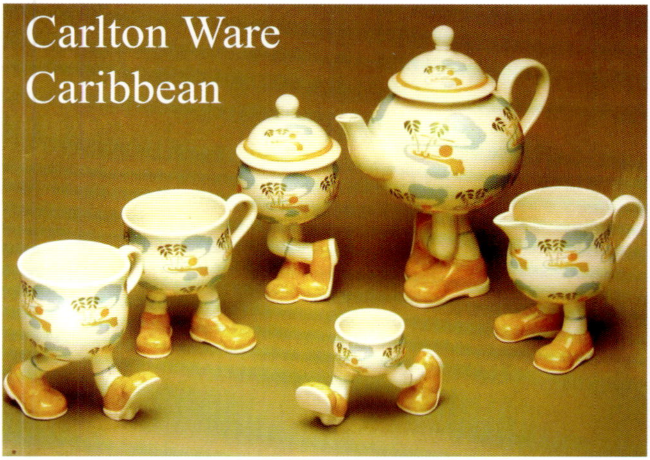

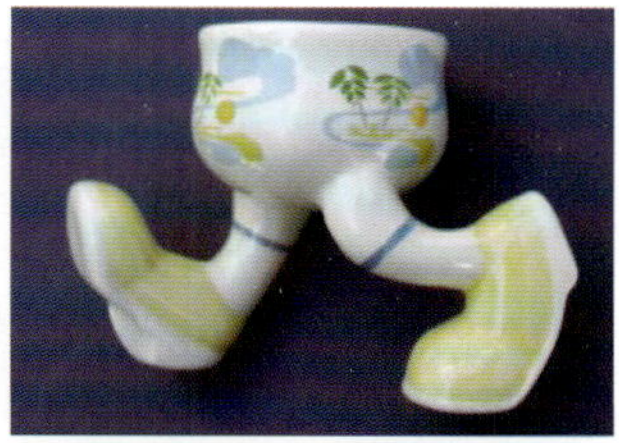

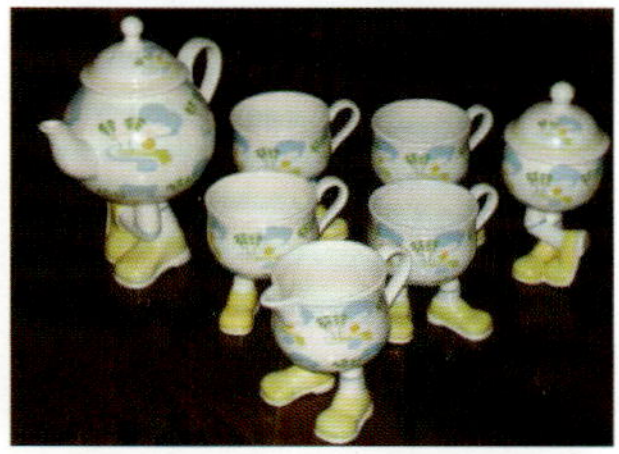

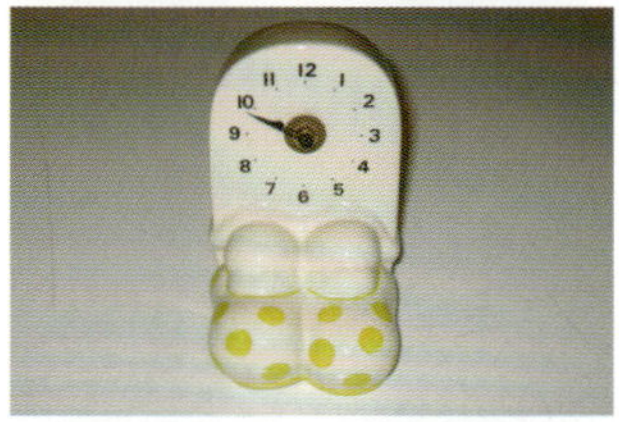

Big Feet

The fourth series was Big Feet, which had oversized feet with coloured polka dots.

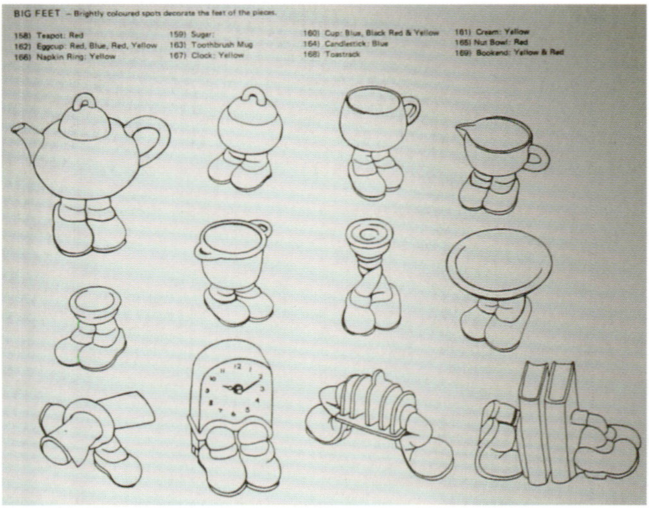

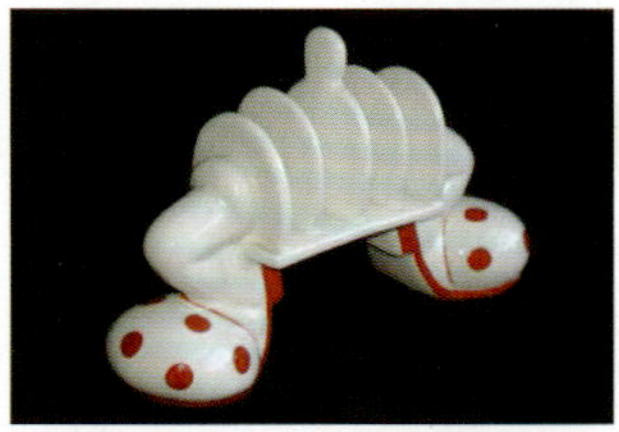

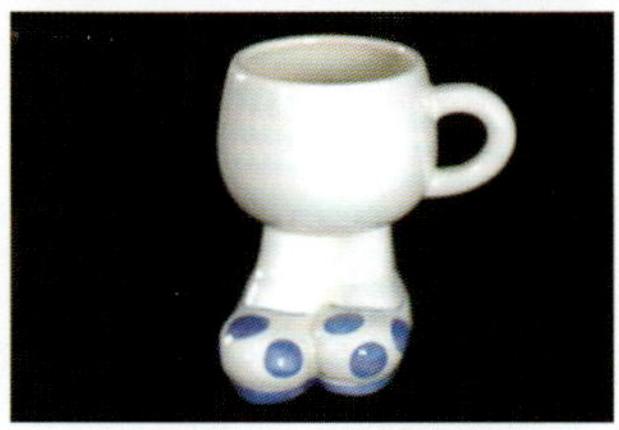

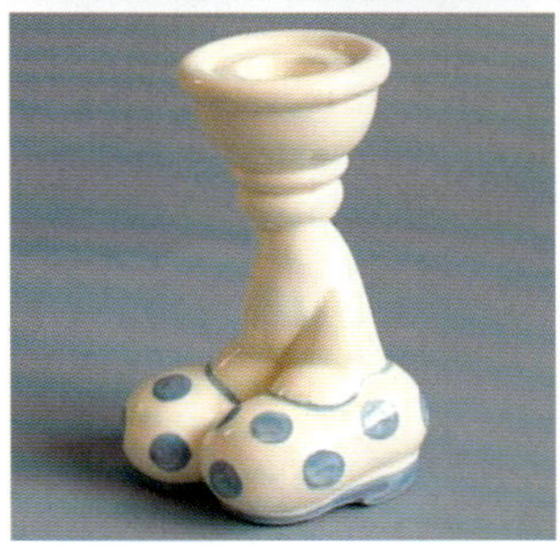

3373 Bookend £50 - £90
3373 Candlestick £55 - £90
3373 Clock £70 - £110
3373 Cup £30 - £55
3373 Egg Cup £25 - £45
3373 Cream £35 - £60
3373 Napkin Ring £25 - £40
3373 Nut Bowl or Soap Dish £40 - £70
3373 Sugar with lid £45 - £70

3373 Tea Pot £80 - £150
3373 Toast Rack £80 - £140
3373 Toothbrush Mug £30 - £55

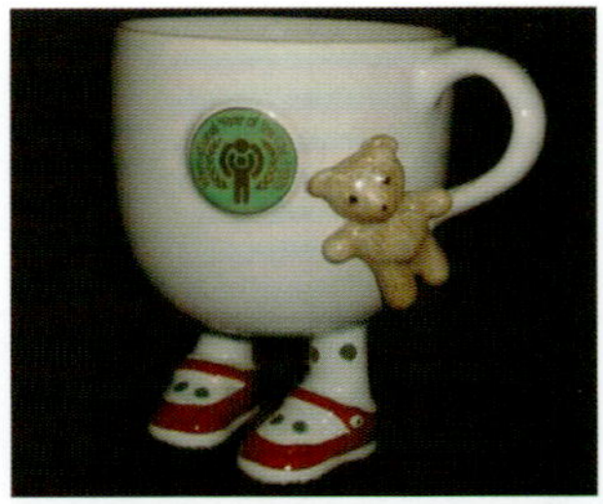

Other Walking Ware Items

Other items produced included Birthday Mugs and Royal Commemorative Ware such as the Queen's Silver Jubilee kneeling mug of 1977.

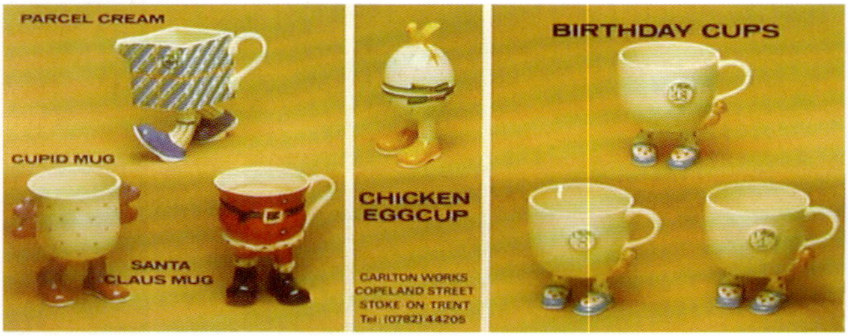

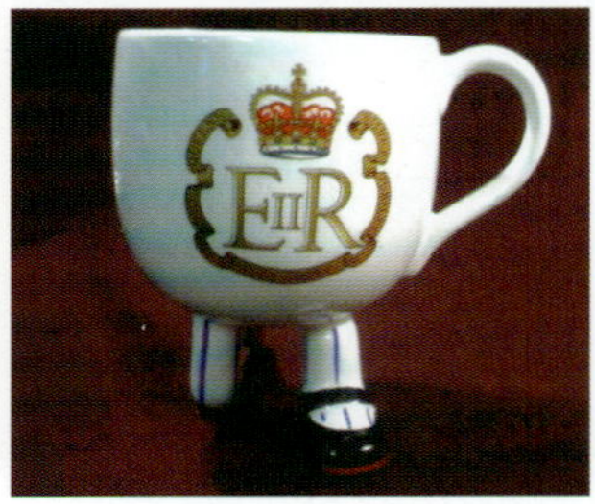

3227 Kneeling Jubilee Mug £60 - £90
3281 Child of the Year Mug £35 - £70
3294 Santa Cup £60 - £90
3301 Birthday Cream £35 - £55
3304 Valentine/Hearts Cup £45 - £75
3308 Easter Egg Cup £45 - £70
3309 Birthday Cup £35 - £55
3332 Charles & Di Cup £45 - £70 each
3345 Wellington Cup £50 - £80

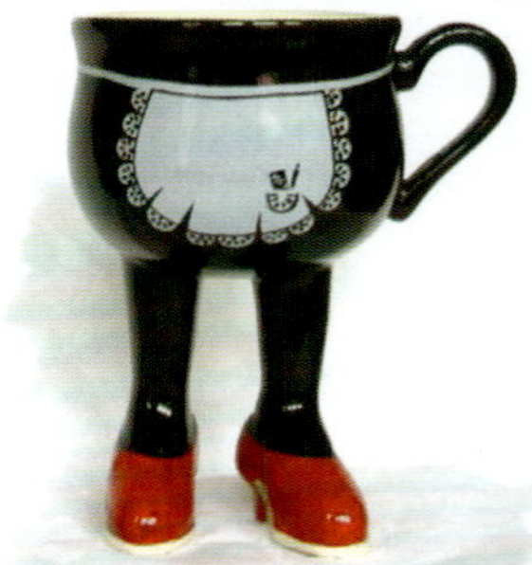

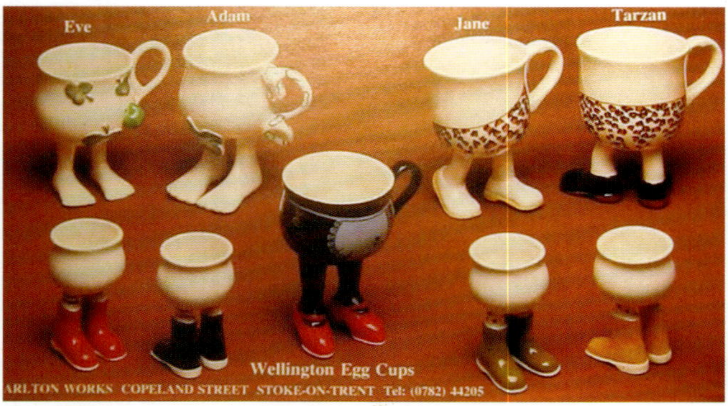

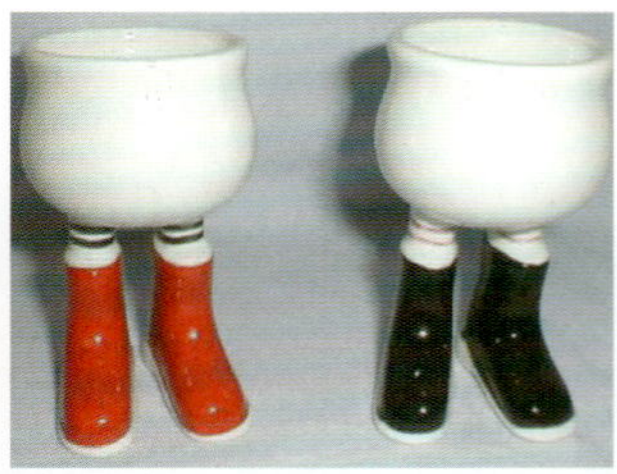

3346 Maid or Waitress Cup £80 - £110
3350 & 3356 Adam & Eve Cup £75 - £110

3219 Cow in Bath Butter £40 - £60
3240 Cow Milk £30 - £50

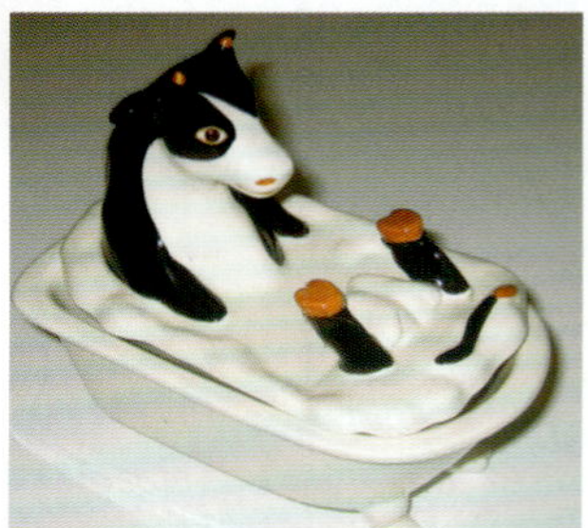

The shape numbers of the *Walking Ware* are rarely visible.

Flow Blue - AW

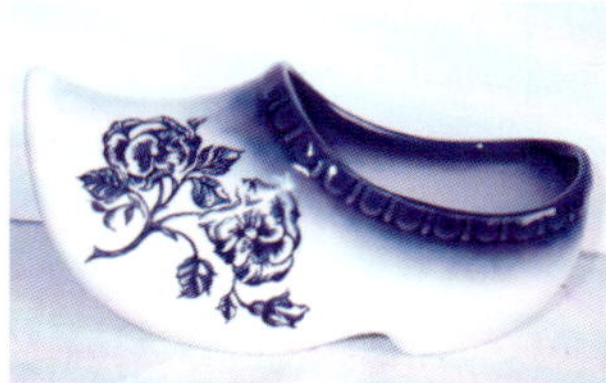

Flow Blue is a type of blue and white pottery in which the blue pattern deliberately flows into the white background. The process has been used mainly since 1840 and Carlton Ware produced a number of *Flow Blue* patterns in their early days. *Flow Blue* in general is very popular in the USA.

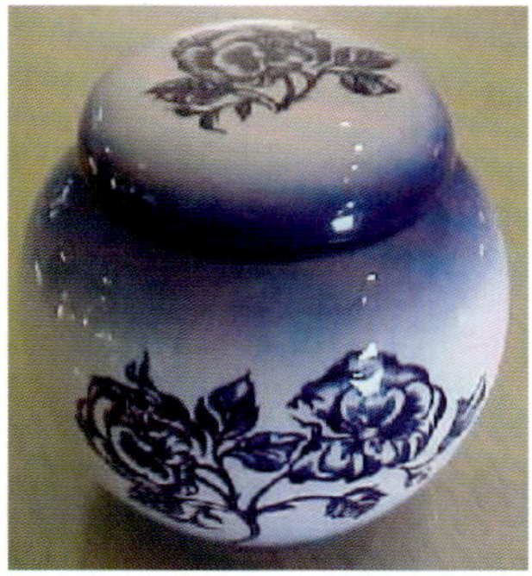

In the mid 1970's Carlton Ware, under the ownership of Arthur Wood, introduced a new range of ornamental sized *Flow Blue* pieces. The list of shapes is given below. Occasionally you may find some of these shapes with other patterns which were produced as advertising ware.

3177 Toothbrush Jar £10 - £20
3181 Candlestick £15 - £25
3184 Heart Box £10 - £20
3187 Footed Box £10 - £20
3190 Tray £5 - £10
3191 Soap Dish £5 - £10
3193 Chamber Pot, 2 sizes £5 - £15
3200 Clog £5 - £10
3202 Apothecary Jar £10 - £20
3203 Tankard £5 - £10
3204 Basin and Ewer £25 - £35
3205 Kettle £10 - £20
3206 Trinket Box £5 - £10
3216 Iron £5 - £10
3224 Caravan Cigarette Box £10 - £20
3233 Tumbler or Goblet £5 - £10
Tea Caddy, 3 sizes £5 - £20

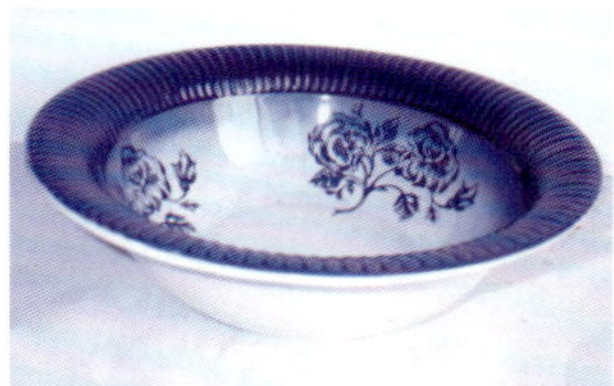

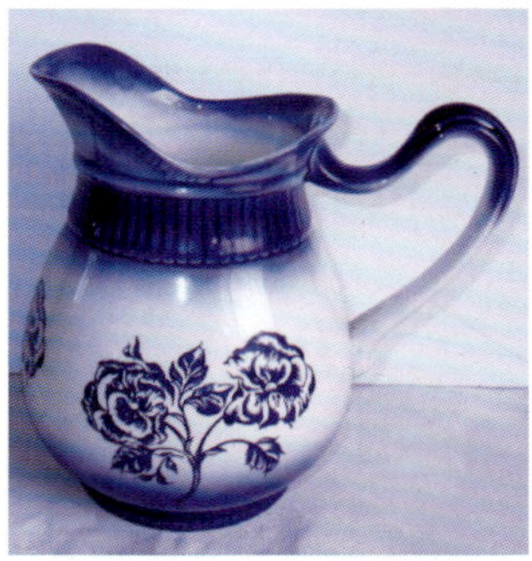

Pig

Two different sizes of *Pig* Water Jugs were made by Carlton Ware in the 1970's. They were designer by Roger Michell and Danka Napiorkowska (see Walking Ware) and have the Lustre Pottery back stamp.

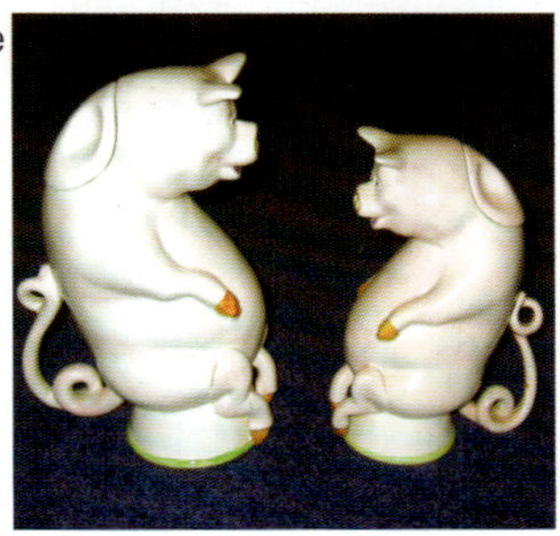

The two in the picture are about 9.5 ins (24 cm) and 8 ins (20 cm) high with the Lustre Pottery 1973 back stamp. The pink body has a green band at the base, purple coloured eyes and orange trotters.

3271 Water Jug, 2 sizes £45 - £75

Hovis

Another range of Advertising Ware made by Carlton Ware in the late 1970's and early 1980's. An advertisement for the range appears below.

3273 Toast Rack £15 - £30
3306 Plate £10 - £20
3449 Mug £10 - £15
3488 Egg Cup £5 - £10 each
3498 Covered Sugar £10 - £20
3499 Cream £10 - £20
3500 Tea Pot £25 - £40
3501 Salt & Pepper £10 - £20
3521 Storage Jar or Biscuit Barrel £20 - £30

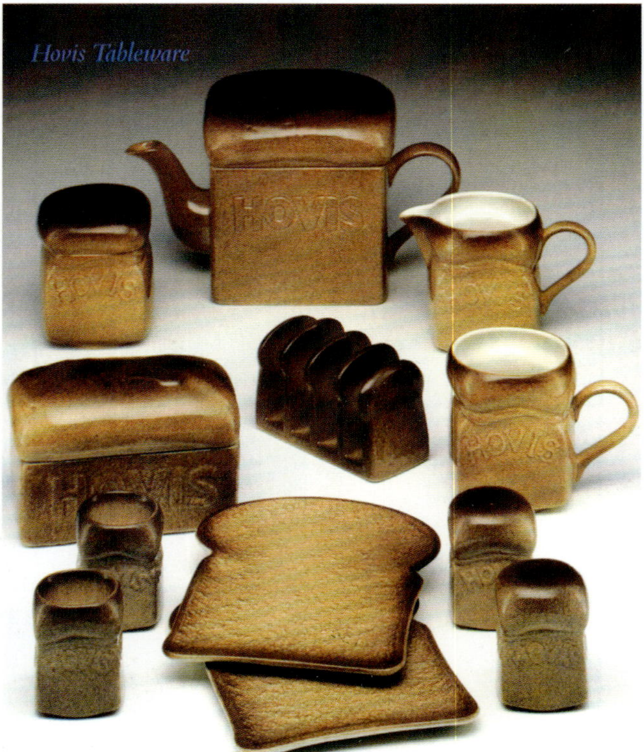

CARLTON WARE LTD
468 King Street, Fenton, Stoke-on-Trent ST4 3DH Tel: 0782 599544, Fax: 0782 599382, Telex: 367144

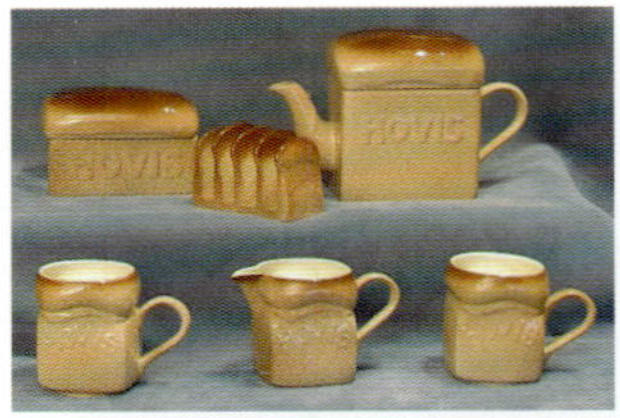

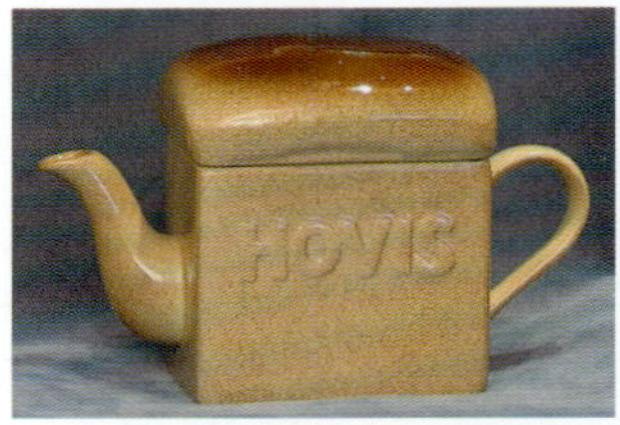

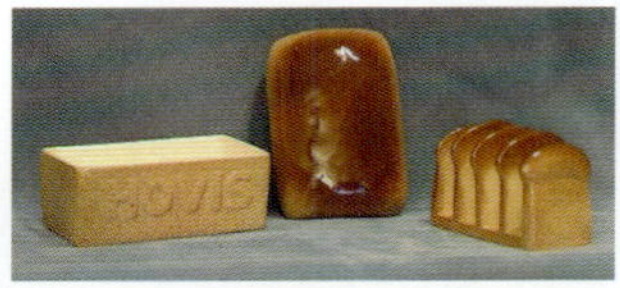

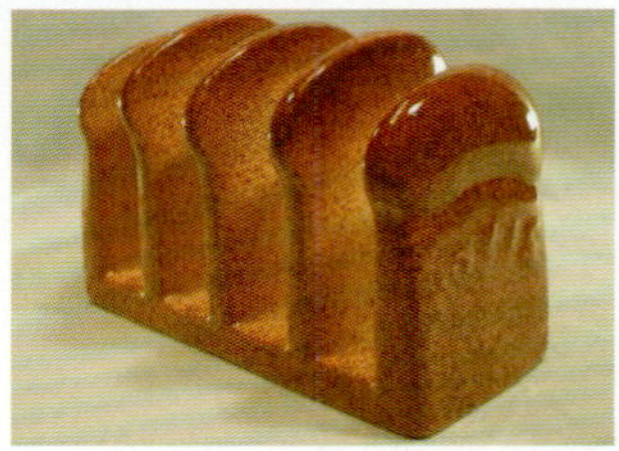

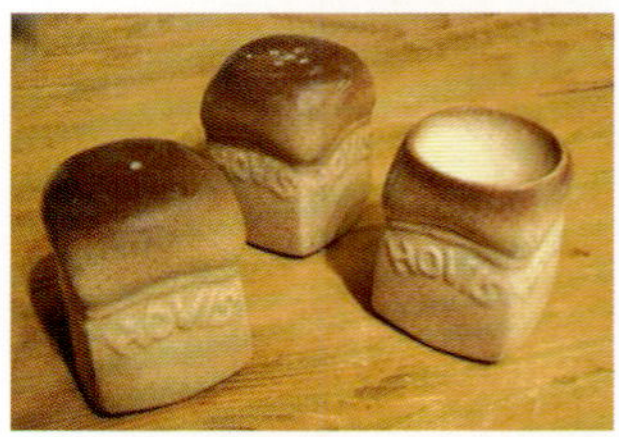

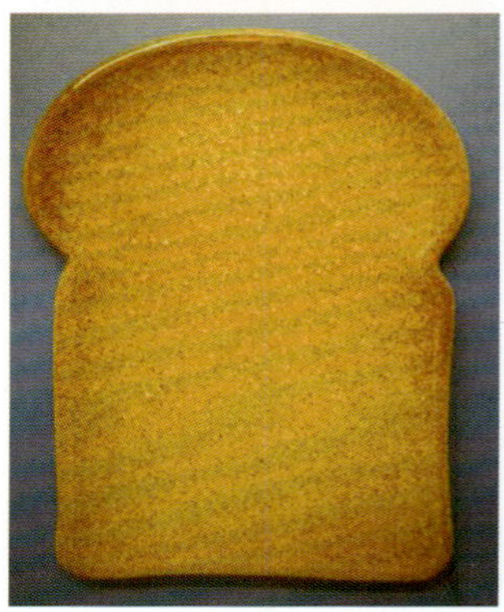

Novelty Tea Pots

3442 Rolls Royce Range ?
3511 Face ?
3512 Maid ?
3547 Bi-plane, Red Baron, Lucy May, Blue Max £60 - £120

The Black & White photographs show some of the stages in the manufacture of the *Bi-plane*.

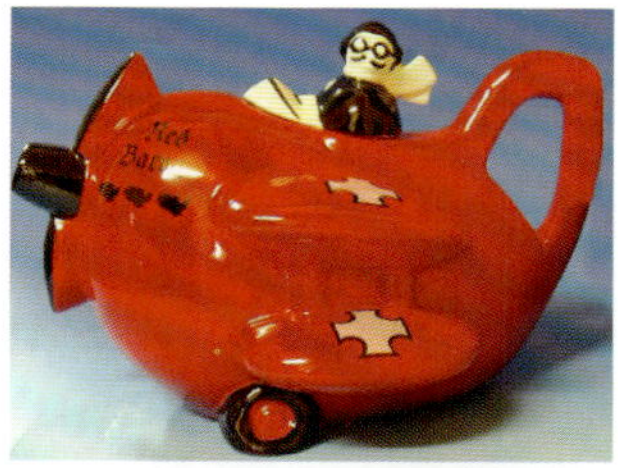

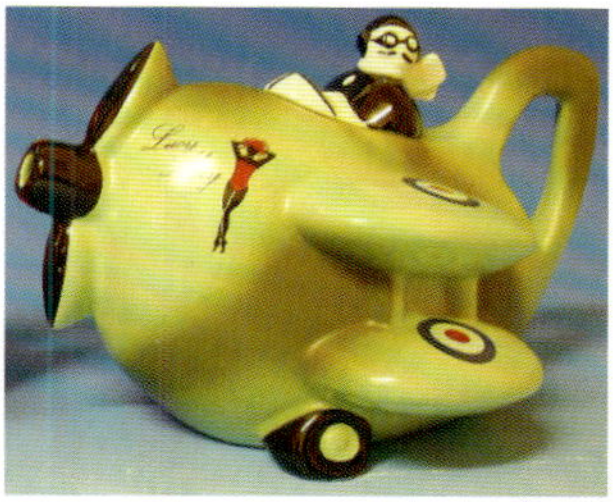

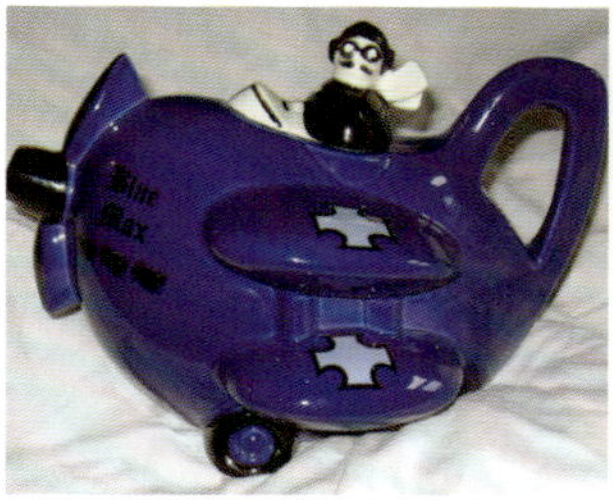

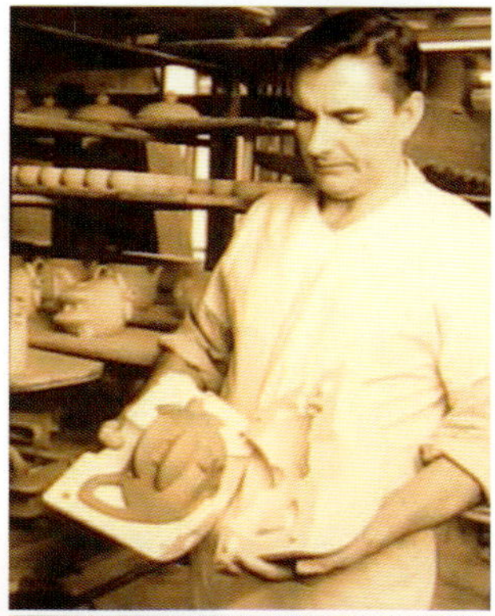

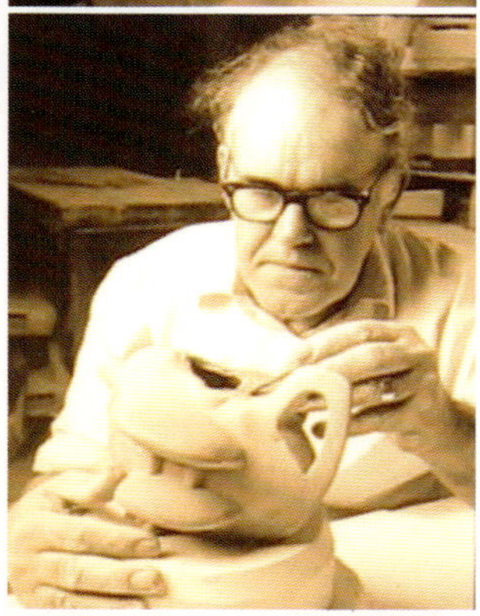

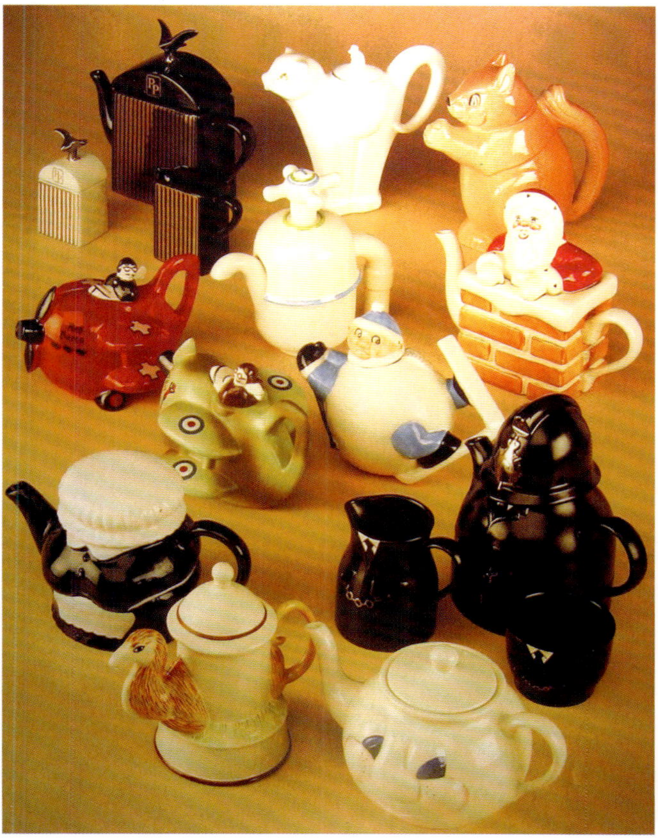

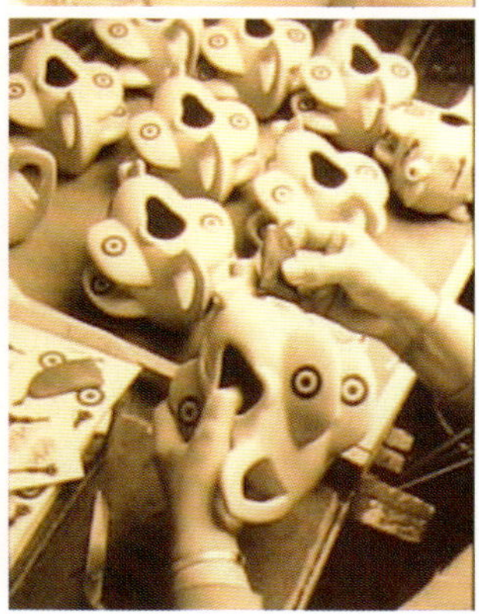

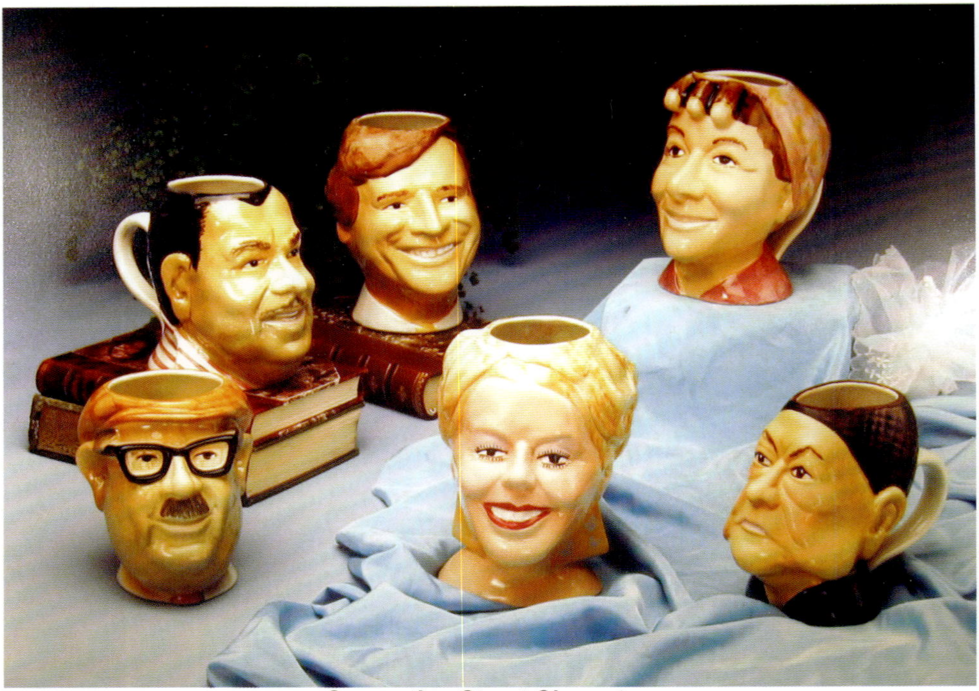

Coronation Street Characters

Original Prices - £6.00 each. Clockwise from bottom left:

Albert Tatlock, Stan Ogden, Mike Baldwin, Hilda Ogden, Ena Sharples, Bett Lynch.

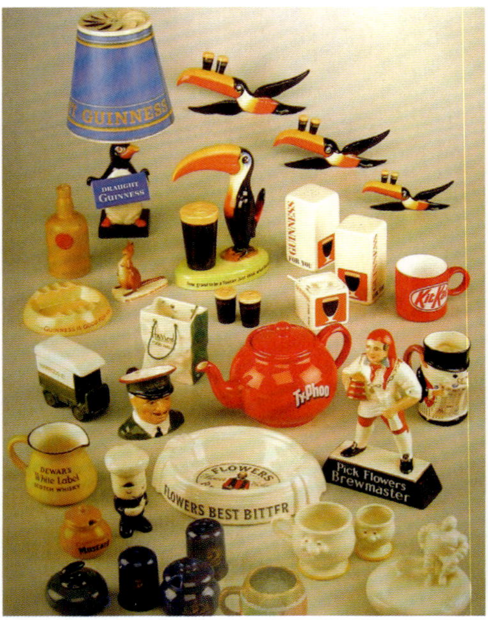

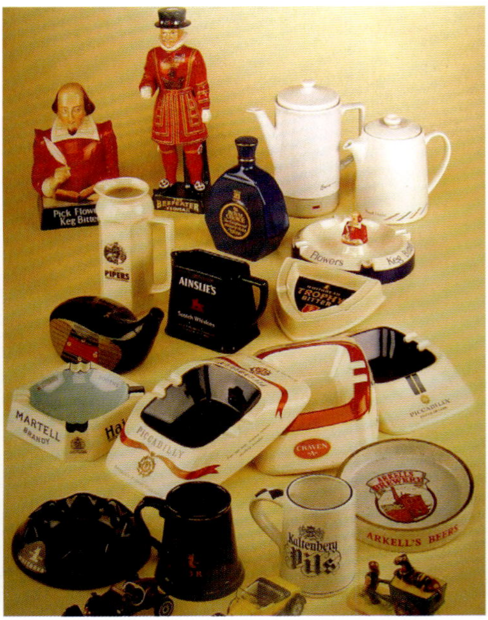

IMPORTANT - PLEASE READ CAREFULLY

Conditions of Sale

As delivery may be affected by circumstances beyond our control, we cannot give any binding delivery dates and the order is booked on this understanding. All orders are accepted at prices ruling at date of despatch.

Retention of Title over Goods Supplied

Note well that Title of Ownership does not pass until all monies due to the company have been received.

Carlton Ware Ltd

From the Authors:

We have done our best to present the information about Carlton Ware in a correct way. Occasionally mistakes may occur and we apologise in advance for any errors. We make no representation or accept any liability for the accuracy or completeness of the information in this book. We will not be held responsible for any losses that may occur in the purchase, sale or other transaction of items because of any information contained in this book.

1997 - A New Beginning

A note from Frank Salmon

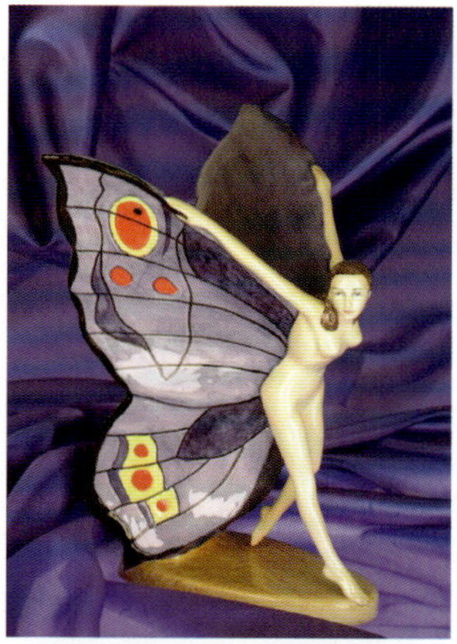

Czes and Yvonne have kindly asked me to provide a little information in regard to Carlton Ware. It was nine years ago, in 1997, that I purchased the rights to Carlton Ware, the trade name, and a good number of original moulds. I have been publishing books on English pottery - mainly price guides - for twenty years and in1993 I published my first Carlton Ware book. The sales of this book were phenomenal and easily outstripped all the other titles I had - titles on Royal Doulton Figures, Bunnykins and Character Jugs, Clarice Cliff, Susie Cooper, Shelly, Poole, Wade, Pendelfin - even Beswick! I realised the trade name and history was extremely valuable. Having previously been a partner in the Kevin Francis Pottery, I felt I could lift Carlton Ware from it's malaise under the ownership of John McCluskey of Grosvenor Ceramics in Staffordshire. We made a deal and I commissioned a number of figurines to be made under the Carlton Ware brand. I wanted a series of female figures, set in flowers, the idea being that the flowers would be inspired by previous Carlton Ware designs. This was hugely successful, but as consumer tastes changed to a more minimalist outlook, I decided to cast the net further.

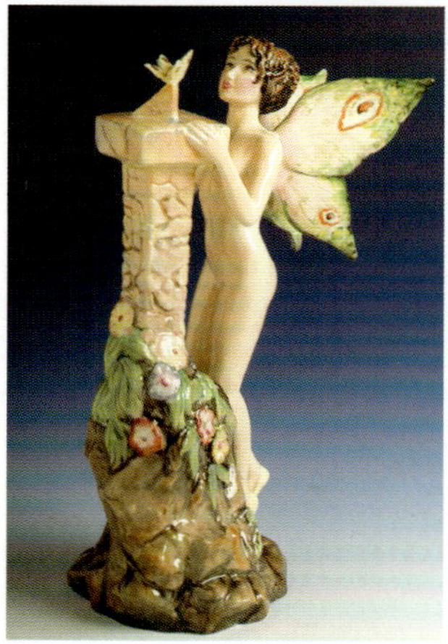

I had some samples made of the moulds I had bought, but decided quickly against reproductions. I introduced the 'Carlton Kid' series, a collection of children dressed in war uniform that was shelved during the war, and was now seeing the light of day for the first time. I also decided on using the 'Red Baron' teapot with a series of celebrities in the cockpit - like Elvis Presley and Winston Churchill.

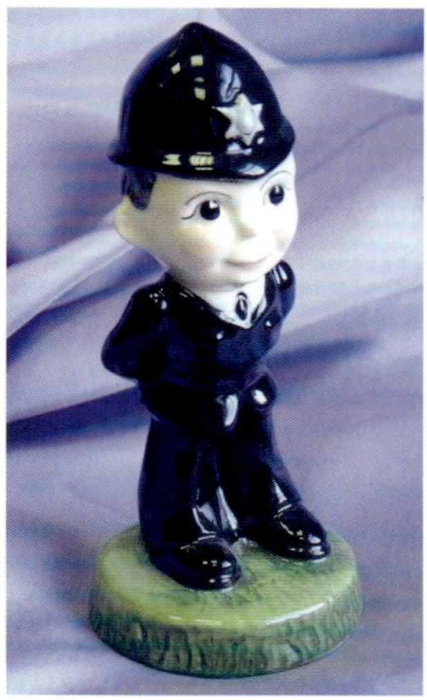

Since then there have been more figurines, teapots and Carlton Kids, and around the turn of the millennium I worked with Marie Graves to make a series of hand-painted designs, some, like the Devil's Copse, from traditional Carlton Ware designs, and other, new designs, like the 'Millennium Eclipse' and the Gustav Klimpt range. It was an exciting time, but we could not continue with Marie because every piece was individually hand-painted, and we just could not keep up with the orders. Marie was so talented but only she could do the work!

Most of the work throughout these years has been undertaken at the Bairstow Manor Pottery in Stoke on Trent. Roger and Brenda have really worked hard to ensure the production of

Carlton Ware, and continue to this day. Our friends at the Moorland Pottery also make tableware for us, and Geoff Ravensdale at the Norcroft Pottery makes the bone china items for us. It is wonderful to know that our orders are helping a number of small potteries in the Stoke on Trent area at a time when the industry is shrinking daily.

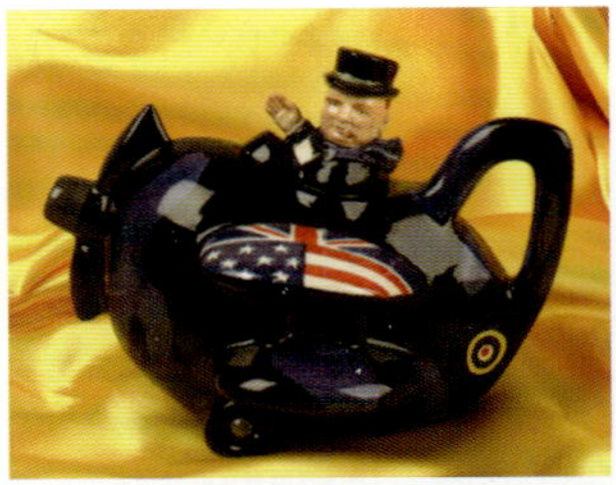

Lately we have also made a quite a number of golly related items. It was only when researching the origin of the golly for a book I was publishing, that I discovered the wonderful world of Florence Upton. It was she who introduced children to a victorian toy town in which toys played with one another in their own world. At the centre of this town was a glove-puppet that had been made for her. She christened the glove-puppet, 'Gollywogg', and the rest is history. She wrote thirteen books and he became a firm favourite with children all over the world. He was also the inspiration for Enid Blyton's Noddy, who bears a similar name, wears a blue jacket and red trousers and is at the centre of Toy Town. Yes, Golly was usurped for a blonde haired blue-eyed boy called Noddy.

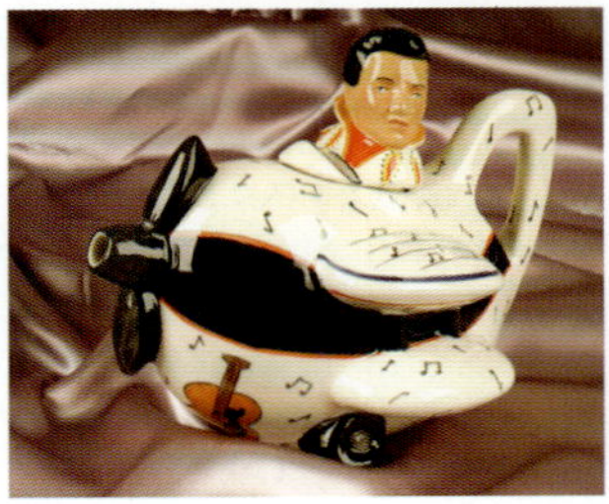

Currently we are working on Snowmen related items, and a range of novelty teapots. All our collectors' editions are now limited to just 100, issued with a certificate. Generally we sell these in one day, so we now launch a product and tell our collectors which day to call us in order to place an order. The response has been phenomenal. This is because there are none of the large numbers associated with other ceramic collectables - 100 is about as low as you can get! But also, being made in England, collectors are latching on the fact that they have the cache that you cannot get from pottery made in India or the Far East. Coupled with the excellent brand of Carlton Ware, our collectables are more successful than ever. Because these items are in such short supply, they do not get to the trade and so you will not find Carlton Ware suddenly appearing on markets at knock down prices. In fact the reverse is the case. For example, in recent months a number of our items have appeared on eBay and have sold at a premium over the retail price.

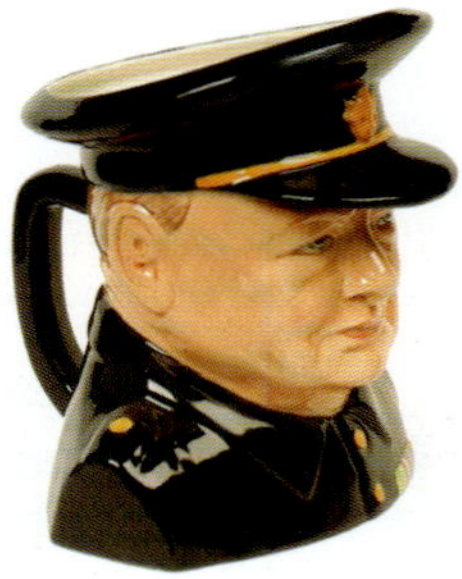

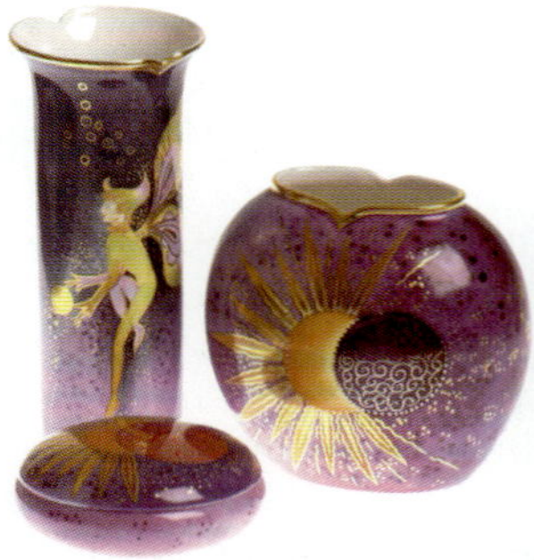

Just a note on backstamps. The new EEC rules imply that if a backstamp is not in use, it can be taken up by any one else. In order to prevent use of the W&R mark, I have registered the 'Swallow Device' and the use of 'Royale' on my Carlton Ware. I now have a warrant to use these marks. The 'Swallow Device' is the same as the pre 1928 mark - BUT, to save confusion there are some amendments: the mark contains 'Est 1890' within it. Also, there is no use of 'W & R'. It is often accompanied by the prefix, 'Genuine' Carlton Ware. This is to

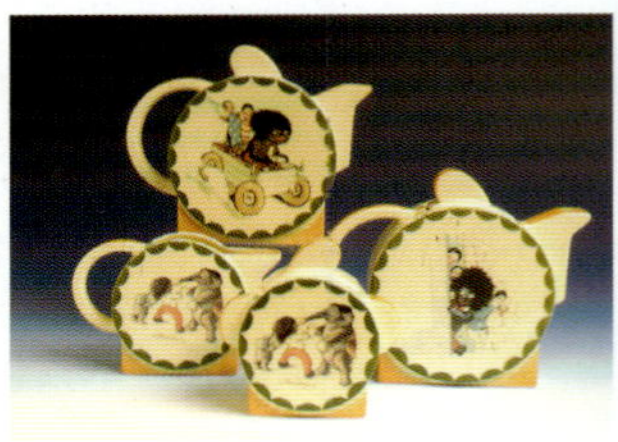

distinguish it from fakes.

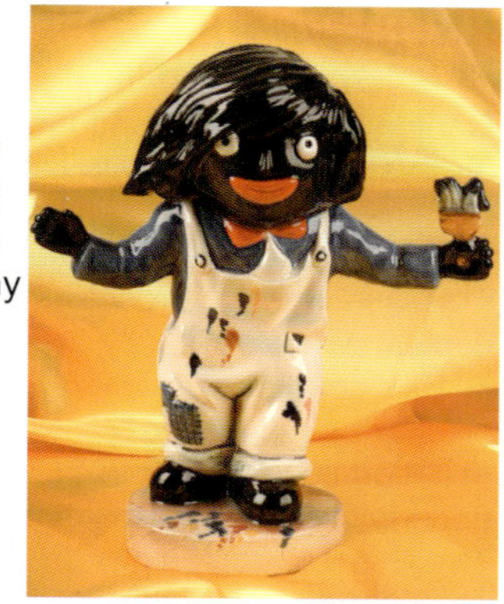

Did you know that Norman Williams was sent down last month for 8 months for faking Carlton Ware and other items? He has also produced Guinness ware with CARLTON WARE LTD on it. He accompanies this with the 'Swallow Device', so people will not be duped, as it is an early mark, but this is why I have taken the action I have. By registering the mark I am protecting the integrity of the Carlton Ware brand.

We constantly strive to live up to the reputation of Carlton Ware and develop new ranges, always with an eye to the character and good humour that has been a hallmark of Carlton Ware in the past. We wish all collectors of Carlton Ware, old and new, the very best for the future, and happy collecting!

Francis Joseph.

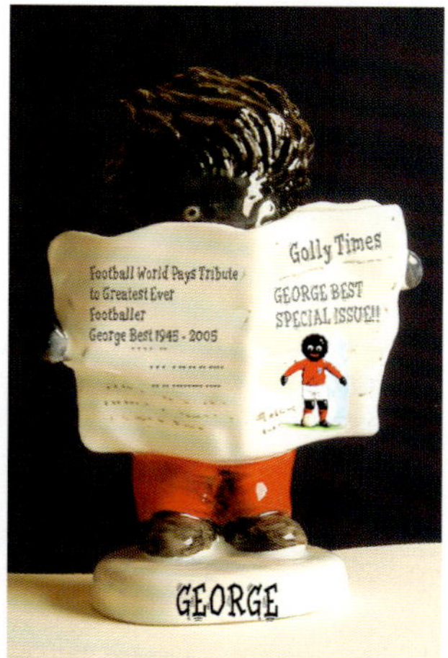

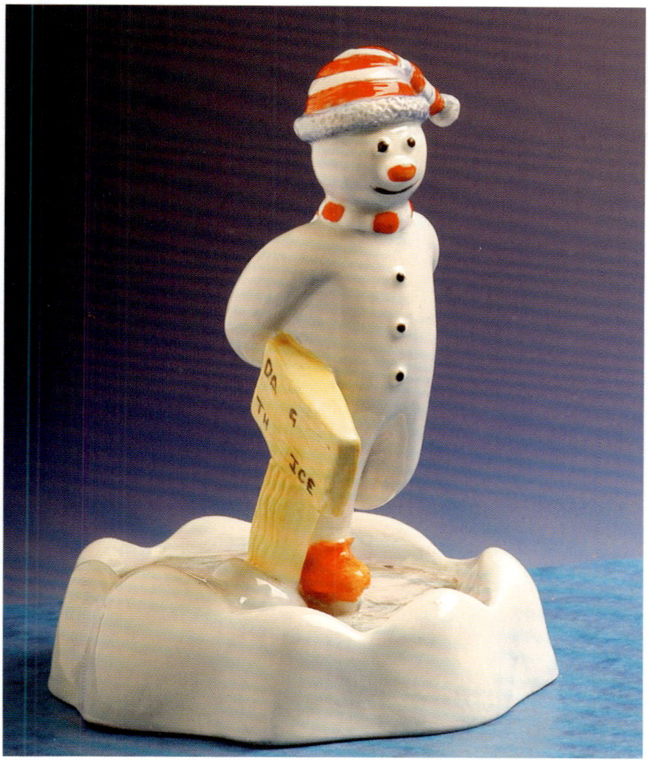

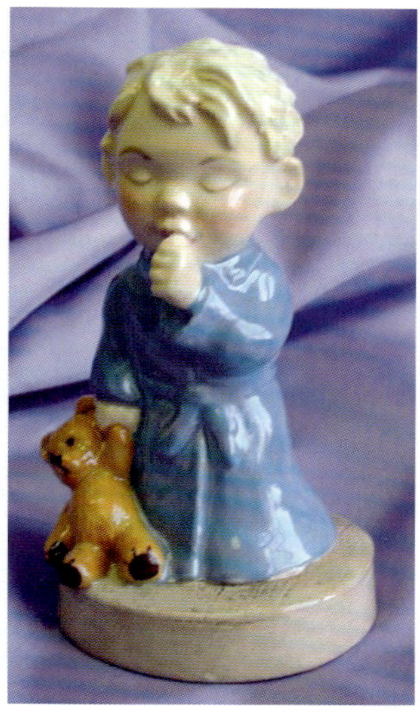

Identifying Fakes

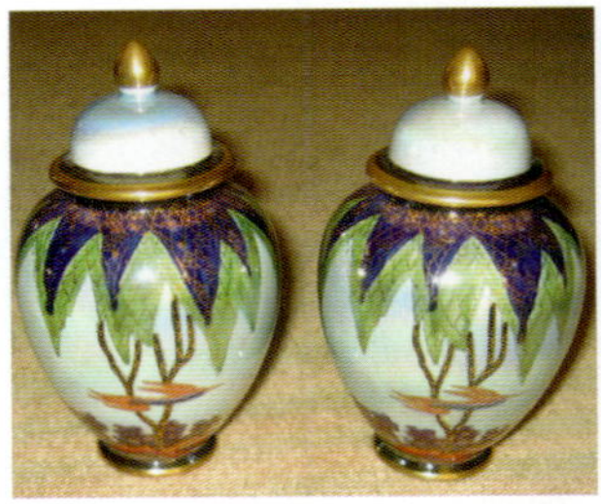

Carlton Ware has a long and varied history but the name was always synonymous with high standards of quality. The designs it created were finished with great attention to detail. Standards remained constant throughout the production run. This is in stark contrast to the contentious issue of fakes and copies, which obviously are not quality items, but illegal inferior counterfeits.

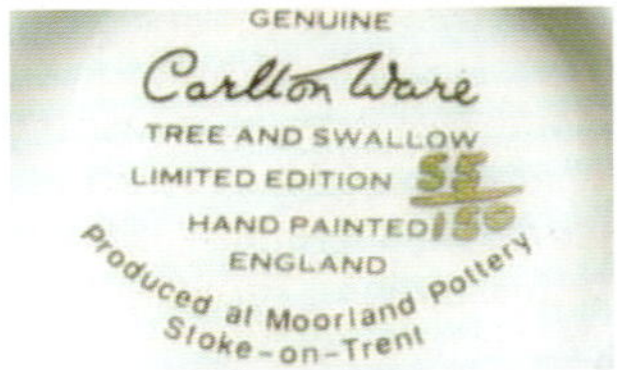

Imitation is supposed to be a form of flattery but the uncertainty and disappointment of deception outweighs this. The lustre ware designs created by Carlton Ware seem to be untouched by the fakers; probably because it's more difficult to emulate some of the complex and intricate finishes.

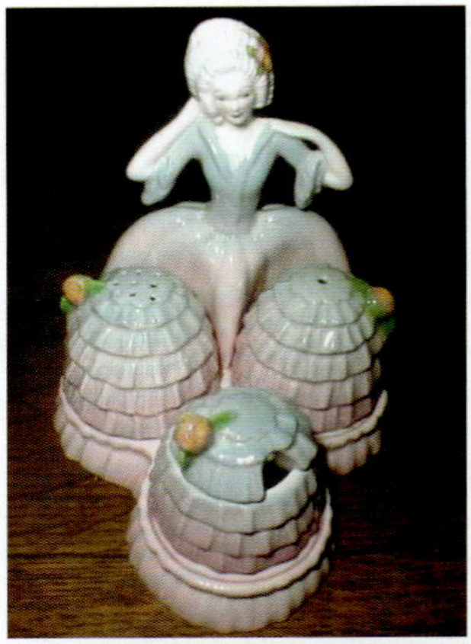

Identifying fakes is not always easy, especially, for unsuspecting new collectors. Fakes can be found at collector's fairs, car boot sales, the Internet and even at auction houses. Unfortunately identifying fakes is not a simple science.

Some fakes are slightly more obvious to seasoned collectors because they are shapes that Carlton Ware never made. But these often have a Carlton Ware back stamp on the base and this can create uncertainty for many. Other fakes are actual replicas or copies and as such are made with some of the original Carlton Ware moulds that were probably stolen when the factory closed down. These are not to be confused with pieces that are made legitimately by the current owner of Carlton Ware, *Francis Joseph*, who does have some of the original moulds, some of which Carlton Ware never used, but these more recent pieces are identifiable by their own distinctive back stamp.

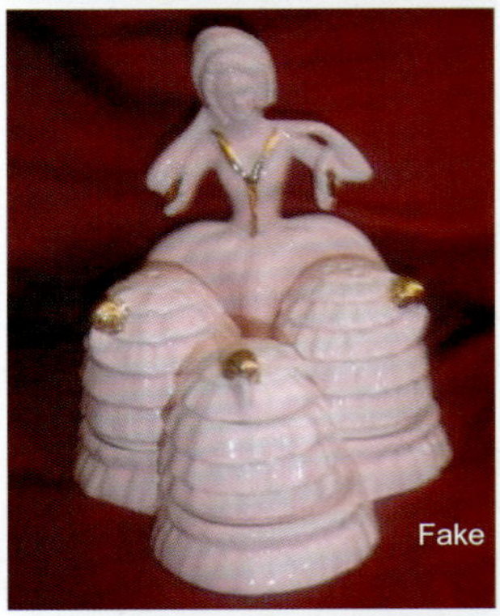

Fake

Apart from obvious errors such as incorrect shapes and incorrect back stamps you should look at the finish of the items. This is not too difficult once you have become a collector or lover of Carlton Ware as the care and attention usually lavished on wares is not in evidence with the fakes, which are inferior and often shoddy. Also be aware of all the colour variations that the original pieces were produced in, as this can be a very good indicator of a fake. Often the colours used on copies are often very loud and not as subtly defined and blended as the originals, which is easy to see when comparing one against the other.

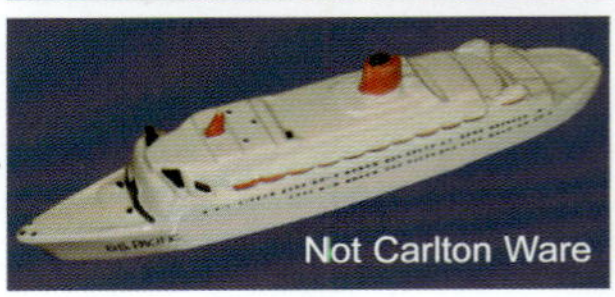

Not Carlton Ware

Prices can be a factor and an indication of authenticity, inferior fakes are often sold more cheaply but this is no guarantee to authenticity as some fake *Guinness* pieces have been sold at very high prices. So, it is a case of buyer beware and if purchasing from a dealer or auction house and in any doubt always get a receipt with a description that states it is Carlton Ware. Other selling mediums are more of a risk.

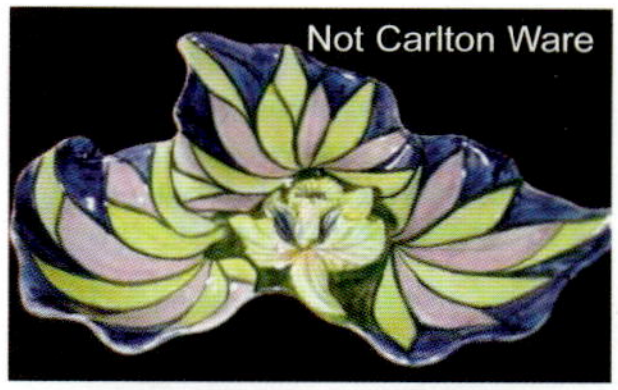

Some details of fakes are provided in this chapter.

The fake *Crinoline Lady* pieces are usually painted in just one colour and have no facial or hair details on the lady.

Some pieces for sale come with a Carlton Ware back-stamp such as the SS Pacific and the three section dish pictured. Neither was made by Carlton Ware. Some war memorabilia are fakes. For example, the *Tank* shown here, is a fake.

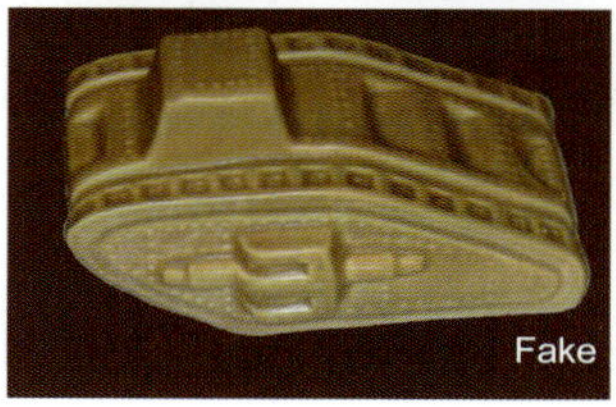

You may see pieces with the back-stamp *Carltons Fantasia Ware Burslam* often advertised as Carlton Ware - they are not!

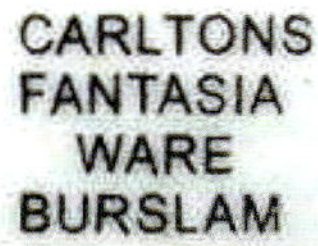

Fakes have been produced of the embossed *Hydrangea* range. Many of these are easy to spot because the four-petal flower heads have a mixture of pink and blue petals.

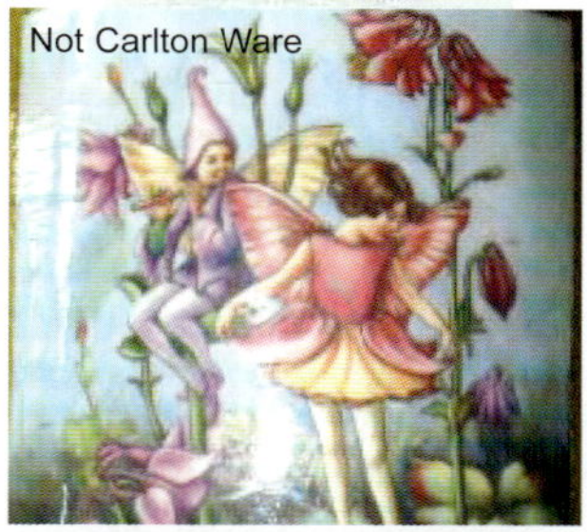

Walking Ware should have a lustre back-stamp unlike the fake in the picture overleaf.

The *Guinness* range is very desirable and has an enormous following of collectors in the UK and internationally. The originals are extremely valuable and consequently the forgers have flooded the market with fakes. The following is a list of the pieces that are known to have been forged with a brief description of how to recognise the originals made by Carlton Ware.

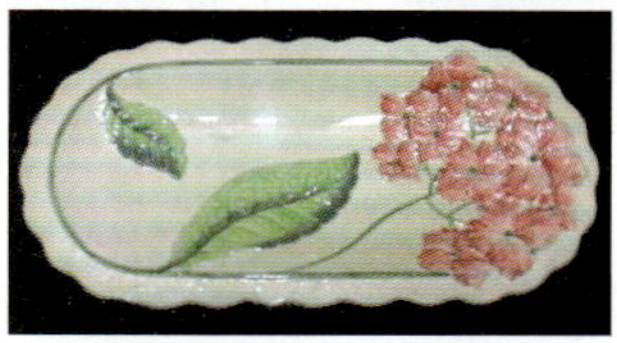

The *Zookeeper* stands on a cream base and his face and hands have a pinkish flesh colour. His dark green uniform and hat contrast well with his white apron and the straps at the back should be white. The little kangaroo in his pocket should have paws and ears clearly visible.

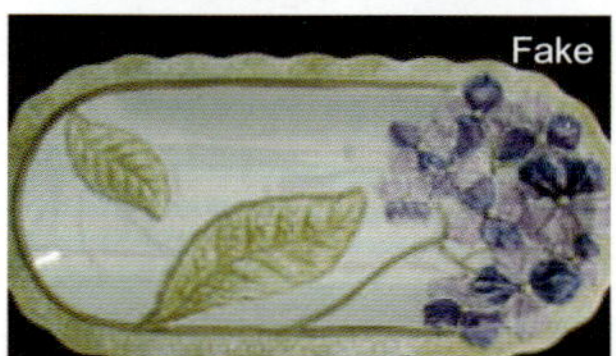

The *Kangaroo* with cream base is rich chestnut brown colour, which shades lighter down his chest. His features such as toes and nails, eyes and brows, mouth and nose are detailed in black. The pouch contains a detailed Guinness bottle.

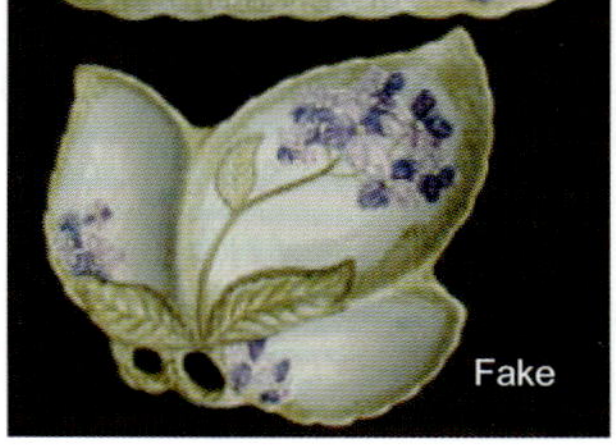

The *Ostrich* on cream base has pinkish tinge to tail feathers, legs, face and neck with swallowed pint. There are lovely realistic details to the feathers and the yellow beak has a black line to detail the mouth.

The *Tortoise* on cream base has good black details to face and feet along with markings on the shell and a 5mm froth on the beer glass.

The *Sealion* is perched on a rich brown stand upon cream base. It is black with white eyes and the beer has 1mm of froth on the beer.

The *Penguin* on pale blue tinged base is black with white front, which has a bright blue plaque with yellow statement *Draught Guinness*. There is good detail to the eyes and the beak is bright orange and yellow.

The *Penguin lamp* has a black base and bright orange neatly painted feet and beak. The eyes are lovely and and there is a blue plaque stating *Draught Guinness*.

The *Drayman* on cream base has rich brown hat, trousers, horse and cartwheels. The cart is dark green with yellow straw and a red and white painted scarf contains a bottle of Guinness hanging from the cart. The horse is happy looking and finished with lots of detailed livery.

The *Toucan* range in general always has a rich orange beak, which shades to yellow above as with markings on chest, which should not be just stripes of colours. The eyes are always detailed in blue/green as are the feet and the tail is highlighted in red streaked with black and white. The *small Glass and Toucan* on cream base has 5mm of froth on the beer glass.

The *Flying Toucans* details are similar and there should be 4-6mm of froth on beer. The *Toucan Bar Decoration* and *Lampbase* are as above but with feet stood on circle of brown, the beer has 15mm of froth on top.

The *Toucan Wall Plaque* is as above but with a realistic and detailed base to the glass of beer with the word *Guinness* and a harp logo as well as 15mm of froth.

The *Toucan Jug* has two variations of base, green rock effect and plain beige. They both have the inscription on the glass *My Goodness My Guinness*. Another variation has a beige base with harp logo and *Guinness* below. The pint has 15mm of froth.

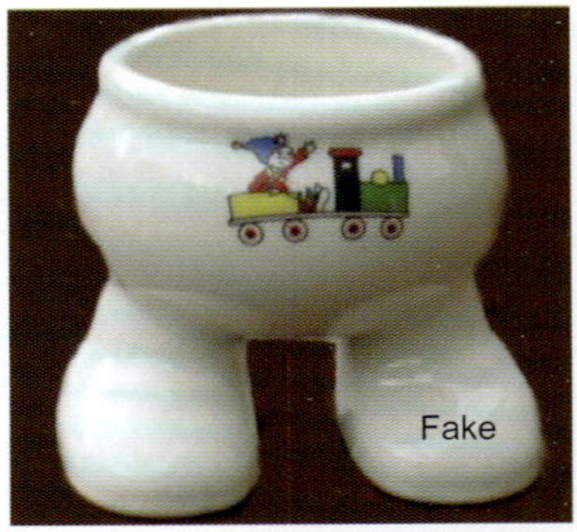

Fake

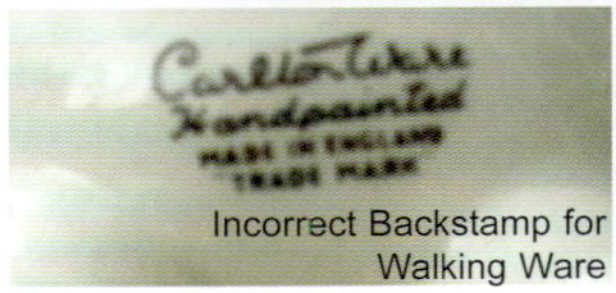

Incorrect Backstamp for Walking Ware

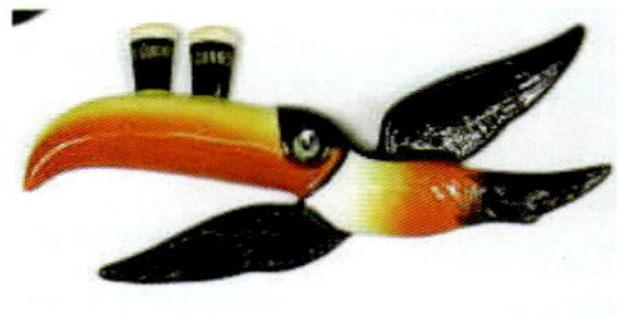

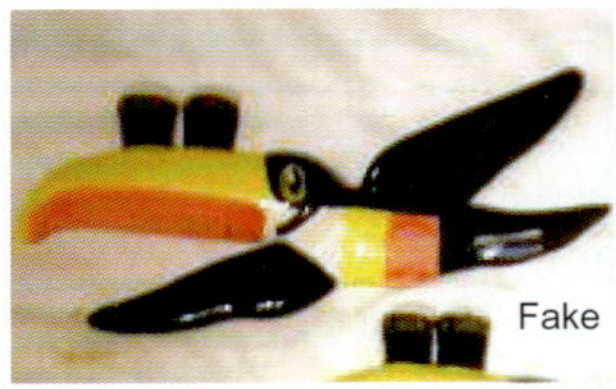

Fake

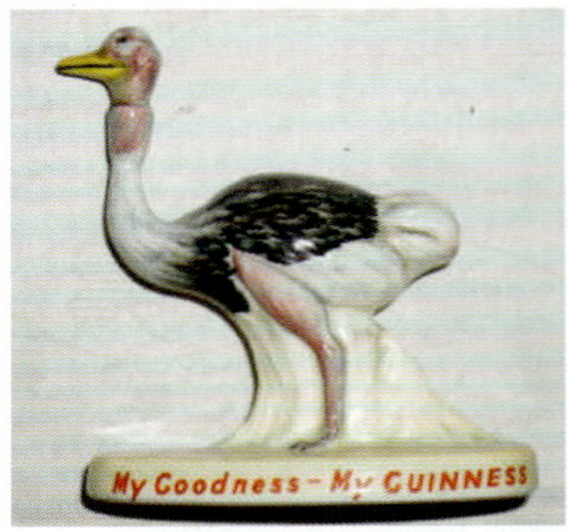

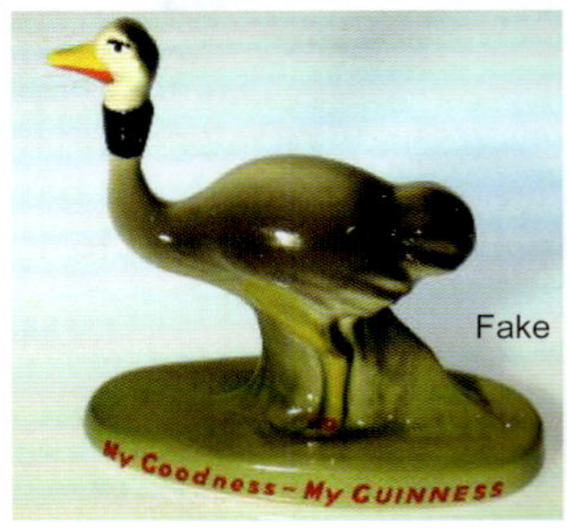

Fake

Carlton Ware - 100 Club

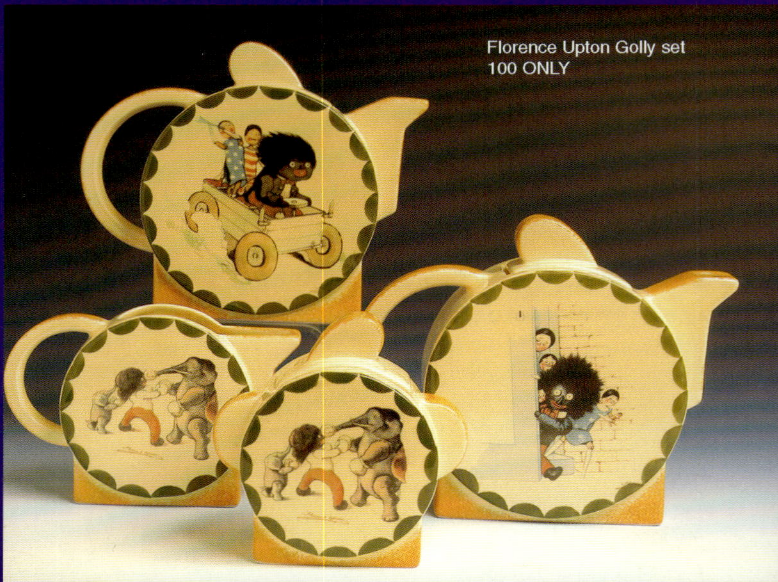

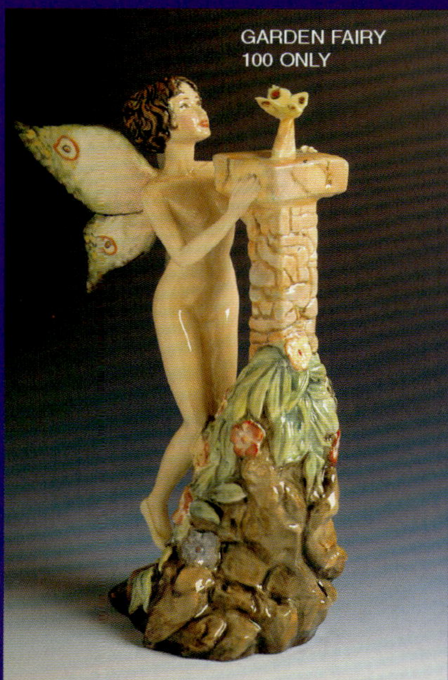

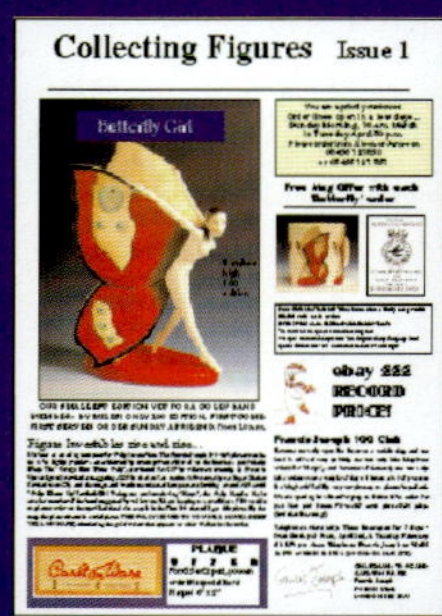

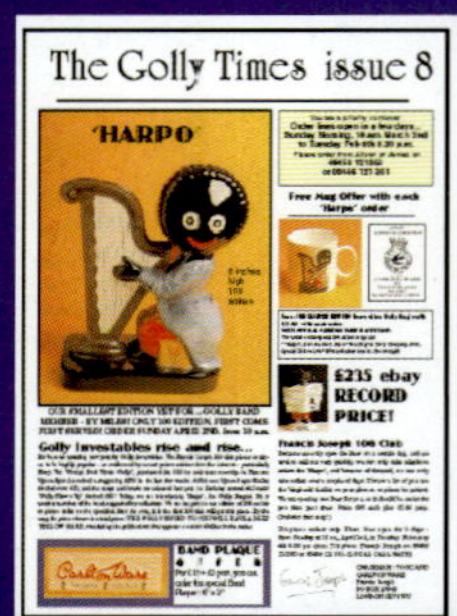

Carlton Ware has been synonymous with quality, hand-made wares, made in England, for over a century. It is a household name that has endured and is highly prized at a time when other English manufacturers are making their pottery in the Far East. To join our mailing list simply call **0208 856 8592** - our newsletters are free. Also, you can email us at info@carltonware.co.uk and just type **free newsletters** in the subject line.

A guide to help you identify Carlton Ware patterns and shapes. It contains over 500 pictures of Carlton Ware.

The introduction covers topics such as Pattern and Shape numbers, a brief history of Carlton Ware and Dating Carlton Ware.

The book is a full and comprehensive guide to identifying Carlton Ware patterns.

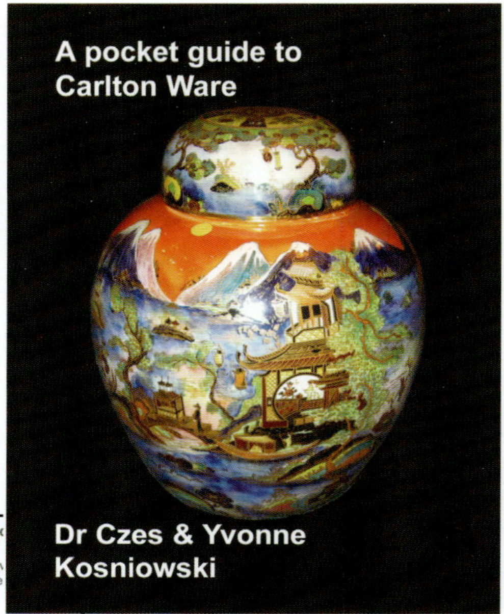

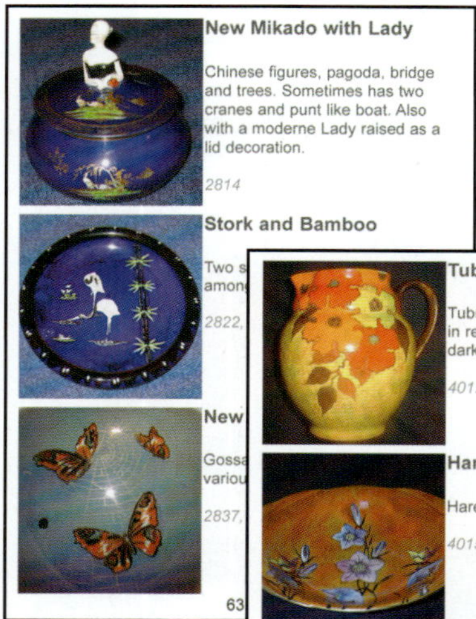

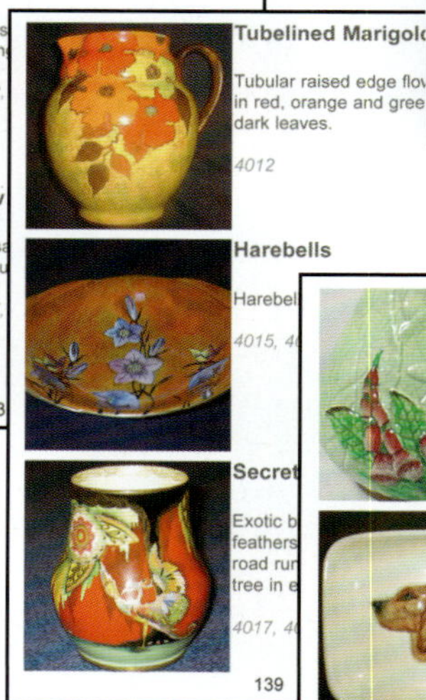

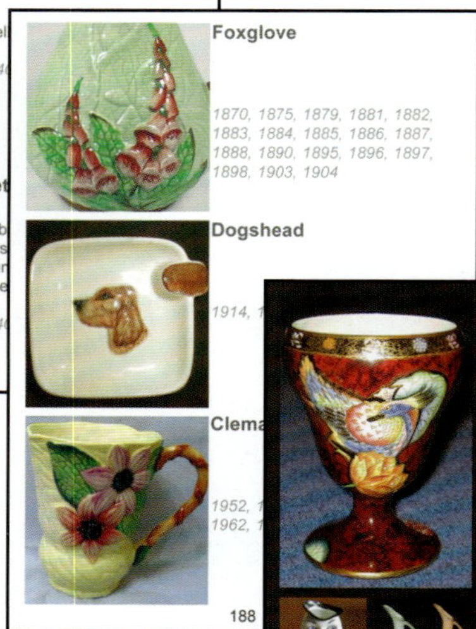

A pocket guide to Carlton Ware

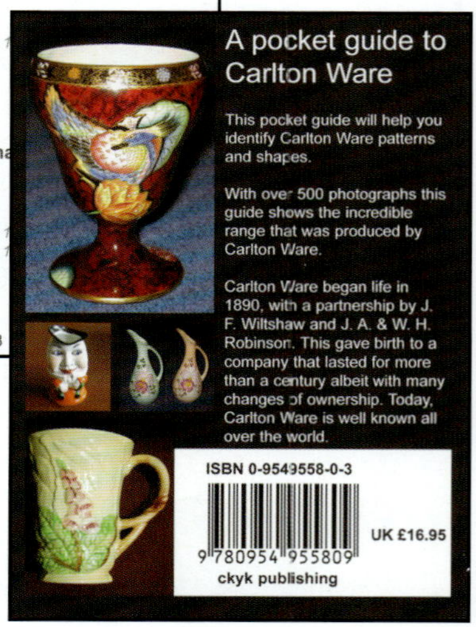

224 pages, soft cover, 106mm x 146mm
Published by ckyk publishing,
a division of ckyk ltd. www.ckyk.com
ISBN 0-9549558-0-3 Price £16.95

Buy the book at discount from www.ckyk.com

Index by Shape Numbers

If you know the Shape number you can check the possible patterns from this list.

Index by Name

Resources: